Vaqueros, Cowboys, and Buckaroos

Vaqueros, Cowboys,

Number Twenty

M. K. BROWN RANGE LIFE SERIES

and Buckaroos

by

LAWRENCE CLAYTON

JIM HOY

and

JERALD UNDERWOOD

UNIVERSITY OF TEXAS PRESS AUSTIN

Cover image: Nail Ranch, 1985. Sonja Irwin Clayton photo.
Photo insets, left to right: Unidentified King Ranch vaquero, courtesy
King Ranch archives; George Peacock, Nail Ranch, courtesy Sonja
Irwin Clayton; Waddy Mitchell, widely known buckaroo, courtesy
Lawrence Clayton.

COPYRIGHT © 2001 BY THE UNIVERSITY OF TEXAS PRESS

All rights reserved

Printed in the United States of America

First edition, 2001

utpress.utexas.edu/about/book-permissions

♾ The paper used in this book meets the minimum requirements of
ANSI/NISO Z39.48-1992 (R1997) (Permanence of Paper).

LIBRARY OF CONGRESS CATALOGING-IN-PUBLICATION DATA
Clayton, Lawrence, 1938–
  Vaqueros, cowboys, and buckaroos / by Lawrence Clayton, Jim Hoy,
and Jerald Underwood.— 1st ed.
      p.   cm.
Includes bibliographical references and index.

ISBN 978-0-292-71240-9
  1. Cowboys—West (U.S.)—History.   2. Cowboys—West (U.S.)—Social
life and customs.   3. Cowboys—West (U.S.)—Pictorial works.   4. Ranch
life—West (U.S.)   5. Ranch life—Southwest, New.   6. Ranch life—
Mexico.   7. West (U.S.)—Social life and customs.   8. Southwest, New—
Social life and customs.   9. Mexico—Social life and customs.   I. Hoy,
James F.   II. Underwood, Jerald, 1931–   III. Title.
F596 .C437   2001
978—dc21   2001027992

This work is dedicated to all of those

VAQUEROS, COWBOYS, AND BUCKAROOS,

past and present,
who have made a living
doing the only thing they want to do—
work cattle while sitting
on the back of a good horse.

The coauthors also wish to dedicate this book to the memory of

LAWRENCE CLAYTON
(1938–2000)

teacher, scholar, author, and friend.

CONTENTS

ACKNOWLEDGMENTS   xiii

INTRODUCTION   xv

The Vaquero   1
JERALD UNDERWOOD

The Cowboy   67
LAWRENCE CLAYTON

The Buckaroo   155
JIM HOY

CONCLUSION   223

GLOSSARY   225

COMPARATIVE CHART
  Vaquero, Cowboy, and Buckaroo Characteristics   245

BIBLIOGRAPHY   251

INDEX   261

ABOUT THE AUTHORS   275

LIST OF ILLUSTRATIONS

1. Victor Amezquita   1
2. The Longhorn   16
3. A vaquero in South Texas   17
4. A King Ranch vaquero   18
5. Braided rawhide reins   19
6. A typical group of South Texas vaqueros   20
7. A brush country chuck wagon   21
8. A chuck wagon in the brasada   21
9. A vaquero washing up for mealtime   22
10. Camp bread   23
11. Vaqueros in a saddle shed   23
12. A vaquero separating a calf from the herd   24
13. A group of vaqueros in Mexico   24
14. An old Mexican sombrero   25
15. A rawhide riata   26
16. A lariat made of maguey fibers   27
17. A lariat of lechuguilla fibers   28
18. A horsehair rope   29
19. A rawhide riata at the base of the saddle horn   30
20. An intricate knot on a horsehair hackamore   31
21. A vaquero saddle   32
22. Saddles in a tack room   33
23. A modern vaquero saddle belonging to Frank Graham   34
24. A modern vaquero saddle owned by David Huerta   35
25. Rear view of the Huerta saddle   36
26. Tapadero on the Huerta saddle   37
27. A modern charro saddle   38

28. Overhead view of the charro saddle 39
29. A traditional pair of Chihuahua spurs 40
30. A girth of twisted horsehair 40
31. Side bars on an old pair of vaquero bits 41
32. An old pair of vaquero bits with high port 41
33. A high port bit with roller, slobber bar, and slobber chains 42
34. The *formando* 43
35. Pepe Díaz 44
36. Victor Amezquita at the ranch in Jalisco, Mexico 46
37. A house in Jalisco, Mexico 47
38. The stable gates at the ranch in Jalisco, Mexico 47
39. Individual stalls for horses 48
40. A *caballo trabajo* in Jalisco, Mexico 48
41. Horses in a set of pens in Jalisco, Mexico 49
42. Barbed wire fencing 50
43. *Corrales de leña* in South Texas 51
44. A belt with leather-covered buckle and painted design 52
45. The intricate geometric design of a *pita* belt 52
46. David Huerta 53
47. A rawhide honda 54
48. A vaquero shoes a horse 55
49. David Huerta's chaps 56
50. David Huerta's quirt 57
51. Ismael Sánchez and Justin Brent Sánchez 59
52. Benny Peacock 67
53. A crew of cowboys in West Texas 76
54. The reason for cowboys—Longhorns 77
55. Cowboys holding a bunch of Herefords 78
56. Cowboys roping and dragging calves 79
57. Cowboys finished with a freshly branded calf 80
58. A branding-iron heater 81
59. Chuck time around the wagon 82
60. Two bedrolls beside the chuck wagon 82
61. Cowboy tepees 83
62. A horseman penning cattle 84
63. Cowboys loading cattle into a cattle car 85
64. A restored cattle car 85
65. A modern cattle van 86
66. A variety of fencing types 87
67. Modern welded-steel fencing 88

68. Terry Moberly using a hoolihan loop   89
69. Part of a remuda   90
70. Two cowboys, about 1930   91
71. George Peacock   92
72. Horses headed to work in a trailer   93
73. Two ropers heading and heeling   96
74. A crew working a calf on a working table   97
75. The working table in its upright position   98
76. A lariat half-hitched hard and fast   99
77. A variety of hondas for securing hard and fast   100–101
78. A mule-drawn chuck wagon   102
79. A series of cowboy belt buckles   108–109
80. A typical cowboy boot with spur attached   110
81. A montage of cowboy spurs   112–115
82. Lawrence Clayton dons his shotgun chaps   116
83. Examples of cowboy chaps   118–119
84. A pair of hobbles secured to the rear cinch ring   120
85. Details of cowboy saddles   121–122
86. A plain metal oxbow stirrup   123
87. An oxbow stirrup decorated with a ranch brand   124
88. The most common type of cowboy tapadero   125
89. Bridles in a cowboy tack room   126
90. Side bars on a pair of bits showing ranch brands   127
91. Three styles of hackamore   128–129
92. A shallow port bit   130
93. A snaffle bit   131
94. A rawhide bosal   132
95. Charlie Cone with his wife, Delia   138
96. G. D. London   142
97. Barney Baldeschwiler   144
98. A herd of buffalo   146
99. Glenn Leech   148
100. George Peacock   149
101. Benny Peacock   150
102. Sonny Edgar   151
103. Jack Pate   152
104. Dwight Hill   155
105. Early-day buckaroo   160
106. Three styles of buckaroo hats   162–163
107. Newt Dodge   164

108. A pair of Paul Bond boots   165
109. Waddy Mitchell   166
110. A pair of woolies, long chaps with the hair side out   168
111. A typical buckaroo saddle   171
112. Another buckaroo saddle   172
113. A third buckaroo saddle   173
114. The post horn and secured lariat of the buckaroo style   174
115. Two styles of stirrups   175
116. Details of a buckaroo's tack   176
117. A single-rigged saddle   177
118. An ornate horn cap with ranch brand   178
119. A decorated horn cap with playing-card emblems   179
120. A pair of dropped-shank Garcia spurs   180
121. Two pairs of ornate buckaroo spurs   181
122. An ornate snaffle bit   182
123. A high port or spade bit with decorative side bar   183
124. Two varieties of slobber chains   184
125. A long shoo-fly   185
126. Buckaroos working cattle   189
127. Mackey Hedges tosses a hoolihan loop   190
128. Early-day buckaroos branding horses   194
129. Paiute buckaroo Tex Northrup   195
130. Mackey Hedges and his son, Ben, working a horse   196
131. Mackey Hedges working with a young horse   197
132. Two versions of knots in horses' tails   210
133. George Smiraldo   211

ACKNOWLEDGMENTS

We wish to acknowledge the caring support of our wives—Sonja Irwin Clayton, Catherine Thompson Hoy, and Dorothy Eads Underwood— and thank them for patience during the preparation of the manuscript and tolerance during the research trips, some of which took us to remote areas where luxuries were scarce. Many of the individuals who contributed to our understanding of the cultures involved are cited in the notes. Of especial value, however, are the following, all in Texas: George and Sue Peacock of the Nail Ranch; Benny and Treca Peacock of Green Ranches; G. D. London of Throckmorton; W. W. Jones II, Dick Jones, and Frank Graham of Hebbronville; Victor Amezquita of Rotan, José "Pepe" Díaz-Sánchez of San Antonio; David Huerta of Alpine; Ismael Sánchez of Odessa; and Mary Jo Beard of Abilene.

Special thanks go to Arturo Alonzo, Cirildo Ortiz, Ramiro Ramírez, Felix Vásquez, and Erasmo Rodríguez, vaqueros of Uvalde, Texas.

Others who were particularly helpful are Charley Amos of the Garvey Ranches, Paradise Valley, Nevada; George Smiraldo and Stanley Griswold of Elko, Nevada; Sue Wallis and Rod McQuery of Nevada; Carl Hammond, Hot Springs Ranch, Golconda, Nevada; Mark Galyen of Jordan Valley, Oregon; Byron Johnson of Murphy, Idaho; and Mackey and Candy Hedges of Deseret Cattle Company, Woodruff, Utah.

The editorial assistance of James Ward Lee is gratefully acknowledged.

Finally we gratefully acknowledge the assistance of our typists, without whose help this manuscript would not have materialized—Ann Baugh Giddens and Peggi Gooch.

INTRODUCTION

I see by your outfit that you are a cowboy.
"THE COWBOY'S LAMENT"

The *outfit* or appearance of members of a bona fide folk group—principally the clothing but also other personal accoutrements associated with the work and daily life of the individuals in that group—is distinctive enough to be identified at a glance, even by a novice. This is certainly true of the cattle herders in the American West. The tall hat, the scarf, the brightly colored long-sleeved shirt, the faded blue denim jeans, the leather chaps, the high-top cowboy boots, the jingling spurs, and other such items have long been recognized as the distinguishing marks of this Western America folk hero. Certainly similarity exists in the outfits of the mounted herders in various regions of the West, but variations in appearance show distinct regional preferences in the choice and style of the items themselves.

How the hat is styled or *crushed*, and whether the scarf is cotton or silk, the shirt is cotton or wool, the chaps are long and full or knee-length, the boots are lace-up packers or tall stove-pipe types, the spurs sport large rowels and jingle-bobs or small rowels and little decoration—these factors determine whether the individual is a vaquero, a cowboy, or a buckaroo. Also important is whether his saddle has a slick or swelled fork, is rim-fire or seven-eighths or three-quarter rigged, and has a rolled or straight cantle. If his rope is thirty feet long, he is a cowboy. If it is sixty, he is a buckaroo.

The outfit preferred by these men in their geographic areas developed over a long period under many different influences. The life of these men was controlled by cattle and horses; it took both to make their world turn. By 1600, there had emerged a distinct class of men who herded and worked cattle in North America. By the early 1700s, Longhorn cattle and these herders were common in northern Mexico, southern Texas, and southern California. They were Mexican vaqueros, who lived in poverty and who no doubt dressed themselves in whatever nondescript garb and worked with whatever equipment they could find to meet their needs. Gradually, however, they developed distinctive clothing, gear, techniques, and annual routines, much of which bore similarities to the vaquero's South American cousin, the gaucho of the broad and grassy Argentine Pampas.

More than two centuries later, when Anglos took up the practice of herding cattle in what was to become California and southern Texas, they adapted the vaquero pattern into a culture that can be divided into two distinct versions related to specific areas of the United States—the cowboy and the buckaroo.

In 1927 Charles M. Russell, the noted painter and interpreter of the West, revealed the common thought about the origins of the cowboy and the buckaroo. Speaking through the dialect of Rawhide Rawlins, he gives the following history: "By all I can find out from old, gray-headed punchers," he drawls, "the cow business started [in the United States] in California, an' the Spaniards were the first to burn marks on their cattle an' hosses, an' use the rope," thus confirming the early influence of the Spanish. Then, he says, "the men from the States drifted west to Texas, pickin' up the brandin' iron an' lass-rope, an' the business spread north, east, an' west, till the spotted longhorns walked in every trail marked out by their brown cousins, the buffalo."

He then delineates the differences between the buckaroo and the cowboy: "Texas an' California, bein' the startin' places, made two species of cowpunchers; those west of the Rockies rangin' north, usin' center-fire or single-cinch saddles, with high fork an' cantle; packed a sixty or sixty-five foot rawhide rope, an' swung a big loop." He depicts with the keen eye of the artist their penchant for fancy gear: "These cow people were generally strong on pretty, usin' plenty of hoss jewelry, silver-mounted spurs, bits, an' conchas." Their tack also caught his observant eye: "Instead of a quirt" they "used a romal, or quirt braided to the end of the reins. Their saddles were full stamped with from twenty-four to twenty-eight-inch eagle-bill tapaderos. Their chaparejos were made of fur or hair, either bear, angora goat, or hair sealskin." He identifies the bits used by these men as the "Spanish spade." He had them pegged: "These fellows were sure fancy, an' called themselves buckaroos, coming from the Spanish word *vaquero*."

In contrast, he notes, the cowboy "originated in Texas and ranged north." Unlike the buckaroo, "he wasn't much for pretty; his saddle was low horn, rimfire, or double-cinch." He identifies another of their salient characteristics and the reason for it: "Their rope was seldom over forty feet, for being a good deal in a brush country, they were forced to swing a small loop. These men generally tied [hard and fast], instead of taking their dallie-welts, or wrapping their rope around the saddle horn. Their chaparejos were made of heavy bullhide, to protect the leg from the brush and thorns." He goes on to note that they protected their feet "with hog-snout tapaderos," those with no flaps. These characteristics are still typical of cowboys, although the tapaderos are found only in brush country.

Russell seems to have preferred the flashy buckaroo to the plainer cowboy, or at least he described the California type more fully. His use of "lass-rope" reflects the dialect of the buckaroo. Without doubt, however, he understood the differences he observed.

The regional differences in the herders of the North American West are discussable only in general terms because there was, and is, no complete uniformity. In fact, any effort to say for certain what style was or was not present in a given region at a specific time is futile, for styles have changed with time as preferred modes of dress have done for centuries with people in all walks of life. The men adopt and then perhaps adapt the customs of their regions. Something different in clothing and technique is initially looked upon with distrust or even with disdain. For example, men of a culture that dallies its lariats when roping will tend to stay clear of a roper who ties off, and the reverse is just as true because tie-off ropers are suspicious of "dally men." There was, however, enough similarity, and there still is, to discuss these types of herders in different regions in general terms.

The first section, by Jerald Underwood, traces the vaquero from his formative background in North Africa and Spain into Mexico, where the Mexican frontier molded an already expert horseman into a consummate range hand. The cowboy section, by Lawrence Clayton, deals with the evolution and current life and work of the cowboy. Jim Hoy's final section on the buckaroo traces the development, life, and work patterns of the range hands of the Northwest United States. The journey to compile this material and collect the photographs has been enjoyable to us; we wish the same pleasure for our readers.

Vaqueros, Cowboys, and Buckaroos

Victor Amezquita on a ranch in Jalisco, Mexico, 1999. Note the hat, the short jacket, and the long chaps, clothing resembling that of a charro. The horse's bits are equipped with slobber chains, and the reins are formed from a single strand of twisted horsehair. Victor holds them with one finger at the point at which the reins would fit behind the saddle horn. The saddle is double rigged and has a fork with little swell and a large horn for dally roping. The stirrups are two-and-a-half inches wide and covered with leather. If Victor carried a lariat, it would be either rawhide or nylon, likely thirty to forty feet in length. The arched neck and conformation of the horse indicate a *caballo fino*, a horse of fine breeding and training. In the background is some of the stabling facility for the rancho. *Victor Amezquita photo.*

The Vaquero

JERALD UNDERWOOD

THE VAQUERO WAS—and is—a man on horseback who works cattle, a "cow worker," the word appropriately derived from the Spanish word *vaca*, meaning cow. Behind both the cowboy and the buckaroo, in the shadows of history, stands the vaquero, a descendant of the Old World horse culture. A vaquero is not to be confused with the Mexican *charro*, a performer who participates in the *charreada*, or Mexican rodeo, nor is he a *caballero*, a *gentleman* on horseback. He is a *paisano*, or country man, a tough, working man, not a genteel sort of fellow.

In the United States there are black vaqueros, white vaqueros, red vaqueros, mestizo or Mexican vaqueros, and some who defy description. J. Frank Dobie, in his classic book *The Longhorns*, describes vaquero Henry Beckwith as passing "for a Negro, but mixed in him were strains of Indian, Mexican, and white blood" (p. 324).

For most people, the vaquero is the forgotten man of history. Texas writer and artist Tom Lea, in his magnificent novel *The Hands of Cantú*, says of vaquero Joaquín Ripalda:

> Gazing at the cow brutes in our charge, he was fond of using a country word, *vaquero*, to describe our work. He used it with pride, like a badge, describing himself. "I am *vaquero*," he would say, as if it explained all, "Not *caballero*, God knows it. . . ." He would glance mildly at me. . . . "but *vaquero. Vaquero* of the North, where the cows grow." (p. 58)

This kind of life is a tradition in many families. Bill Wittliff, whose revealing photographs capture the vaquero's spirit, questioned one whose grandfather and father also were vaqueros. Finally the vaquero answers, "Vaqueros siempre . . . desde el comienzo" or "Vaqueros always . . . since the beginning" (p. i).

Most people today would consider the early-day vaqueros brutal, but a person should be judged in the context of his times, not by modern-day standards. Anyone who has faced an angry stallion charging with his mouth open to bite, ears laid back against his head, or faced the charge of an enraged bull will understand. The vaquero lived in a harsh, brutal environment; he had to be tough to survive.

The unique skills, gear, tack, and character of the vaquero developed on the northern frontier of Mexico, its borderlands. And the tradition is still alive in areas of Texas, New Mexico, Arizona, and California, the states on which this study focuses. These states make up a large region, but they possess similar flora, fauna, and geography. Working cattle and living in that region demanded that the vaquero develop special skills in order to thrive, and he did so. This development caused the cattle herding "Man of the North" to differ from the farmers of southern Mexico. The vaquero of the North bore many similarities to other American mounted herdsmen—the "Man of the West" (the cowboy) and the "Man of the Northwest" (the buckaroo). There are many interesting parallels, but also many differences.

The vaquero tradition has a long history, and its beginnings can first be seen in Morocco, in North Africa, where the Moors established a culture in which the horse played a pivotal role. The seeds of Moorish horsemanship can be seen in the early days of the Islamic religion. Mohammed, born in Arabia in the sixth century, established as a part of his religious practice taking the faith to nonbelievers by any means possible, even by the "Jihad," or holy war, in which armies of men on horseback proved to be overwhelming. In 642 the Arabs had conquered Egypt and were on their way into North Africa, where they spread their influence among the fierce desert tribes there, notably the Berbers on the northern edge of the Sahara Desert. The Berbers, an ancient tribe of North Africa, were and still are farmers and herdsmen who raise dates, grain, and olives and herd sheep and goats. In the summer they drive their herds to high mountain pastures, then bring the animals down before the winter snow flies. The Berbers are an unusual people in that they are masters of both mountains and deserts. For centuries Berber camel men have guided caravans through the vast wastes of the Sahara Desert.

Berber men are sometime called "The Blue Men of the Desert" because they wear blue robes of cotton cloth. These robes are colored with a blue dye that rubs off on skin and beard, giving the men a bluish appearance. In the Berber culture exists a custom that is the opposite of one well known among the Arabs: the men keep their faces veiled; the women do not.

In an age-old story, repeated many times down through the ages, a warrior tribe, superior in some way, overpowers other people. In the middle of the seventh century, this pattern occurred when Arab horsemen swept out of the east and invaded the land of the Berbers in North Africa. The Arabs were tall, bearded, and hawk-nosed. Ferocious fighters, they carried great, sharp swords and shouted the name of their god, Allah, as they fought. They were fired with religious zeal and rode swift, tough horses of the desert that could turn quickly on a fast run and carry their masters all day without tiring.

The Berbers were not easily defeated. They deserved their reputation for being good fighters who were accustomed to privation and danger. In fact, the Berber word *ribat* means "one who pickets his horse on a hostile frontier." They were, however, no match for the Arabs. The religious zeal of the Arabs, which was close to fanaticism, and their expert methods of fighting on horseback allowed them to overcome the Berbers. After the battles had ended, the two cultures merged. The Arabs and Berbers intermarried, and many Berbers were converted to the Moslem religion to solidify this culture.

By 700 the name Moors was used to describe those mixed Arabs and Berbers of the Moslem faith in the western part of North Africa. They were called Moors, from the Latin *mauri*, because they came from the Roman province named Mauritania. Although most sources explain that Moors are a mixture of Arab and Berber blood, the word Moor came to be used to describe Black Africans who came to Spain and to North America: Shakespeare's "Noble Moor," Othello, was a black man, as was the famous Moor of North America, Estevan, sometimes called Estevanico, the companion of Cabeza de Vaca in his wanderings across the southwestern part of the present-day United States (1528–1536).

In 711 the Moors of North Africa conquered Spain and brought their horseback culture with them. Because they were in Spain for almost eight hundred years, the Moors had a strong impact on the country in many ways. Perhaps the best-known influence was in architecture, in the graceful Moorish building styles and beautiful fountains that still exist in Spain today because of the Moorish occupation. Nevertheless, the Arabian and Berber horse culture had the greatest impact there and later in the New World.

The Moors rode "la jineta," like a modern-day jockey with their knees pulled up high because of their short stirrups. In battle the Spanish knight, on the other hand, rode "la brida," with the legs straight, encased in the saddle, with armor on himself and his horse. To carry all this weight, the horse had to be a draft-type animal. To the Spanish, the best fighter in battle was a knight on his horse looking very much like a fortress. There was a major problem with this—the swift desert-bred horses of the Moors could outmaneuver the big draft horses of the Spanish, and the slow-moving Spanish were vulnerable. The Moors rode around the Spanish like circus riders and speared their enemies in vulnerable spots at will. Once the knight in his heavy armor was toppled from his draft horse, he was helpless on the ground. The Spanish learned a great deal from these defeats in battle. They adopted some of the Moorish methods and even improved upon them.

In addition to techniques for fighting on horseback, the Moors introduced to Spain techniques used by men on horseback hunting wild animals. Great contests were held in which men on horseback fought wild bulls. These remained a part of Spanish life.

By the mid-1400s, change in the long Moorish influence in Spain was on its way. In 1469 Spain was unified by the marriage of Queen Isabella of Castile and King Ferdinand of Aragon. Before this marriage, Spain had been a series of independent states, with Castile and Aragon the largest and most powerful. In 1469 all of the independent kingdoms of the Iberian peninsula except the kingdom of Portugal came under the rule of Isabella and Ferdinand. The two monarchs ruled together and established Catholicism as the state religion of Spain in 1478. The infamous Spanish Inquisition purged all elements of Moslem religion from Spain.

The Spanish turned the tables on the Moors and began their own holy war. Spain developed the concept of the "Christian knight" in order to drive out the invaders. This new fighting man was to become one of the great glories of Spain, indeed one of the greatest warriors of history. He had a new type of horse now and a new style of riding. All of this the Spanish had learned from the Moors.

By 1492 the Spanish had driven all Moors from Spain and were looking for new fields to conquer. They turned to world exploration and conquest. Many of the Christian knights came to the newly discovered America as conquistadors. They brought their love of horses and their knowledge of Arab horsemanship with them, along with their horses and the breeding stock of cattle and other animals that would eventually provide the stock for ranching in the newly discovered land. The North American stage was being prepared for the vaquero, who would establish a culture built upon the care of these cattle.

The vaquero is a creature of frontier existence—first in North Africa, next in Spain, then in North America. The Arab or Berber who staked his horse on a hostile frontier had much in common with the vaquero, who also staked his horse on the hostile frontier of New Spain— both on the borderlands of northern Mexico and the Spanish Borderlands of the United States. These were wild, dangerous, and unsettled places, wide-open country peopled with hostile Indians and with wild animals on every hand.

The Spanish invaders of Mexico gave rise to the vaquero tradition on this continent. No one is more responsible for the horse culture in America than the conqueror of Mexico, Hernán Cortés, who was an expert rider and fighter on horseback. Cortés and many of his men were from Extremadura in Spain, where they had ridden the wide-open spaces and developed a special relationship with their horses. Cortés thought of himself as a caballero, a gentleman on horseback. He also considered himself a Christian knight who would seize the New World for God and King. Most historians, when writing about the motivations of the Spanish conquistadors, mention the three G's—God, Glory, and Gold. All were important to Cortés, but glory was the most important to him. The desire for fame dominated his life. Cortés once said he did not come to the New World to work with his hands as a common laborer. He had a clear vision in his head of what he wanted: to conquer native Americans, to dominate them and govern them. Cortés also wanted to get rich along the way.

Cortés was a member of the *hidalgo* class of nobility, low on the social and economic scale. With nothing to gain by remaining in Spain, he struck out boldly for the New World to find his fortune. Cortés first landed in Cuba and became a sugar grower for a time; later the governor of Cuba selected him to lead an expedition to Mexico. The governor did not trust Cortés completely, and at the last minute changed his mind about the leader of the expedition. Learning of this development in advance, Cortés left Cuba with his men, one jump ahead of the governor's forces, to launch his planned expedition into Mexico.

Cortés landed his cavalry on the eastern shore of Mexico in 1519. He had with him the famous sixteen horses of the conquest. One of the mares had a colt on board the ship, so some historians say there were seventeen horses. This exact number is unimportant. The conquistadors remarked, "For, after God, we owed the victory to the horses" (R. Graham, p. 11).

Graham also comments on the relationship of the Spaniard with his horse: "If the conquistadores (after God) owed their conquest to their horses, there was an intimate companionship between them that is well nigh impossible to understand today." He goes on to say that it was "a companionship and pride at the same time, such as a man might feel for a younger brother who has accompanied him in some adventure" (p. 12).

In the diary of Bernal Díaz Castillo, a member of the Cortés expedition, is confirmation of the fact that the conquistadors and their horses shared a common bond: the Spaniards lived with their horses, they endured together the heat, the cold, and other aspects of the harsh life of the frontier. Díaz Castillo writes in his diary:

We slept in our armour and sandals with our weapons close beside us. The horses stood saddled and bridled all day, and everything was so fully prepared that at a call to arms we were already at our posts and waiting (p. 280).

The native Americans who first met Cortés as he entered Mexico had never seen a horse. The Aztecs who first saw a mounted Spaniard thought horse and man were one animal. When the Spaniard dismounted, it was magic; the animal came apart, they thought. The horse proved not only an important physical instrument of war but also a psychological weapon arousing great fear among native Americans.

To the development of ranching, this introduction of the horse was crucial. The Spanish inadvertently brought one of the major parts of the coming ranching industry to North America in their horses of the conquest.

The Spanish also brought the second ingredient—cattle. The first came to North America in 1521, when Gregorio de Villalobos landed on the coast of Mexico. He brought them from Santo Domingo in the West Indies, where Christopher Columbus had first introduced cattle on his second voyage to the New World in 1493. Cattle were essential to the survival of the Spaniards in Mexico; the animals furnished meat, leather, and tallow. The cattle that became the Longhorn breed in the United States were actually crossbred from three original breeds—the Barrenda, a spotted bovine with white body and black patches on neck and ears; the Retinto, a large bovine characterized by a red to tan color; and the Ganado Prieto, the black cattle that produce the fierce bulls made famous in the fighting ring.

Horses and cattle needed keepers—commoners to take care of the stock, work to which Cortés and the other conquistadors never stooped. The conquistadors were soldiers first and then governors, landowners, and ranchers. Spanish gentlemen did not take care of horses and cattle; they had servants or slaves who did that. These servants and slaves became the vaqueros.

It is probable that the first vaquero in North America was a Moorish slave belonging to Cortés. He has been called a *Morisco* or half-Moor, a black slave. Many of these half-Moors, slaves to the Spanish, were brought to North America to take care of cattle and were the first true vaqueros in North America. Only black slaves were vaqueros at first because the Spaniards did not want native Americans to learn to ride horses. In fact, Spanish law decreed that an Indian who rode a horse would be put to death. This was done for an obvious reason: to the Spanish the horse was an instrument of war and should be kept from the Indians. The Indian was a captive of the Spanish, and the horse was a means of escape. If the Indian mastered the horse, he would in battle be equal to the Spaniards. The Spanish foresaw the threat that later developed with the mounted Plains tribes.

Once the native Americans in southern Mexico had been conquered, the conquistadors established great estates and began raising cattle and horses. Since the herds increased rapidly, the Spanish found it necessary to ignore or rescind the law prohibiting Indians from riding horses. The first change in the law allowed an Indian to ride a horse but not with a saddle. A saddle was expensive, but more important to the Spanish, the saddle was a mark of a caballero, or gentleman. In this arrangement, the Spaniards unwittingly made the Indian an excellent rider. The best way to learn to ride well and get the feel of a horse is to ride bareback. At a later date, Indian vaqueros, though still at the bottom of the social scale, were allowed to use saddles because of the necessity of roping cattle with the *lazos.*

On the plains of Querétaro outside of Mexico City, cattle multiplied by the thousands. Here, more than any other place in Mexico, the cattle culture was born. Black, Indian, mulatto, and mestizo horsemen began to work large herds using methods similar to those used in Spain.

Imagine, if you will, a situation in which a Spanish conquistador takes as his wife an Indian woman. To this couple is born a little boy. He rides on a horse in a cradle strapped to his mother's back. Later he rides in front of her, clinging to the horse's mane with his little hands. His mother holds him to keep him from falling off. This little boy absorbs the feel and smell of the horse. As he grows larger, the boy rides with his father and later gets his own horse. By the age of ten the boy becomes an accomplished rider. He is part of the horse; the horse is part of him. The boy is neither Spanish nor Indian. He is a member of a new bronze race: he is Mexican. This young man can ride as no one in North America has ever ridden before; he is the true centaur of the New World.

Of the four great migratory streams that led to the settlement of the United States—the French in Canada who moved southward, the English who came directly to the East coast, the Spanish who came directly into Florida, and the Spaniards who conquered New Spain (Mexico)—only the last group is of special importance in the development of the vaquero tradition.

From 1540 to 1776 the Spanish launched several great expeditions to the far northern frontier of Mexico. Historians of the Spanish Borderlands use the expressions *near north* and *far north* to describe these frontiers. Some of these Spanish expeditions, or *entradas*, would result in settlement; some would not.

The first major expedition to the far northern frontier of Mexico was that led by Francisco de Coronado from Compostela, near the eastern shore of Mexico. Coronado had with him three hundred armed soldiers and a larger group of native Americans, some of whom herded the cattle taken along for food only. Coronado returned to Mexico two years later (1542) and was considered a failure by Spanish authorities because he had not found gold. Sandoz notes, however, that Coronado had done something tremendously important: he had taken the first cattle and horses to present-day Arizona, New Mexico, and Texas. A number of his cattle escaped into the brush, and others were run off by Indians. These cattle multiplied rapidly, and twenty-five years later these wild herds numbered in the thousands on the far northern frontier of Mexico (p.9).

The next important expedition by the Spanish was in 1596 and resulted in the founding of the permanent settlement of Santa Fe. This *entrada* was led by Juan de Oñate and began near Parral, Mexico, in southern Chihuahua. Oñate recruited colonists from Zacatecas and Santa Barbara and started north with about 130 armed men and their families. The expedition had more than 1,200 horses and mules and 6,000 other animals, including cattle, sheep, and hogs. Vaqueros herded and watched over these large herds of livestock. With so many animals, the soldier-settlers also had to take their turns herding livestock.

The Spanish had gone north in a series of small leaps from Mexico City. One result was the discovery of silver mines at Zacatecas (in 1548), at Guanajuato, and at San Luis Potosí. To settle Santa Fe, the Spanish made a *giant* leap of eight hundred miles to the north. Juan de Oñate established a settlement on the east side of the Rio Grande about twenty miles north of present-day Santa Fe. The Spanish gave the settlement a curious name, which reveals much about the Spanish culture of that time. They called the little town San Juan de los Caballeros, which means in English "The Saintly Place of the Gentlemen on Horseback." In those days, a horseman and a gentleman were the same thing in Spanish culture. There is an old Spanish legend that tells of a country woman who sees a caballero behaving badly. No doubt he had had too much to drink. The country woman scolds him saying, "Why are you acting this way? You are a horseman."

In the fall of 1598, the first Spanish settlement in New Mexico was moved to a new site named San Gabriel, on the west side of the Rio Grande. The Spanish settlers occupied adobe apartments that had been built by native Americans. Because these Indians lived in houses in town, the Spanish called them *pueblos*, the Spanish word for *town* or *village* that can also indicate the common people.

In 1610 the governor of New Mexico, Pedro de Peralta, moved the settlers of San Gabriel twenty miles to the south and founded present-day Santa Fe. The Indians revolted in 1680, but the Spanish reclaimed the settlement in 1694 after battles with the Indians. Santa Fe became not only a main center of trade for the Southwest but the most important place where Indians of the plains could obtain horses.

Another exploration of the northern frontier of Mexico began at Guaymas, near the eastern coast of Mexico. In 1687 Padre Eusebio Kino, a Jesuit priest, led an expedition to present-day Arizona and California. His work in the decade to come would be very significant to the development of the vaquero.

The next expedition to the far northern frontier of Mexico began at Loreto, in Baja, California. In 1769 two parties of Spanish soldiers marched north and entered present-day California. One group was led by Fernando de Rivera y Moncada, commander of the fort at Loreto. This military party was followed by a second group, led by Gaspar de Portolá and a priest, Junipero Serra. Both parties reached present-day San Diego, and later Portolá marched to the north as far as present-day San Francisco Bay. This party had horses and pack mules; unfortunately they had no cattle with them and almost starved.

Two significant Spanish expeditions to Texas occurred in 1689 and 1690. In 1689 the Spanish captain Alonso de León was ordered to East Texas because the French had established a fort there. The French had named this place Fort St. Louis, and the Spanish saw this as a major threat to their claim on Texas. De León found Fort St. Louis decimated by disease and Indian uprisings and La Salle, the founder of Fort St. Louis, killed by his own men. De León visited with local Indians, who invited the Spanish to return later to provide religious instruction. In 1690 De León returned with a major force and established the mission San Francisco de los Tejas in East Texas. After two years, the mission suffered a major disease epidemic and failed as a permanent settlement. Other missions established near present-day San Antonio survived to become centers of the ranching industry.

The 1774 expedition to the far northern frontier of New Spain

(Mexico) was led by Juan de Anza. This party was launched from Tubac, Arizona, and had 165 head of horses for transportation and 65 head of cattle for food. Juan de Anza entered present-day California, traveled as far as Monterey, and then returned to Tubac.

As the Spanish moved into the frontier north of Mexico City, they encountered a kind of Indian quite different in temperament and aggressiveness from those in Central America. The Chichimeca, Tarahumara, and Yaqui tribes proved adept at war and attacked the invaders with a fury that stymied the Spanish at first. These tribes were so hostile that the Spanish called them *Indios bárbaros*, unpacified Indians. These confrontations only foreshadowed the problems that would come later from the Apaches and Comanches.

At first the Spanish tried their previously successful tactics of subduing these tribes with military force. This strategy failed because the Spanish had too few soldiers to defeat the large numbers of attacking warriors and control the vast stretches of arid, mountainous land. Clearly a new approach was needed.

The new strategy was to establish missions to try to convert the Indians to Catholicism. Each location had a presidio or fort with a contingent of soldiers to defend it and to protect the religious workers living at the mission. The padres, or priests—Jesuits, Franciscans, or Dominicans—were more successful than the soldiers had been at establishing a Spanish presence, because the religious men attracted members of several tribes to the Catholic rites. The pattern proved fruitful, especially in present-day Arizona, California, New Mexico, and Texas.

Many of these priests died unsung heroes in this distant land and left their marks on the culture established in the North American Southwest. The most outstanding of these men was Padre Eusebio Francisco Kino, who did most of his work in present-day Arizona, which the Spanish called Pimería Alta, the upper land of the Pima Indians. In 1687 Kino establish Mission Dolores, his first mission and the headquarters for his work in the area. He eventually established a total of twenty-nine missions. The most famous of these was San Xavier del Bac, founded in 1700 about nine miles southwest of present-day Tucson. Part of the founding included a trail drive of seven hundred cattle from Dolores to San Xavier del Bac. The mission, known as the White Dove of the Desert, is now restored.

Kino and his followers brought cattle, horses, mules, sheep, and goats to Mission Dolores, and, as their numbers increased, the settlers moved stock to the other missions to form herds there. Kino trained mission Indians to be vaqueros to care for all kinds of livestock. These vaqueros drove the new herds to each mission as it was founded. Bolton, in *Padre on Horseback*, described Kino in this way: "Eusebio Francisco Kino was the most picturesque missionary pioneer of all North America —explorer, astronomer, cartographer, mission builder, ranchman, cattle king, and defender of the frontier" (p.49). Kino was true to his priestly vows; no hint of improper behavior marred his remarkable life. He died in 1711, a few hours after saying his last mass. Without Kino's leadership, the missions of Arizona, and the cattle industry there, declined.

Two efforts placed a Spanish influence in California. In 1769 the Spanish ship *San Carlos* landed with several head of cattle. In *The Longhorns* J. Frank Dobie refers to this ship as the "Mayflower of the West" (p. 5) because the colonists aboard were destined to found towns.

Also in 1769 a land party led by Gaspar de Portolá entered California from Loreto (Lower California). A very important person was in this party—the Franciscan priest Fray Junipero Serra, the leader in founding a chain of missions above San Diego. All of these had livestock, including cattle. Serra and his fellow priests trained vaqueros to care for the animals. By 1820 hundreds of Indian vaqueros served Serra's efforts, and herds of up to 15,000 head of livestock around each mission were common. Serra founded nine California missions and baptized more than 6,000 converts during his work in California.

New Mexico proved a challenge to the system. The Spanish founded missions there, but the cattle industry did not prosper at first. Ramirez notes that the Pueblo Indian Revolt of 1680 was a serious blow to the efforts to raise livestock because the rebel Indians ran off much of the stock (p. 3). Drought, epidemics, and raids by Apaches took their toll on the stock as well. When the Spanish regained control of the area many years later, they reintroduced cattle, but sheep seemed much better adapted to the region. Not until after the American Civil War in the 1860s did the livestock business thrive in New Mexico.

Texas, on the other hand, was explored early but settled late. Soldiers and missionaries brought the first European cattle into Texas in the 1690s and early 1700s. The first mission to have cattle was San Francisco de los Tejas, established by Alonso de León between the Sabine and Neches rivers. The Spanish there, however, would suffer the same fate as the French at Fort St. Louis; within two years the effort failed because of disease.

A number of other successful and important Texas missions were established along the San Antonio River, and all had cattle. Mission

San Antonio de Valero—which later gained fame as the Alamo—was founded in 1718 and eventually had 1,200 cattle, 2,300 sheep and goats, and 300 horses. The leading mission in the production of cattle was Espíritu Santo at La Bahía, located at present-day Goliad. According to Myres, in 1758 the mission at La Bahía had 3,000 head of cattle; by 1768 the number had increased to 16,000 head (pp. 12–13). Eventually, all of the missions in Texas had large herds of cattle and became centers for ranching. The primary purpose of a mission was religious conversion of the natives, but these settlements were also political and economic units. Only the missions had the free labor, the organization, and the political support to succeed in the ranching industry in early Texas.

By the late 1790s another phase loomed in the pattern of development. The missions were secularized and the lands distributed to important people. The buildings were turned over to the military, and the mission as an institution in the ranching business passed away. The mission-presidio complex as a means of settling the country was replaced by the *encomienda* system, one similar to the feudal system in Medieval Europe. The Spanish crown intended the *encomienda* to be a "people" system—a grant of land, along with the land's native inhabitants, to a person important to the king. Under this system conquistadors were made responsible for the welfare of their Indian charges. The king wanted these Indians to be brought into the Catholic faith and all good things done to civilize them. The Indians could be used as free labor, but they were not to be mistreated. The Spanish priests were an important part of the plan: they were the teachers of trades and ministers of the gospel. Even the most devout priests did not question the Spanish right to dominate the Indians; the priests believed that Spanish civilization was superior, and they believed in saving lost souls.

The plan was well intentioned, but reality fell far short of the dream. The *encomienda* system became something the Spanish crown did not want: a land-people system in which the Indians became slaves and in most cases were viciously mistreated. Many Spanish priests vigorously protested this mistreatment. The first bishop of Mexico, Juan de Zumarraga, preached openly against the abuse of Indians and sent secret messages to the Spanish king informing him of these wrongs. Bishop Zumarraga's ancestry was Basque, a people of Northern Spain who had a long tradition of not fearing or being dominated by anyone. His life was threatened many times by wealthy landowners, but he was never intimidated.

Because of the abuses and because of men like Zumarraga, the *en-*

comienda system in Mexico was abolished officially in 1720. Part of the reason was that in addition to the government's concern about the abuse of the Indians under the old system, officials knew that the Indians on the northern frontier were more hostile toward the Spanish, less easily forced into a docile slavery. The new system was that of the *hacienda*. In this system, the king awarded large land grants to people who had served his interests well. These large estates were generally thousands, sometimes millions, of acres. The peonage system provided workers. Under Spanish law these workers, the peons, had to be paid, but owners found a way to circumvent that rule: they kept the workers in debt by issuing food and other needed items on credit and paying low wages. Peons were always in debt and had no way to escape their plight. If they fled the estate seeking freedom, Spanish law allowed them to be forcibly returned because of their debt.

A development that changed the nature of ranching in Mexico was Mexican independence from Spain in 1821. The Mexican government continued to emphasize the raising of livestock, even to expand it. Some of the Spanish grants were continued by some of the families, but others were offered to people friendly to the Mexican cause.

The frontier promised a fruitful return, but not from the farming that flourished in the humid south. The frontier was, instead, almost ideally suited for raising livestock. The Spanish established estates with huge herds of cattle and large numbers of vaqueros. A very large estate was called a *latifundio,* a term that denoted several haciendas owned by the same family. The largest of these was founded by a Catholic priest, Father José Miguel Sánchez Navarro, in 1765. At that time the province of Coahuila in northern Mexico extended north of the Rio Grande as far as the Medina River in what is today Central Texas. The headquarters of this ranch was in Monclova, Mexico, in the state of Coahuila, and its holdings extended into Texas. According to Charles H. Harris III in his *A Mexican Family Empire,* the Navarro family *latifundio* was Mexico's largest, about the size of Portugal (pp. 1–11).

One of the other large haciendas established in northern Mexico included that of Luis Terrazas. During the French occupation of Mexico from 1864 to 1867, Terrazas supported the forces of Benito Juárez in their fight against the French. The Terrazas family controlled over six and a half million acres of land. The hold of this family was strong for many years, and in 1910 the haciendas of the Terrazas family branded 140,000 calves. According to Machado in his *The North Mexican Cattle Indus-*

try, this number marked the family as the largest single cattle owners in North America.

Some of these large ranches were not owned by Mexicans. One, San José de Bavicora in north-central Mexico about 175 miles south of Arizona, was founded in 1770 by Jesuit priests and was later owned by Americans. The original ranch failed after 1840 when the founders were killed by Apaches and the cattle stolen or run off. In 1882 Americans from Arizona came to the property and re-established the ranch. The new owners hired vaqueros to work the cattle and fight off the Apaches.

In the late 1880s Frederic Remington, the famous painter, visited the ranch and recorded his experiences in both written form and in paintings. In his views, recorded in *Frederic Remington's Own West,* he called this hacienda "an outpost of civilization" (p. 137). His vivid pictures show the clothing, equipment, and skills of the hacienda's vaqueros. In the early 1900s, William Randolph Hearst, wealthy American newspaper magnate, purchased the operation, consisting at that time of 860,000 acres.

Ranching, as developed on the large estates of northern Mexico, evolved in large measure in response to the land on which the livestock grazed. The Aztecs had founded Mexico City on a mountain lake centuries before. North of the city two large mountain ranges jut toward the sky as they spread to the north. On the east stands the Sierra Madre Oriental and on the west the Sierra Madre Occidental. The higher elevations of the city descend to the *bajío,* or lowlands, to form a vast, arid plain between the two mountain ranges. The mountains allow few rain clouds to reach this inland area, and few streams flow out of the mountains to water the sparse vegetation. The major stream is the Conchos River, which meets the Rio Grande near present-day Presidio, Texas, and its counterpart in Mexico, Ojinaga. The Spanish called the area La Junta de los Ríos, the juncture of the rivers. To the southeast along the Conchos River is a great plain called Llano de los Caballos Mesteños, the Plain of the Wild Horses.

On these vast northern plains, cattle multiplied rapidly after being introduced by the Spanish. Here the character of the vaquero was developed as the men worked the cattle in the open country. This new method of working cattle in North America spread to the northern frontier, spurred by the discovery of rich mines of silver at Guanajuato, San Luis de Potosí, and, especially, Zacatecas, which proved to be the richest in Mexico. The mining operations required large amounts of meat to feed

The backbone of the early cattle business in North America, the Longhorn, seen here in the dense brasada of South Texas. *King Ranch Archive photo.*

the workers, leather bags to hold the silver ore, and tallow for candles to light the mines. These were the main products of the herds on the haciendas.

In the 1700s the most energetic, most adventurous, and most courageous of the people of Mexico moved to the far northern frontier and established settlements on the south bank of the Rio Grande (called the Río Bravo in Mexico). The leader of this migration was José de Escandón, sometimes called the "Colonizer of the Lower Rio Grande." For the more than twenty settlements he established, Escandón recruited inhabitants from the ranks of veteran ranchers and vaqueros in central and southern Mexico. In the 1850s the people of one of these settlements followed Captain Richard King across the Rio Grande to Santa Gertrudis Creek and became the *Kineños*, the people of the King, the first vaqueros of the King Ranch in South Texas.

Vaquero on the King Ranch in South Texas. Note the brush jacket and the long chaps. The horse wears a bridle with bits as well as a hackamore. The reins for the hackamore are still around the horse's neck; the single looped rein, made of twisted horsehair and attached to the bits with slobber chains, hangs from the bits. The short tapaderos are typical of South Texas and northern Mexico. *King Ranch Archive photo.*

Unidentified King Ranch vaquero. Note the horsehair bridle rein on the horse on the left. The horse on the right is being held in place by the rein looped behind the saddle horn. *King Ranch Archive photo.*

On the King Ranch and the ranches of northern Mexico, the vaquero flourished. The vast space of the Borderlands has a dramatic effect upon people, and to ride a spirited horse in a wide-open country adds another dimension to the soul. "Room, room to turn round in, to breathe and be free / To grow to be a giant, to sail as to sea," (p.247) says the poem "Kit Carson's Ride" by Joaquin Miller in an appropriate description of this concept. This space and the horse culture allowed men the opportunity to achieve the "Centaur Wish," to be one with the horse, to live the life of the gods. True, the vaquero's life was very hard, and he was generally very poor, but when he was in the saddle with the sun on his back and the wind in his face, he was free.

The vaquero rode his horse great distances, working cattle but also defending the hacienda against hostile Indians. In this struggle, the vaquero had only his lance, knife, and rope, since guns were expensive on the frontier. It was common for a vaquero to use *la riata* (the rawhide rope) as a weapon. It took great courage for a man to ride down an Apache warrior, rope him around the neck, and drag him to death. Because of this and other dangerous feats, the vaquero became a folk hero on the frontier of northern Mexico. Noyes notes that the Indians learned the use of the rope from captured vaqueros (p. xxv). The Mexican cowhand could ride down any wild cow and rope it; he could catch, ride, and break wild mustangs; he could dance all night; he was a ladies' man, and a fighter who scorned danger. He had a determined look in his eyes—one that looked far off to the horizon. Few people have looked more at home on a horse than a vaquero. He rode with his hands feather-light on the reins, and sat down in the saddle, whereas the cowboy tended to stand up in his stirrups. The vaquero rode in a kind of balance that is the mark of a true horseman.

Not only did the vaquero develop a style of riding and roping that fit his land, his clothing was suited to the geography of northern

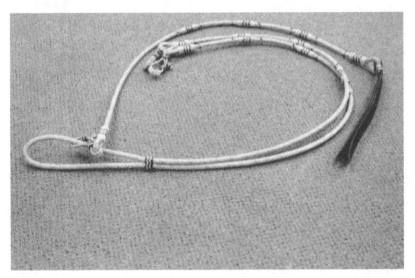

A finely made set of braided rawhide vaquero reins from southern Mexico. These differ from similar reins used by the buckaroo in that the reins are actually the one-looped rein preferred by the vaquero, not the two separate reins preferred by the buckaroo. The mecate is held in place by being attached to the rein. The small honda near the rider's end of the rein will slip to allow the rider to adjust the length of the rein to fit over the saddle horn and hold the horse in place. *Lawrence Clayton photo.*

A typical group of South Texas vaqueros at one of the King Ranch camp houses. *King Ranch Archive photo.*

Mexico and the southwestern United States. The vaquero's clothing not only protected him from the elements he faced daily but also gave him a unique appearance. In the hot climate in which he worked, he had to protect his head. He adopted the *sombrero,* a hat with a "low flat crown and straight brim . . . constructed of leather, cheap felt, or woven palm fiber" (Dary, p. 13). Because of the poverty of the vaquero, these hats rarely if ever sported the ornament found on the hats of wealthy Spaniards.

Vaqueros' shirts were usually made of cotton or wool, depending upon the climate in which the vaquero lived and the season. Wool was readily available because of sheep brought to the region from Spain, and cotton had long been cultivated in the area. Leather was no doubt used as part of the wardrobe as well, since a ready supply was available. Eventually, a bolero-style jacket was adopted, along with pants that laced up the sides and fit tightly round the vaquero's thighs and waist. Often at the waist the vaquero wore a sash of red or green silk or cotton (Rollins, p. 109). Leather leggings called *botas* covered the lower part of the legs. The high-heeled boots, which enabled later herdsmen to keep their feet securely in the stirrup, were not available to the early vaqueros. These

A brush country chuck wagon with a six-mule hitch to pull the wagon in deep sand. *King Ranch Archive photo.*

A chuck wagon at mealtime in the brasada. *King Ranch Archive photo.*

A vaquero washing up for mealtime. Note details of the brush jacket. The water barrel is lashed to the rear of a pickup with a lariat. *King Ranch Archive photo.*

early herders wore crude sandals; only the rich could afford the boots of supple leather. Since the climate was warm most of the year, protective footwear was not required. Dary notes that those who could afford to do so strapped large-roweled Spanish spurs, much like those the conquistadors wore, to whatever footwear was available (p. 14). These gave the rider better control of the horse. But even these were luxuries that many of the poor vaqueros could not afford.

Because the vaquero spent much of his time away from other people, he built temporary shelters. The huts at these cow camps usually consisted of crudely constructed lean-tos built near sources of water and wood. The men erected two forked poles in the ground and laid another pole across the forks to form a ridge pole. Other poles were then leaned against the ridge pole with the lower ends resting on the ground. Cattle hides, straw, or shingles were laid on the sloping poles, thereby complet-

Camp bread cooked over a mesquite fire. *Sonja Irwin Clayton photo.*

Two King Ranch vaqueros in a saddle shed. Note the tapaderos, hats, and chaps. *King Ranch Archive photo.*

A hard-riding vaquero separating a calf from the herd. *King Ranch Archive photo.*

A group of vaqueros in Mexico with cattle roped by the head and heels in a large stone corral. *Texas State Library and Archives Commission photo.*

An old Mexican sombrero. *Lawrence Clayton photo.*

ing the shelter, the back of which faced the prevailing wind. Straw or grass was sometimes spread on the ground to form a soft floor, but, as often as not, the bare earth sufficed. At the front of this crude shelter, the vaqueros built fires and cooked simple meals, principally cornmeal mush and small game.

In this primitive existence, the vaquero had no access to manufactured items and used his spare time and limited resources to fashion his gear. One of his most important "tools" was his rawhide riata, the rope the vaquero made with his own hands from dried cowhides. It was, therefore, more than a rope; it was an extension of his own arm. He "reached out" and snared an animal with incredible skill and accuracy. To a vaquero, to rope something was as natural as breathing. Malcolm D. McLean wrote about catching wild mustangs in early-day Texas and recorded the fact that many were caught with the "lazo" or lariat. McLean quoted an article from the *Arkansas Gazette* of 1839 which said that the "skill of the Mexican in the use of this instrument exceeds belief. He will dart like a falcon into the midst of a drove of mustangs, single out one that pleases his fancy, and at the distance of twenty or thirty paces, throw the lariat with unerring certainty" (pp. 75–76).

The roping skills of the vaquero are legendary and come from generations of skilled vaqueros passing their abilities on to their offspring.

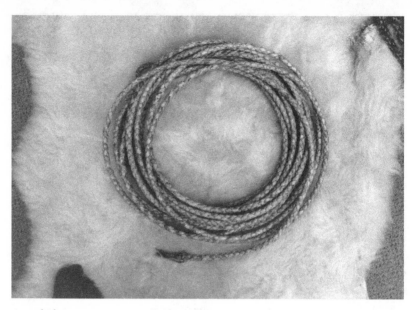

A rawhide riata. *Lawrence Clayton photo.*

Most Indians of northern Mexico would "snare" small game such as rabbits with short ropes made from bark or plants. Combine this native ability to "snare" with superb Spanish horsemanship, and one can see the results.

Many ropers can rope well from the ground (the author included) but find it very difficult to rope on horseback. Roping from the back of a horse requires the rider to perform two major skills at the same time: first, control a powerful, plunging animal, and second, throw a rope accurately. The Mexican had the innate skills to rope expertly from horseback. The environmental conditions to stimulate the development of these skills were present on the northern frontier of Mexico: a vast area, numerous cattle, no fences, and the need to catch and hold cattle. In this vast openness, the vaquero developed the tradition of *lariata larga*, the very long rope (Ramirez, p. 96).

German pioneer Ferdinand Roemer traveled through Texas between 1845 and 1847, observing and recording life on the frontier. A trained geologist who has been called the "father of Texas geology," he observed with a scientist's eye. When he visited Torrey's trading post near the Brazos River, he saw two Mexican boys, ages seven and nine (he called them "lads"), roping wild mules in a corral. These young boys had been captured by the Comanche Indians but had been ransomed. Roemer refers to their "dexterity" in roping mules as "excelling even adult Americans who tried." Roemer states further, "Among the Mexicans the practice in the use of the lariat, which in a great measure serves both as a tool and a weapon, begins in the earliest youth, and this accounts for the unbelievable dexterity they display."

Roemer further quotes Kendall, who in his report on the ill-fated Texas Expedition to Santa Fe, New Mexico, said that he frequently saw Mexican boys lassoing chickens. "They were even able to lasso the particular leg desired" (p. 193).

The best ropes were made from the hides of cattle. These skins were allowed to dry and then cut into strings. The tools used in this process were primitive, often no more than a notched block of wood and a sharp knife. The vaqueros prepared the strings by stripping off the hair and winding the long strings into balls for ease in handling, for the plaiting required the crossing of the strings numerous times. When enough suitable strings were prepared, the vaquero plaited his rope of six strands of hide to fifty or sixty feet or more in length. When he had finished, the vaquero stretched the rope and rubbed it with raw beef liver or fat to give the proper combination of rigidity and flexibility. These ropes

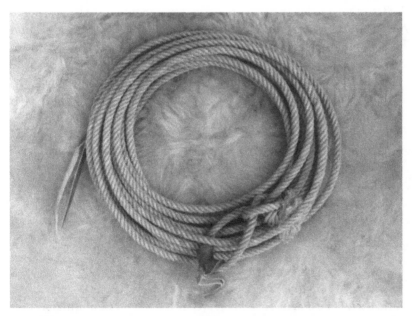

A lariat made of maguey fibers. *Lawrence Clayton photo.*

A lariat of lechuguilla fibers. Note the replaceable rawhide honda to save the expensive rope. *Sonja Irwin Clayton photo.*

had to be guarded from moisture, and when rain threatened, the vaquero wrapped the rope around his body beneath his shirt. At night, he kept it in his bedding in order to ensure that the rope did not get wet (Perkins interview).

Ropes were also made of native or natural fibers such as maguey, lechuguilla, and horsehair. Both the maguey and lechuguilla plants contain tough fibers that when separated from the plant and dried serve to make a fine lariat of sufficient stiffness to make an excellent lasso. The vaquero strips the fleshy part away and collects the fibers. He then separates them and lets them dry. Then he twists them together into ropes, usually combining three or four single strands to fashion a lariat. The loop, or honda, in the end of the lariat is typically fashioned from rawhide and attached to the lariat. In that way the honda can be replaced without damaging the rope. In using these ropes, the early vaquero developed the technique called *dar le vuelta,* wrapping the rope around the saddle horn, rather than tying it off in the fashion called "hard and fast." This Spanish phrase later served as the source for the anglicized form *dally.* The practice of dally roping originated in California, according to Mora (p. 56). In California the ropes were longer than those used in Texas. In Texas, the thirty-foot rope served well for the technique of tying hard and fast to the saddle horn. Hence, the buckaroo's long-standing practice of dallying while the Texas cowboys tied hard and fast, as Ramirez points out (p.96). By wrapping rather than tying the rope, the horseman can give slack to keep the strain from being excessive, thus prolonging the life of the valuable riata (variations in this practice are discussed later).

The men made ropes for other purposes from twisted horsehair. This kind of rope served as bridle reins and lead ropes, not as rope for catching livestock. To make these ropes, the vaquero used a twisting device. He fashioned this tool, originally, from the shoulder bone of a steer, with one of the straight leg bones as a pivot. He twisted the hair collected from the horses' manes or tails by inserting the straight bone through a hole made in top of the shoulder blade. The hair was attached to the top of the blade, and the twirling device then twisted the horse-hair much in the fashion of a spinning wheel. Later, metal rods bent into cranks served the same purpose. The vaquero had to make the piece twice as long as the final product needed to be. Once the twisting was

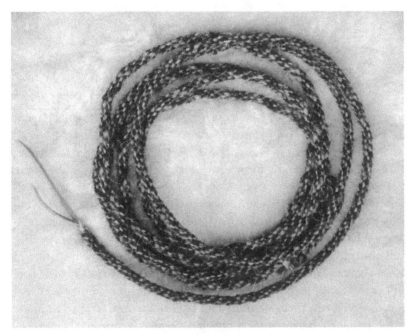

A horsehair rope. *Lawrence Clayton photo.*

A rawhide riata in the groove made to accommodate it at the base of the saddle horn. *Lawrence Clayton photo.*

complete, the rope was doubled over and allowed to twist against itself, thus ensuring that it would not unravel.

Since the vaquero was adept at herding and roping from horseback, the horse naturally forms the basis of the vaquero culture. Some of the best horses came from Randado, a ranch located in the brush country about seventy-five miles southeast of Laredo. It was at one time the greatest horse ranch in Texas. These horses were descendants of the original horses brought by the conquistadors in 1519. They were mostly duns and grullas with black manes and tails and a black stripe running down their backs. Many of them had black zebra stripes on their legs and a black stripe across their shoulders. They were incredibly tough. Vaqueros would ride them a hundred miles without unsaddling. The spirit of the vaqueros' horses mirrors the qualities of their masters' natures—or was it learned, one wonders, the other way?

The gear with which the vaquero controlled his horse was also made from available materials, especially rawhide and twisted horsehair. This was particularly true of horsehair reins for bridles and halters. Rawhide was often used for the head stalls; braided rawhide *bosals* frequently served as a means of controlling a horse, especially a young one. Generally, the vaqueros broke their horses with hackamores, and only several months or years later would they use a bit in a horse's mouth to control the animal. Still common is the use of the bosal with two bridle reins and the tie rope, now found in the buckaroo culture.

A style of saddle ridden by many vaqueros in the last century was light in weight and scantily covered with leather. Inexpensive to construct, its base features a fork utilizing the fork of a tree, usually mesquite or oak for strength, hence the name of this part of the saddle regardless of the culture. The tall horn may be cut at an angle slanted back toward the rider or may be rounded. The groove cut around the base of the horn facilitates the dally style of roping used by most vaqueros. No rawhide covers the horn because the riata cuts it off as the rope is drawn rapidly around the horn, often with enough speed and friction to cause the wood to smoke.

The side bars, to which the stirrup leathers attach, are fastened to the fork, usually by nails. The cantle is a piece of wood fastened, usually

An intricate knot on a horsehair hackamore. *Lawrence Clayton photo.*

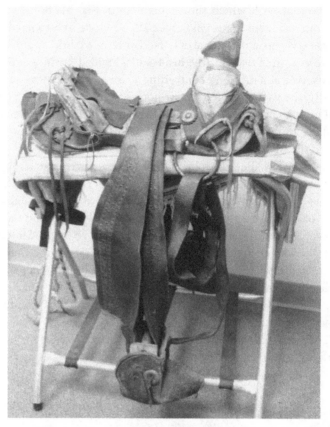

A vaquero saddle thought to be over a hundred years old. *Lawrence Clayton photo.*

with nails, to the rear of the side bars. Rawhide is often, but not always, added to this tree to provide strength. The seat may be partially covered with leather. Some use of nondescript leather such as the top of a boot or other such cast-off material may be used to cover the seat to protect the rider.

The rigging that holds the saddle on the horse is arranged around the fork and held in place by leather straps that reach around the rear of the cantle. Single rigging in the front is common. In this way the weight of the rider holds the saddle on the horse's back when the pull of the lariat is to the front. Flank or rear cinches are rare. The dally technique allows the rider to give slack to the roped animal and keep the strain off the saddle and rigging.

The stirrup leathers are adjustable by a series of holes held together with leather thongs. The stirrups are wooden and held together at the top with a steel bolt or rod, sometimes run through a rounded wooden piece to shield iron from leather. Short tapaderos to protect the rider's feet from thorns are standard on these saddles. These are tied to the stirrup by leather strings run through holes in the stirrup sides and the leather. Usually a concho or rosette secures the ties.

The underside of the saddle is a sheet of leather covered with a felt-like fabric, not fleece as the cowboy and buckaroo prefer. Little decoration is found on most of these saddles because they are strictly utilitarian, easily constructed from native materials. In recent years, most have been replaced with sturdier saddles built on the Texas-cowboy model, though Pepe Díaz, whose story appears later, says that any vaquero worthy of his name makes his own gear, including his saddles.

The modern saddle of David Huerta, a vaquero who learned to work cattle and horses on a ranch in Coahuila, Mexico, resembles the

Saddles in a tack room. Note, on saddle on the left, the snakeskin covering on the cantle and the sword attached to the rigging. Also note the quirts tied to the saddles. *Victor Amezquita photo.*

A modern vaquero saddle belonging to Frank Graham of Kingsville. Note the swell in the fork and the bare horn resembling those of the old vaquero saddles. *Joy Graham photo.*

Texas cowboy saddle with some unique variations. This style of saddle has gained significant prominence among today's vaqueros, and the trees have even been imported into the United States. Frank Graham of Kingsville, for example, owns one of these saddles, which a local craftsman completed for him. The horn is about four inches across and smooth on the top, with the angle descending to the rear at about forty-five degrees. A channel for the riata to run in when the rider is dallying his rope is cut around the base of the horn. The reason is obvious—the dallied lariat must be kept at the base of the horn and not allowed to run over the top. The rest of the tree is covered with rawhide.

The swell of the front fork of the saddle extends past the rider's legs in a style known in some parts of the United States as a "bronc saddle." The cantle is straight and stands six or more inches above the seat, a height typical of cowboy and buckaroo saddles with straight cantles. The stirrups are attached to thick leather straps about four inches wide at the narrowest part. The sweat leathers are cut as part of the stirrup leathers. The saddle is double rigged in the rimfire or Texas fashion with front and back girths. The saddle shows definite influences of cowboy saddles in design and materials.

One of the unique features of the saddle is the style of tapaderos used. Unlike the earlier plain ones on older vaquero saddles, the tapaderos on these saddles are short, have flaps that extend below the stirrup some six to eight inches, and are formed from sewing together two pieces of leather, not from the single piece usually found on the older vaquero models.

The underside of this saddle is lined with fleece, not the fabric found on many of the older saddles. The saddle has full leather covering, another trait that distinguishes it from the older style of saddle. Saddlebags behind the cantle are common.

An interesting historical note from Barney Baldeschwiler of Heb-

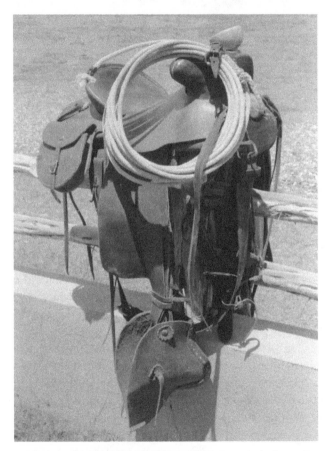

Another modern vaquero saddle, owned by David Huerta of Alpine. *Sonja Irwin Clayton photo.*

Rear view of the Huerta saddle. *Sonja Irwin Clayton photo.*

bronville, Texas, is that the older style of saddle was used in Texas by early vaqueros but was usually discarded on the demand of Texas ranchers if the often shorter Mexican saddles galled the backs of the horses. Then the vaquero was required to buy an American saddle or quit the job.

The charro saddle is more ornate than the vaquero saddle and is built on a rawhide-covered tree that sports a round horn six to eight inches in diameter, much larger in size than that of the vaquero saddle. Much of the tree is visible. The saddle may be ornamented with colorful tufts of cloth. The stirrups sometimes lack tapaderos, for these saddles are not for riding in the brush. The saddles sport a type of saddlebag on the rear. Also found is a leather covering tied onto the seat of the saddle to pad this area for the rider. Like the vaquero saddle, the charro saddle is covered on the underside with felt. No sweat leathers protect the rider's legs, and the stirrups hang on leather straps about four inches wide.

As a vaquero rode through the brush chasing cattle, he needed protection from scraping limbs and puncturing thorns. An early version of chaps developed by the vaqueros was based on a method of protection used by soldiers, who wore heavy leather *chaparreras* to protect their thighs and lower legs from the projectiles and blows of their enemies.

Tapadero on the Huerta saddle. *Sonja Irwin Clayton photo.*

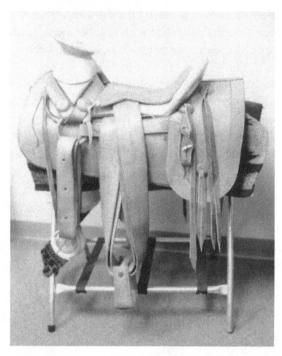

A modern charro saddle also ridden by vaqueros in Mexico. *Lawrence Clayton photo.*

Thus the use of chaps to protect the rider's legs developed early, and the leg coverings served admirably to protect from cactus and thorny brush and even, when adapted appropriately, from cold weather.

Although the vaquero way of life formed the basis for that of the other mounted herdsmen in North America, some of the techniques remain unique to the vaquero. One of these unusual practices involves the method used to catch horses when the men are preparing to ride. Evidence of a superior kind of horsemanship is amply provided by this remarkable activity, the *formando*. The term for this practice comes from a Spanish word that means "to form up" or "to line up." The formando is an ancient art among vaqueros. It was used on ranches in Mexico for centuries before it came to what is now the United States, and it can be traced back at least as far as early Spanish ranching in Cuba.

A common practice for catching horses is to rope them, usually in a corral. When on open range, the men modify this practice by driving the horses into a makeshift pen of a single strand of rope held up by the crew. One or two men then go in and rope the horses selected for riding that day. When a ranch uses the formando method, however, the men stretch between two fixed objects a rope about hock high on the horses. On command of the man in charge of the herd, the horses gather at the rope and back into position, their rear legs touching the rope just above the hocks. The animals then stand patiently as each man goes to the horse selected for riding that day and catches it. Then he leads the horse to the rider's tack and saddles the mount. When the man in command is ready, he releases the remaining horses with a signal recognized by the animals.

This system saves time and avoids confusion as the men catch their mounts from herds that may number sixty or more horses on some ranches even today. Once trained in this method by a patient vaquero, the older horses in the herd teach the younger ones by showing backed ears and bared teeth, a sure sign of anger on the part of one horse to another. No halters or other devices are on the horses when they line up for this ritual. Each horse in the line likes the same partners, so the ani-

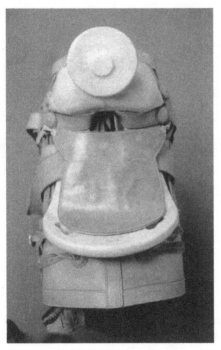

Overhead view of the charro saddle. Note the leather seat covering and the large horn. *Lawrence Clayton photo.*

A traditional pair of Chihuahua spurs with spoke rowels. *Lawrence Clayton photo.*

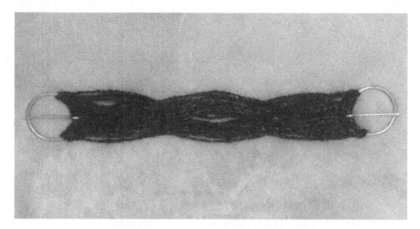

A girth of twisted horsehair. *Lawrence Clayton photo.*

mals assume the same position in line each time. I observed this practice on a ranch in South Texas where the horses had been trained by Félix Vásquez, a master horseman and vaquero. In response to my inquiry about this tendency, Vásquez replied, "When you go to church, don't you always sit in the same pew?"

Another technique is simply to gentle the horse and train it to come to the vaquero's whistle or to stand in order for the vaquero to catch it.

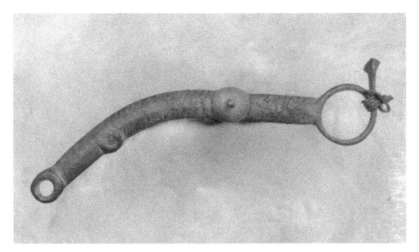

Side bars on an old pair of vaquero bits. Note the bent horseshoe nail in the top ring. The hole in the bottom of the bars will handle only a slobber chain, not a leather rein. *Lawrence Clayton photo.*

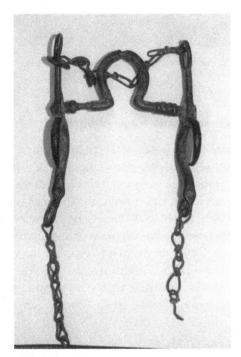

An old pair of vaquero bits with high port and a groove for a copper roller, now lost. Note the use of old nails to attach slobber chains, the right one of which is broken. *Lawrence Clayton photo.*

A high port bit with roller, slobber bar, and slobber chains. *Lawrence Clayton photo.*

SOME CONTEMPORARY VAQUEROS

The vaquero culture still exists in northern Mexico and southern Texas. Only in the past decade or two has the vaquero come to be influenced by the same forces of modernization that have changed the lives of his two United States counterparts, the cowboy and the buckaroo. The vaquero has consequently been forced to change at a far slower rate in some areas than have the other two. Similarly, poverty and lack of economic development have caused life in Mexico to proceed at a slower rate than in neighboring areas such as California and Texas. Today ranch life in Mexico still moves at a slow pace, with poverty and isolation the rule rather than the exception in some areas. However, the spirit and verve of the vaquero continue unabated.

PEPE DÍAZ

José "Pepe" Díaz Sánchez was born in 1919 on a ranch in Jalisco, Mexico, and grew up working alongside his father, a seasoned vaquero. Today on his small horse ranch on the outskirts of San Antonio, he still works every day to train horses just as he has throughout his lifetime.

His childhood memories of Jalisco are strong. Díaz remembers that the houses of the vaqueros were made of adobe with grass roofs and had only thin cloth curtains to cover the windows and doors. These simple structures were in contrast with the houses of the rich, which were made of stone and had roofs covered with packed clay and rounded to turn water. People traveled by natural means, the rich on horses and the poor on burros or on foot. Few of the poor had horses. The pens in which the men worked the cattle were typically constructed of limbs woven around posts set upright in the ground.

Díaz speaks plainly, however, about the work of the vaquero: "The life of a vaquero is to work for a wealthy person who owns the land, the cattle, and the horses. The main work for the vaquero is with horses." Speaking of the pride the men had in their skill in training their mounts, Díaz says, "The vaqueros made the horses." In his day the horses were born from the ranches' own bands of mares and were raised and trained specifically for ranch work. They were what Díaz calls *caballos corrientes*, or common horses. He remembers that later ranchers began incor-

The *formando* on the B. K. Johnson Ranch near Uvalde. *Dan Talbot photo.*

"Pepe" Díaz getting a kiss from a horse he trained to do this "trick." *Lawrence Clayton photo.*

porating Quarter Horse blood into their herds to improve the quality. The men spent long demanding days working cattle and horses, usually for fifty cents a day. But this work was the life of the men.

When not working, the vaquero engaged in sports related to his life. One of these was to fight roosters. Díaz, in fact, raises roosters to honor his father, who loved his fighting chickens. Another of the sports that Díaz remembers seeing is *corella de toros*, in which a rider runs behind a charging bull, wraps the bull's tail around his (the rider's) leg and the stirrup leathers, and then turns the horse to the side in order to trip the bull. One other sport that Díaz himself engaged in as a charro later in his life involved the roping of wild horses. In this event the rider ropes the horse by the forefeet, then lies on his back with the rope around his neck in order to throw the horse. It is a dangerous game, requiring great skill.

One of the characteristics Díaz recalls of vaquero life is that the men made, by hand, most if not all of their own gear. All of the men learned how to fashion what they needed from the hides of cattle and horses or from horsehair. These items included whips, quirts, bridle reins, and head stalls. From iron they made bits, spurs, and branding irons. Being made by hand from readily available materials was particularly true of the saddle, even to making the tree for the saddle from forks of trees that grew on the ranch.

The lasso that Díaz grew up learning to use was made of maguey fibers, not lechuguilla or rawhide. The lariat was sixty or more feet in length to allow the vaquero plenty of room to let the wild horse or cow play at the end of the rope. Díaz recalls that all of the vaqueros around whom he worked were dally ropers. Often he has seen the smoke rise from around the saddle horn as the rope plays out with the charging animal on the other end. In fact most of the saddles in Díaz's tack room showed signs of the heat generated by the friction of these ropes around the base of the saddle horn.

Because horses were central to vaquero life, breaking horses was an essential activity. Díaz recalled that the first step usually was to rope the horse and saddle it, but several men might be involved in getting this "simple" operation accomplished. One of the men then mounted the horse while another opened the gate on the pen to allow the rider to take the horse out into open country. This was done to prevent the horse from hurting itself in the confines of the corral. Another man might follow along to help the vaquero, should he require assistance.

The marketing of cattle required driving them to Guadalajara, a trip that often took a month or more. No chuck wagon was used on these trips; the men carried all of their supplies on horseback.

The clothing he remembers for the vaqueros was usually gabardine or cotton. He has seen vaqueros wearing sandals because they could not afford to buy boots, but even these men wore spurs.

Díaz's recollection of this life is that it gave him his beginning, and he admires it. After he had moved to the United States, he began competing in charro contests, and he went on to become one of the greatest charros in North America. The trophies in his tack room attest to his proficiency in the complex skills of these exquisite horsemen. The basic difference between a vaquero and a charro is that the charro must have all the skills in riding and roping of the vaquero but also have fine clothes, excellent gear, and a fine horse. Above all, according to Díaz's wife Rosa, "He must be a gentleman."

Victor Amezquita in front of the stables of the ranch in Jalisco, Mexico. *Victor Amezquita photo.*

VICTOR AMEZQUITA

Victor Amezquita, like Díaz, grew up in the state of Jalisco but more recently, in the 1970s and 1980s. He has seen many changes in the half century from Díaz's time to his. He remembers seeing some of the farmers in the area use tractors but recounts that most of the men who farm still use mules, and they still irrigate their fields from cement-lined canals. The houses they live in also have changed somewhat. Some are still made of adobe but have flat roofs fashioned by laying sticks across large beams, or vigas, and pouring a layer of cement on the lattice of sticks. The barns are made of bricks and covered with tin roofs. Straw, or thatched, roofs are infrequently found today.

Many of the remote ranches are still lit only by power from generators or by kerosene lamps or even candles. Amezquita recounts that in many cases the walls of existing buildings have been incorporated into the pens in which the livestock are worked. A sign of affluence may be found in some corrals made of pipe welded together or of barbed or net wire. Some of the corrals, however, are simply pits dug several feet into the ground: the steep walls hold the cattle effectively.

Both Díaz and Amezquita recount similar details in the typical ranch diet. Principal foods consist of corn tortillas, potatoes, rice, beans,

A house in Jalisco, Mexico. Note the tile roof. *Victor Amezquita photo.*

The gates on the stables at the ranch in Jalisco, Mexico. *Victor Amezquita photo.*

Individual stalls for horses. Note the domed cement roof. *Victor Amezquita photo.*

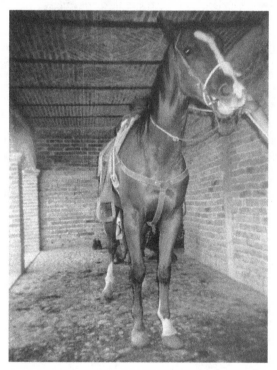

A *caballo trabajo* in Jalisco, Mexico. Note the single rein and slobber bar and chains but the absence of tapaderos. *Victor Amezquita photo.*

Horses in a set of pens in Jalisco, Mexico. Note the whitewashed stone fence with the dwelling on the left forming part of the wall.

and beef, goat, pork, and lamb. The rural people slaughter their own meat and prepare the hides for use in their work. The meat that cannot be cooked and eaten before it spoils is covered with salt and either hot peppers or lemon juice and dried. In the cool climate of Jalisco, however, the meat will keep for a long time before it spoils.

Some things have changed in the lives of vaqueros in the fifty years that separate the lives of these two men. Now when the men ride into the mountains to gather cattle, they carry their tortillas and other foods packed in a tin container, called a *pocillo*, and put it in a sturdy bag made of plastic fibers. In a thoroughly modern touch, the men often carry bottles of Coca Cola to drink. At mealtime the men build a fire of dry wood found in the mountains, let the fire burn down, and place their lunches in the ashes to warm.

The cattle in the mountains are referred to as *vacas sierras*, or mountain cattle, a type of beef animal usually showing some Brahman blood. To work the cattle, the men ride into the pastures for the roundup

Barbed wire fencing with a water tank and an outbuilding in the background. *Victor Amezquita photo.*

(*junta de vacas*) and drive the animals to the corrals at the headquarters. There the men separate the calves from the cows and wrestle the calves down for castrating the bulls and branding the animals. The branding irons usually carry the initials of the owner of the ranch and are purchased at a store that stocks ranch supplies, or are made by the vaqueros themselves.

The young horses are broken to ride, often beginning as young as one year of age, with the bosal and hackamore arrangement. The bridle with a snaffle or hinged bit attached is also used on the young horses, but all direction is given with the bosal. This technique varies somewhat from Díaz's practice, in which he lets the horse wear the bridle with the bit in his mouth with no reins attached to it. Amezquita also recounts using another technique, in which the rider mounts a young horse held by a strong lead rope to the horn of the saddle on a mature horse. If the young horse attempts to pitch, the rider of the mature horse can snug the rope to the saddle horn and control the pitching.

The bits for the mature horse (from four to five years old) have a high port with rollers, and the side bars are decorated, often with flowers of tin or silver. The reins are usually two pieces of rope made from cotton fiber or horsehair or some other strong material. Amezquita remembers particularly that these are knotted together about six inches from the end so that the rider can manage the reins with one finger inserted in front of the knot. In some cases the rider may choose to put on the horse a halter with a lead rope attached. This lead rope is helpful if the rider intends to tie the horse during the day for an extended period. If the rider dismounts for only a brief time, however, the knotted reins are slipped behind the saddle horn and are adjusted to just the right tension to hold the horse in place.

The spurs Amezquita describes range from early models with three-inch rowels to more modern ones with rowels half that size. These are decorated with flowers and other designs made of tin or silver and held to the riders feet with buckled leather straps. The men use the spurs to control the horses to some degree, but more commonly the rider carries a stick for controlling his horse. These sticks are usually decorated with carvings. The rider also carries a quirt tied to his saddle but rarely uses it. This quirt is a form of ornamentation.

Other items of gear have remained consistent. The lariats are still made of maguey, though Amezquita remembers ropes about thirty feet in length, much shorter than those of Díaz's time. The chaps are still long and made of tough, pliable leather, but they close on the back with small plastic pepper-shaped buttons that slip through the loops.

Corrales de leña located in South Texas. *Sonja Irwin Clayton photo.*

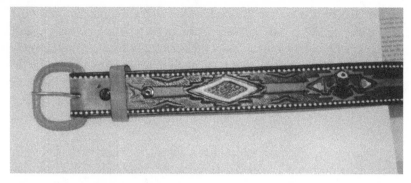

A belt with a pass-through, leather-covered buckle and painted geometric design. *Lawrence Clayton photo.*

The intricate geometric design of a *pita* belt. *Sonja Irwin Clayton photo.*

Over the years, plastic has replaced the wooden buttons that Díaz remembered.

Sports have broadened to include bull riding—often with no rope to hold on to—and roping steers. Amezquita does report that *corella de toros* is still a favorite, as is fighting roosters.

The clothing of a vaquero has changed little. The hats worn by the men are usually straw with five- to six-inch brims and a tightly fashioned string going under the wearer's chin. The belts worn by the men usually sport painted designs, not tooling, and a large flat buckle with fighting roosters represented on it. An exception is the expensive belt that Díaz wears. It is finely stitched from the natural fibers of a desert plant. This an art know as *pita.*

The pants the vaquero wears are of heavy cotton. Shirts, always with long sleeves, are of cotton and in bright colors. Riders may have boots with tall tops, but a popular style, which Díaz prefers, has the bottom of a boot but a top that stops at the wearer's ankle with an elastic band to hold it snug. This style allows the rider to move his foot comfortably in the stirrup during long days of riding. Since the lower legs are protected by *chaparajos* and the feet by *tapaderos*, the rider does not need his lower leg protected by the boot top.

DAVID HUERTA

David Huerta, a vaquero originally from the Rancho Ojo de Agua, San Louis Potosí, Mexico, recalls in that area adobe houses with straw roofs, as they have had for centuries. At the age of fourteen he moved to the Rancho Nuevo in Coahuila, Mexico, and has been working with cattle and horses ever since. He is an especially effective horseman.

He remembers working cattle on the Rancho Nuevo by gathering them usually in a dry tank or depression in the ground and having a ring of vaqueros hold the cattle in place while one man rode into the herd to rope a calf by the head and pull it toward a crew ready to

David Huerta. *Sonja Irwin Clayton photo.*

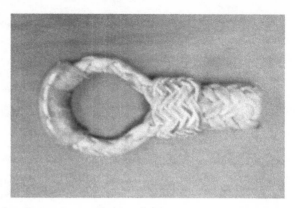

A rawhide honda. *Lawrence Clayton photo.*

work it. Another man then roped the hind legs and threw the calf to the ground. Dragging a calf by the heels is not common in this area because rocky, abrasive soil cuts off the hair and scratches the hide of the calf dragged along the ground. He recalls no vaccinations, but the calves were branded, their ears notched, and the bull calves castrated.

The ropes he remembers are made of lechuguilla. The honda is made from plaited rawhide, which saves the rope from excessive wear and can be replaced. Huerta is a dally roper and commented that many times he has seen smoke rise when the lariat twists around the wooden horn of the saddle as a large animal pulls away from the man on the horse. His lariat is usually sixty to seventy feet long, like that of Díaz, not the thirty- to thirty-two-foot variety of the cowboys or that preferred by Amezquita.

In the Rancho Nuevo region it was common to have a cook with a chuck wagon. The foods included cornbread (not corn tortillas), beans, potatoes, rice, and goat meat. When the men ate their meals at the headquarters, they had the same foods cooked in a fireplace in one of the houses.

Cattle in this region were various breeds, but most were Herefords crossed with Brahman, a common combination in the United States. Horses were raised on the ranch. When a man came to work, he was assigned two mounts already broken and several unbroken horses to add to his string of mounts. This way he practiced his skill working with horses. Huerta remembers that skillfully working with these horses determined that the man would be well mounted for the work.

Huerta's equipment shows some influence from cowboy culture. The bits are either snaffle or medium port, not the high port bit reported by Díaz and Amezquita. The reins may be two long leather reins or one single looped rein. These, especially the latter, may be plaited from rawhide. If this is the case, the strings will be very narrow and the handwork very fine. The chaps are typical of those described earlier that close with a series of bone, plastic, or wooden buttons on the back. Huerta does carry a quirt, a thick and heavy tool for teaching a reluctant animal. The spurs he wears have large rowels, three inches or more, and his boots are very much like those of the Texas cowboy, but the tall heels and soles may be rubber rather than leather.

In typical vaquero fashion, Huerta knows the fine art of plaiting rawhide and horsehair and makes whips and quirts as well as other items of tack, such as breast collars. He did not make his own saddle, however.

A vaquero in Jalisco, Mexico, shoes a horse. Note especially the man's leather leg wraps. *Victor Amezquita photo.*

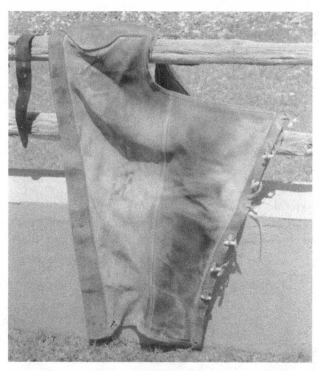

David Huerta's chaps. Note the plastic buttons on the right side to close the leggings at the back. *Sonja Irwin Clayton photo.*

ARTURO ALONZO

Arturo Alonzo was born and reared in Músquiz, Mexico. His father was a vaquero who taught his five sons this way of life on the Papalote Ranch owned by Amelio Acosta, a retired army general. By the time Arturo was twelve, he was working regularly with cattle and horses.

In 1948, Alonzo came to the United States and began working on ranches in South Texas around Uvalde. He spent many of his years working for B. K. Johnson, part of the King Ranch dynasty.

Like the other vaqueros, Alonzo's recollections of horses are quite strong. These were utility horses, the *caballos corrientes* that Díaz remembers, because the Quarter Horse had not yet made its impression on Mexican bloodlines. Though not *caballo finos*, they were nonetheless tough horses, descended from the Spanish Mustang and capable of incredibly difficult and demanding work. The bits used on these horses, as both Díaz and Amezquita remember, often were the high port or spade models with rings and rollers. The men used two bridle reins, often made of twisted horse mane hair, plaited rawhide, or rope twisted from the fibers of commonly available plants, such as lechuguilla. The spurs had large rowels. In this area the men used rawhide riatas, most sixty to seventy feet long. Alonzo recalls seeing some of the best ropers snare cattle and horses at distances up to thirty to forty feet, and the men dallied their lariats. Men became excellent horsemen and took pride in their horsemanship.

In this region the men drove the cattle, usually Herefords, to market. The trip often took two or three weeks to drive the fifty to sixty miles to a city to sell the cattle to the slaughter trade. The men drove the beginning of the herd from ranch to ranch, adding other cattle until a large herd was gathered along the way for the journey.

The clothing the men wore was typical of the period. The hats, called *wairpas*, were made of tule cane and were woven, he recalls, by Kickapoo Indians in the region. The vaqueros wore the large sombrero style hat that had a string descending from the brim under the throat of

David Huerta's quirt. *Sonja Irwin Clayton photo.*

the rider to keep the hat from blowing off when the horse was running. Some of the men wore as well a piece of cotton cloth tied around the head to absorb sweat. Shoes and sandals, not boots, were common. Vests were worn but usually came from a dress suit, rather than being made of leather. This tradition shows up also in the buckaroo culture. The chaps were made from cowhide and closed with leather buttons rather than the wooden, plastic, or bone buttons found in other areas. Trousers were cotton but not name brands such as Levi or Wrangler. The leather belts had metal pass-through buckles, not the flat buckles that Amezquita remembers.

Working with the cattle in this region included roping and dragging the calves, since rocky soil was not a problem. Often, however, the men separated the cows from the calves and simply wrestled the calves down to castrate and brand them.

Alonzo remembers one of his favorite dishes as cornbread, not corn tortillas. He said there was strength in the bread and that if the men had it for breakfast, they could work a long time. They also ate beef and wild game, and he recalls eating a lot of tacos, a common dish among all vaqueros.

ISMAEL SÁNCHEZ

Ismael Sánchez, whose family has ranched in both Mexico and Texas for several generations, knows the life firsthand. The family's Texas ranch is about fifty-five miles from Van Horn, Texas; their Mexico ranch is about fifty miles from Ojinaga, Mexico, in the state of Chihuahua. The ranches are about twenty-five miles apart. The family's access to the Mexico ranch is by horseback from Texas.

Neither housing nor food preparation has been much affected by modernization. Housing for the vaqueros is adobe huts with grass roofs. The windows of these structures amount to little more than shutters that can be closed to cut off the flow of the air. No electricity is found on the remote ranches in the region, and wood-burning cookstoves are still used for preparing the simple foods, which include handmade corn tortillas, beans, potatoes, coffee, and various meats available locally—beef, goat, deer, some catfish from the Rio Grande, and some pork. One of the favorite meals is a stew made from goat. The blood is caught when the animal's throat is cut and then fried and added to a mixture of intestine, liver, heart, and other delicacies from the carcass.

When working away from the ranch headquarters, the men eat whatever can be killed during the day. The meat is cooked over an open

Ismael Sánchez and his grandson, Justin Brent Sánchez, a sixth generation Texas-Mexican rancher. *Sánchez photo.*

mesquite wood fire or on hot rocks, or it may be preserved by drying. The jerky made from the loin of a deer or calf will keep several days for consumption by the men. Another dish is mountain oysters, the testicles of the calves the men work. These are often cooked in the fire used to heat the branding irons. This is supplemented by flat biscuits made with wheat flour and water and little else. The men eat but two meals a day when on these roundups, one before they begin work at daylight and another after dark.

All of the men carry rifles, either .22 caliber for small game or .30-.30 caliber lever-action for deer and mountain lions. These weapons provide protection as well as a means of supplying food.

Working the calves is done in monthly *corridas* in which all the vaqueros in the area gather the cattle to portable pens in the mountains. Once the cattle are gathered, the team captains, the older men, remain on horseback to rope the calves with the lasso. The younger men wrestle the calves to the ground. One man puts his foot on the top rear leg of a calf, and another man then applies the brand with a hot iron. The design of the brand likely will have been in the family for generations.

In this work, the vaquero may still ride mustang horses, which run wild in this part of Mexico. He makes most of his own gear or barters for items with other men working in the same area. Twisted horsehair and braided rawhide are common. Men become known in a locale as makers of particular items, and others bring items to trade with them.

In much of vaquero country, clothing has changed little from earlier times. The sombrero is still likely to be of heavy straw with a drawstring under the chin; felt hats are extremely rare. The boots have a heel more slanted than that of the cowboy. The cotton denim pants are not as tight fitting as the cowboy's are and have no label on the back pocket. No Levis or Wranglers here. The belts are *piteadas*, or painted with designs, rather than stitched. The buckles are not large and shiny; they are instead made of leather. The neckerchief, usually plain and used daily, may be secured with a slide or clasp. The shirt is homemade and may be in a fancy design. The man carries a folding knife in a leather sheath on his belt. Little jewelry is found; often a saint on a chain around the neck to provide protection is the vaquero's only ornament.

The vaqueros' health as well as that of the animals is guarded by the saints and home remedies, or *remedios*. These are concocted from herbs that are grown or gathered for medicinal use and fermented usually with sotol, a 190 proof liquor fermented from the hearts of the sotol plant. Peelings from oranges and nuts as well as other ingredients also may be added to the remedies. Horses and cattle are treated for injuries with ashes and some oils that the men carry with them when working in the mountains. These same oils are used to treat the men's injuries as well. While out on the *corridas*, the men bathe in streams when opportunity presents itself, often at the end of the roundup. For dental hygiene, the men chew on sangregada, an herb found on the sides of the hills.

Smoking cigarettes continues to be common. These are handrolled from Bull Durham or other such bulk tobacco. The men can roll these on horseback in a strong wind without spilling any of the tobacco.

The vaquero's rope most typically is made of plant fibers. Sánchez recalls seeing few rawhide ropes used by vaqueros on his family's ranches, though the braided rawhide quirt is still common. The saddles used in Mexico are those typical of the Mexican culture and feature large horns. Surprisingly, the vaqueros in this area do not dally but tie off "to the death." Hence, their saddle horns are wrapped with strips of rubber to keep the rope from slipping. The saddle blankets consist of layers of leather, but if cloth is used in the padding, it includes brightly colored pieces to decorate and individualize the vaquero's outfit. If a blanket is used, it is a woven fabric similar to that found in serapes and will serve the vaquero as a covering when he sleeps.

Little or no machinery is found on most of these ranches. Frequently, the only tie with the outside world is a battery-powered radio. Battery power also is used to help pump water into the tanks in areas away from natural water sources. Vehicles of any kind are rare. Few pickup trucks are present, so the hauling of horses on the ranch is unknown. Gasoline is scarce and must be hauled to the remote ranches in fifty-five gallon barrels. The men ride their horses to an area where they will work. Horse power is cheaper than gasoline. Tractors are nonexistent. Ranchers rely totally on horses or mules and human muscle for work on the ranch. However, no trail drives take the cattle to market. Instead, despite a poor road system, large trucks haul the cattle to distant markets, as is done in the United States. The earlier practice of slaughtering animals for hides and tallow is no longer seen.

CIRILDO ORTIZ

Cirildo Ortiz, whom I knew personally, was 83 years old when I met him. He was then too stiff to ride a horse, but he still worked hard every day building fences and corrals for ranchers. He built a fence for me that is still tight as a fiddle string after twenty years. Cirildo Ortiz told me this story:

I came to the United States with my family when I was nine years old. We came across the Rio Grande on a barge, pulled across the river by a rope pulled by hand. My father was a vaquero and his father before him was a vaquero. My father gave the barge man a nickel to take us across. I saw my father rope a jackrabbit for food.

I was working like a man by the time I was twelve years old. Later when I was about twenty-three years old, I was working on a ranch near Brackettville, Texas. This ranch had fifty sections [32,000 acres] in it. The ranch had 1,200 sheep, 700 to 800 mother cows, 1,000 Spanish goats and 60 to 70 brood mares.

One day I roped a white-tailed buck deer when I was on horseback. I ran the deer about 200 yards before I caught him. I tied him to a tree and rode to the bunkhouse and told the foreman what I had done. He didn't believe me. He told me the deer had to be sick. I said no, that I had ridden him down and roped him on a dead run. The foreman told me that was not possible. I asked the foreman to go with me to see the deer. He went with me, and I showed him the buck deer. The buck was still tied to the tree where I had left him. He was jumping around.

When Cirildo Ortiz ended his story, I asked him what kind of horse he had used to run down and rope the deer. He said the horse was "part thoroughbred," and then a smile lit up his dark, bronzed face as he recalled the incident. "You have to have a good horse to do that," he said.

A few months later Ortiz passed away. After I learned of his death, I felt such great emotion about this old vaquero. The world would never know what he had done. I decided to write a special tribute to him. Most of what I wrote did not seem fitting, so I finally wrote a poem that I thought might capture his spirit and skill:

> Tribute to Cirildo Ortiz, Vaquero
> Gone, gone forever,
> Vanished like the wild roses of San Juan,
> The wild roses that grow
> On the banks of the Nueces,
> Vanished in the furnace heat
> Of the Texas summer.
>
> Oh vaquero, your grace, your skill
> Will not be seen again.
> Oh how I wish for the power
> To describe the color,
> The wildness
> And the glory
> Of those days.

A COMMONALITY OF EXPERIENCE

These men represent varying perspectives of the life of the vaquero in Mexico. Commonality of experience is great, despite surface variations prompted by traditions, climate, and topography. All of these men fit firmly into the tradition of the vaquero.

The vaquero has stood for centuries in the shadows—not the spotlight—of history. He has lived his life in remote areas doing what he has always done—working with horses and taking care of someone else's cattle, often under primitive conditions. No Hall of Fame touts his accomplishments, as do those for the cowboy and buckaroo. Published photographs recording and interpreting his life are noticeably lacking. The majority of photographs of Mexicans on horseback depict bandolier-laden banditos or revolutionaries with Pancho Villa and other leaders. Many of these men were also vaqueros, but the photographers' interest was in the soldier, not the lowly cattle worker. The images one sees in commercial establishments such as Mexican food restaurants in the southwestern United States are not vaqueros at work. Racial prejudice may be at the root of this neglect, but it stems also from the vaquero's remoteness from cultural centers where photographers worked, and from the poverty that precluded the families' owning cameras to make the pictures. And it probably never even occurred to the ranch owners to record this life for posterity.

Rare exceptions to this general neglect do exist. Frederick Remington on the San José de Bavicora ranch in Mexico produced some excellent art work. The revealing drawings of José Cisneros in *Riders Across the Centuries* depict great detail about many horsemen, including vaqueros. Bill Wittliff's photo essay, published in 1972, is excellent and revealing. But these few works do not fill a noticeable void.

Western fiction sometimes includes the vaquero, but he is usually the subject of scorn or derision and suspected of being a killer or thief. Many of the Mexicans presented in western fiction are cooks and hands accorded the poorest jobs on the trail drives or ranches. *Lonesome Dove* has such a cook, Bolivar, who determines not to complete the drive to Montana with Gus and Call. Po Campo, also a Mexican, replaces him. Benjamin Capps depicts such a figure in his first novel, *Hanging at Comanche Wells,* and uses him as a mysterious but sinister figure who guns down one of the villains at the climax of the novel. He serves almost as the *deus ex machina* for the plot and is not one of the developed characters.

The main literature of the life of the vaquero is found, according to Ramirez, in stories and *corridos,* the folk songs of the vaqueros. She delineates various themes found in this material: fidelity, melancholia, patience, endurance, love of horses, vanity, pride, death and tragedy, buried treasure, and, of course, romance between the sexes (pp. 178–186). Typical of the fidelity of the vaquero is an incident that occurred on the King Ranch in South Texas. A *caporal* named Ignacio Alvarado failed to show up for work one afternoon and was not heard of for several days. Later his son rode into the camp to tell Robert Kleberg, who ran the ranch for many years, that the father apologized for not coming to work because he "had to die" (Lea, 2: 515). The pride of the vaqueros can be seen in another tale from the King Ranch: a vaquero thrown from a horse in front of the other vaqueros was so embarrassed that he vowed to quit the vaquero life and become a cotton picker, a line of work abhorred by the horsemen. Other stories include accounts of roping bears, a common practice in California, as well as wild horses and cattle, buffalo, even elk (Ramirez, p. 181), and as noted above, a buck deer by Cirildo Ortiz.

The material in the *corridos* is abundant. One of the songs, "Las Mañanitas de San Juan," speaks of rain, singing birds, and a new day beginning. Ramirez notes that this song is often sung when the men saddle up in the morning and look forward to a new day in the saddle. The ballad "Mi Querida Nicolasa" tells of a vaquero trying to attract his beloved by showing off his horse. In "El Noviello Despuntado," a steer brags of overcoming four vaqueros who are too vain about their skills to pay attention to their work and have to pay for their lapse.

One story that has attracted considerable attention is that of Gregorio Cortez, a young vaquero who kills a sheriff in South Texas because of a misunderstanding about the theft of a horse. The young man must flee in a fruitless effort to avoid capture. His valiant and skillful ride through the countryside, during which he eludes capture for some days in his dash to the Rio Grande, glorifies the spirit of the vaquero. Américo Paredes's book, *With His Pistol in His Hand: A Border Ballad and Its Hero*, contains a complete discussion of the story. Elmer Kelton sympathetically depicts the story in *Manhunters*, one of his early works.

The paucity of formal literature dedicated to favorable depiction of the vaquero is indicative of the role he has played in the culture. He has no equivalent to *Martín Fierro*, the national epic of Argentina, in which the life of the gaucho is forever captured and glorified. Paul Espinosa, a modern film personality, critiques the limited role that any Hispanic culture plays in modern film and commercial television. When present, he says, the material more often than not presents a negative view of any Mexican (p. B7).

Despite this negative portrayal, the vaquero continues to be a necessary force in the still largely agricultural economy in many areas of Mexico and the southwestern United States. It seems that his presence is a large part of what separates Southwest from West in the United States. Regardless of his image in the public eye, however, his importance cannot be denigrated in the development of the cowboy and the buckaroo.

To the vaqueros, these horsemen whose skills are legendary and whose iron wills are almost mythic, the cowboys and buckaroos owe their existence. Created by Spanish influence in North America, these hearty souls have ridden their way into the pages of history and the fabric of life, even the very soul, of the world. Tom Lea, that great artist and writer of the Spanish borderlands, shared a special insight into the character of the vaquero when he wrote the following in his *Randado:*

> Men of fire riding
> the blood-flecked tracks;
> Men of flint and of steel
> enduring the heat and the cold,
> the hate, the hurt and
> the love of being free:
> Yours is a music that will not die. (n.p.)

The vaquero, his way of life threatened by encroaching civilization, nonetheless, like his counterparts in the rest of North America, continues to fight for his existence and to pass his traditions on to his children. Bill Wittliff, one of the premier writers, film directors, and photographers of the day, traveled into Mexico several times to record the life of this vaquero. In his *Vaquero: Genesis of the Cowboy* (p. 1), he observes that because of the Spaniards' cattle and horses, there emerged the "most enduring legend" of the New World—the vaquero.

Benny Peacock, a cowboy, in Shackelford County, Texas, 1998. Note the hat with extreme crush on top and rolled, wide brim. He wears a scarf tied around his neck but no vest. His saddle has a swelled fork and rolled cantle and is a double-rigged rimfire. The horn is about five inches high and wrapped with rubber. He has no breast collar, though he usually does use one. His lariat is thirty feet of nylon with a metal honda for tying hard and fast and is secured to the horn with a light leather string that would easily break if the rider were thrown and the man's leg caught in the rope. The side bars of his bits, the heel bands of his spurs, and the outside edges of his oxbow stirrups bear emblems and ranch brands in brass and silver. His reins are two split leather reins about seven feet long. *Sonja Irwin Clayton photo.*

The Cowboy

LAWRENCE CLAYTON

OF THE MOUNTED HERDERS of North America, the cowboy is, no doubt, the most familiar to audiences of film and readers of fiction and history. In reality, however, the term *cowboy* is often used in the generic sense to indicate not just someone mounted on a horse who works cattle, but anyone dressed in the clothing we think of as western.

According to the *Oxford English Dictionary*, the term *cowboy* (also *cow-boy* or *cow boy*) was a British term to designate "a boy who tends cows"—and nothing is mentioned or suggested about tending cattle on horseback. In Southwest usage, the cowboy is *always* a man on a horse. A man who herded cattle on foot was no cowboy. In fact, on the unfenced Texas plains and in the brush chasing Longhorn cattle—animals more feral than tame—a man on foot was useless and often in danger of being gored or trampled to death by the cattle.

As used today, the word *cowboy* is known around the world, and the cowboy, usually associated with Texas in the minds of everyone not familiar with the history of the American West, is one of the mythological figures of American history. Those who are concerned with technical distinctions separate the cowboy from the vaquero and the buckaroo, though all three work cattle on horseback and share many of the same folk qualities. The distinctiveness of the cowboy is apparent to those who observe his background, appearance, work, and daily life.

The cowboy has become an American folk hero, an icon of the American West. His emergence on the public scene came with dime novels and, later, B-movie Westerns. He took over prime time on TV in the 1950s and 1960s, but the TV western met its demise in the face of more sophisticated public entertainment.

This uniquely American figure did not begin in America. He had his origins in the Old World. His principal antecedent was certainly the vaquero, who had seen centuries of development in Spanish North America before Anglos and their black slaves moved into the eastern United States. Texas historian Walter Prescott Webb places the birth of Texas cowboy life and ranching in a diamond-shaped area of Texas with San Antonio on the north, Laredo on the west, Indianola on the east, and Brownsville on the south. The Nueces River, once the border between Mexico and Texas, runs through this region. This area, the *brasada*, or brush country, is the home country of Webb's friend J. Frank Dobie, the folklorist who wrote extensively on the cattle industry, the cowboy, the vaquero, and the brush country. Dobie loved this region's unique Spanish-influenced culture and inhabitants. And both Webb and

Dobie agreed that the most important influence on this country lay in its Spanish roots.

To the influence of the vaquero on this ranching culture, Dobie, in his *Longhorns*, adds a second figure, the herd-owning caballero, a Spanish gentleman-owner (p. viii). Some of these men established large ranches and hired cowboys to do the work, just as the Spanish priests and conquistadors had done in Mexico and Mexican Texas.

Early cattle raisers put their herds on "the open range"—public land open to anyone who used it for cattle grazing—and the cattle roamed and survived as best they could with a minimum of care, even in the winter months. The men held periodic roundups to brand and gather cattle for slaughter or market. From this cattle-rich area much of the stock for the trail herds later came.

Two other scholars offer support for Webb's and Dobie's basic theory of the area of origin. Folklorist Joe Graham, whose chief interest is in South Texas ranching, sees the main influence on Texas ranching farther to the west and south, thus acknowledging only part of the diamond-shaped area Webb describes. In his *El Rancho in South Texas*, Graham cites as support for his vaquero theory, among other notions, the more than two dozen terms taken from Spanish to describe items and techniques essential to cowboy life. Some of this borrowing was reluctant because of the deep prejudice of Texans against the Mexicans, especially after the war for independence in the 1830s and the later conflict in the 1840s between the United States and Mexico. Another scholar, photographer and filmmaker Bill Wittliff, has photographs to supplement his argument that the vaquero is the progenitor of the cowboy. He says in *Vaquero: Genesis of the Cowboy*, "When Texas got interested in the cow business, the Texas cowboy adopted most of the vaquero's accoutrements and methodology of working cattle in big country, adapting here and there to fit his particular needs" (n.p.). A traveling exhibit from the Institute of Texan Cultures carries these photographs to a large audience.

The second school of thought is a revisionist view denying the predominance of the vaquero influence and is espoused largely by Terry Jordan in his *Trails to Texas* and to a lesser degree in *North American Cattle-Raising Frontiers*. Jordan, a cultural geographer, holds that the impetus for an early cattle-raising culture in Texas came especially from the South as elements of mostly British culture were transferred to Texas by newly arrived immigrants from Georgia, Florida, and the Carolinas by way of Louisiana, where many of the people had settled temporarily before being allowed by Mexican authorities to move into Texas around the mid-1800s. While it is true that these people had a long history of cattle raising using slash and burn techniques in woodlands with some open areas of grazing in the South, it is also true that they did not have experience raising cattle on the vast, open, treeless plains found in Texas. To these open areas the southerners often applied the word *prairie*, not the Spanish term *llano* or the word *plain* as found in the descriptive name Great Plains applied to the flat, rich, one-time grassland, now given largely to farming, that stretches from the Texas Panhandle into Canada. These newcomers from the South made extensive use of dogs in working their cattle. The English term *cowpens* was used instead of *ranch* from Spanish *rancho*. These southerners used whips to drive their cattle and did not rely upon the lazo used by the vaqueros and, later, by the cowboys. There was little need for the southerners to rope their cattle if the men had pens in which to catch the animals in order to work them. These southerners also used salt licks, which cattle regularly visit, as a means of managing stock. These ranchers had what Jordan describes, in *North American Cattle Raising Frontiers* (p. 367), as a "greater attention to the welfare and quality of livestock" than was common in the open-range culture farther west. Their cattle were better bred than the Longhorn cattle that formed the basis for open-range ranching in Mexico and Texas. The slender conformation of Longhorn cattle was not a negative factor in the beginning years of Texas ranching, because the main market for cattle was in hides and tallow, not beef. The Anglos, according to Jordan, established themselves and the basis for ranching culture in an area in South Louisiana, some four hundred miles east of Webb's diamond in South Texas, and later moved their way of stock raising to Texas. He discusses at some length their tradition of trailing herds of cattle to market.

There is, however, doubt as to the validity of some of Jordan's conclusions, and in some cases he is just wrong. Historian Richard Slatta in his *Comparing Cowboys and Frontiers* criticizes Jordan's errors as stemming from the historical *over-revisionism* of the 1980s and 1990s that sought to rewrite the history of the West along deconstructionist lines. Among the revisionists—or New West Historians as they call themselves—are Patricia Limerick (*The Legacy of Conquest: The Unbroken Past of the American West* [1987]), Richard White ("*It's Your Misfortune and None of My Own*": *A New History of the American West* [1991]) and an exhibit entitled "The West as America: Reinterpreting Images of the

Frontier," housed at the Smithsonian's National Museum of American Art (1991). Slatta correctly links this drive for revisionism to the Deconstruction movement that has dominated the arts, especially literature, during this same period, but he admits that some correcting of the traditional image is overdue. The New West historians have sought to revise the notions that Anglo males were the prime movers in the Westward movement and have emphasized the roles of other ethnic groups and women. However, a general feeling that revisionism has resulted in overcorrection is apparent.

Slatta notes that Jordan "ignores" both linguistic and material culture evidence to draw some "feeble" conclusions. Among the errors of Jordan's early thesis is the claim that *buckaroo* and *corral* derived from the African terms *buckra* and *kraal* and came west with the slaves accompanying new Anglo settlers from the South. Another is that the Africans "shaped" the ranching culture and strongly influenced the development of the cowboy. The most specious of Jordan's claims is that the role Texas culture played in the development of ranching techniques and institutions has been greatly exaggerated (pp. 188–189). In these matters, Webb and Dobie were closer to being on target than is Jordan. Frank Graham, a South Texas cowboy of long years, characterizes the difference between cowboys and vaqueros by saying that the vaquero is the "master teacher. He was here before Anglos came, and he gave his terminology to us." He also taught the British descendants of the South "how to work cattle in the wild, open country. And the vaquero knew the brush; the English did not." Ramirez supports this idea when she notes that in Texas the vaqueros remained behind when Anglos came to dominate ranching there, and those vaqueros taught the newcomers the skill of working cattle in open country and heavy brush (p. 252).

The corrective that Slatta has brought to Jordan's notions is encouraging and may lead to further correction of the notion that the cowboy is dead and gone. My own work in *Clear Fork Cowboys* (1985), *Ranch Rodeos in West Texas* (1988), *Historic Ranches of Texas* (1993), *Watkins Reynolds Matthews: Biography of a Texas Rancher* (1994), and *Cowboys* (1997) presents enough evidence to prove even to the most skeptical that cowboys are still working cattle in one region of the West and, by extension, in a good many others as well.

On the positive side of Jordan's extensive work, however, is his discussion of the fact that there were—and are—Cajun cowboys, some of them black descendants of slaves who worked cattle on horseback and drove herds of cattle to various markets, mostly to the east. Jim

Bob Tinsley, an authority on cowboy songs and cowboy life, notes that the black mounted herders were called "cattle hunters or graziers" and the white ones "cow keepers," (*He Was Singin' This Song*, p. 4), not "cowboys" and certainly not "vaqueros." This southern terminology was carried to Texas, where some early settlers from the South went on "cow hunts," not "roundups." These people, however, came to Texas after vaqueros had been ranching in South Texas for centuries. It seems apparent that Jordan's Louisiana incubator theory for the origin of open-range ranching as an institution in the United States lacks validity.

Even though the deepest debt of gratitude for the origin of Texas ranching goes to the Spanish-Mexican influence, Texas ranching was improved by the British use of breeds such as Hereford, Durham, and Angus, all of British origin and introduced into Texas by the 1880s. These breeds produce carcasses with a much better quality of beef than did the Longhorns. Of extreme importance as well is the introduction into South Texas of the Brahman from India in the 1860s, with large-scale introduction occurring by 1910. The Brahman is desirable because of its resistance to disease and parasites, traits that allowed it and its crossbred descendants to thrive in the hot, humid climate of South and East Texas. The British breeds brought to Texas by ship were hauled inland by wagon to avoid exposure to the Texas fever tick until the legally enforced use of the dipping vat ended this threat. The British breeds had no natural resistance to this deadly parasite, to which the Longhorn cattle in Texas and Mexico were immune.

A revealing analysis of the development of ranching farther north in Northwest Texas serves to illustrate how various influences merged to form a variant culture. Along the rich lands of the Clear Fork of the Brazos River in Shackelford, Stephens, and Jones counties and farther east into Palo Pinto and Parker counties, cattle barons such as Oliver Loving, Jesse Hittson, and others established ranching kingdoms and spread them all over the West. Men like John G. Irwin, Joseph Beck Matthews, and Barber Watkins Reynolds, all of Scottish descent, established significant and long-standing ranching operations and later trailed cattle to distant points on both sides of the Rocky Mountains. They were followed in the trade by George and W. D. Reynolds, John A. Matthews, John Chadbourne Irwin, and others whose descendants have continued their ranching interests into the present. Their early practices were developed on the open range, but as time has progressed, other practices suited to changes in the region have developed. Pastures have been fenced and cross fenced, some land has been put into cultivation (mainly for growing wheat in the winter), and cattle suited to the land have been selected, especially Herefords and Black Angus, often crossbred. In fact, Albany is called Home of the Hereford because of the early introduction of the breed into the region. Similar developments have occurred in other regions; for example, to the northwest of the Clear Fork region, at the once huge Matador Ranch, which was owned for decades by a Scottish syndicate.

In *A Texas Frontier*, Cashion credits Scottish roots for the kind of operation run by these men and cites two paths of entry. One, he says, spread "through the Piedmont and Appalachians into the Ohio Valley and the Midwest" and on "through Missouri" en route to North Texas. The other strand came "through Georgia, the Florida Panhandle, Alabama, Mississippi, and Louisiana before reaching deep East Texas" and coming to the plains of Texas (pp. 59–60). Raiding Indians were still a problem in the early days, and losses of stock and human life on both sides were common occurrences until General Ranald Mackenzie's successful foray against the Plains Indians in Palo Duro Canyon in 1874 forced the tribes onto reservations. The later slaughter of the buffalo herds ended this era of frontier life forever.

A cowboy culture still thrives in this area, especially along the Clear Fork, where the soil is shallow and rainfall scant in most seasons. Despite this environment, however, the area is one of the best cattle-raising areas in the world. There is little doubt, nevertheless, that the cowboy originated farther south.

Whatever the theory of genesis of the cowboy one accepts, it is sufficient to say that in the southern part of Texas developed a ranching culture that spread, along with its cattle, over the western part of Texas and hence on to other areas, especially the Northern Plains, where free grass beckoned to hardy souls that found ranching a promising way of life. The Texas ranching culture was often carried on the heads of Longhorn cattle that had been brought in by the Spanish and allowed to multiply on the open ranges of South Texas. There a man on horseback could look at the horizon and make a living at least as good as the man following a mule with a hand on the plow and an eye on the mule's posterior. The man on horseback had found a way of life that allowed him to rope and work with his cattle, not bend his back to chop weeds and crawl to pick cotton. Each of the basic divisions of agriculture has attracted followers, but the romance of the cowboy has proved the most attractive to the popular imagination. Farming and open-range ranching were the oil and water of frontier life. They did not mix. Cowboys hated plows and the people who plowed up the native pasture.

The chief demand supplied by the cattle on the Texas ranges in the early days was not the demand for beef, because there were no available markets. It was instead for hides and tallow, as it was in the Mexican trade. The tallow furnished candles for work in the silver mines, and one major use of the leather was to construct the bags in which the ore was transported. Some cattle, however, were driven to California to feed miners after the discovery of gold in 1849, and others were shipped through the ports of Indianola—a now-vanished Texas coastal town—New Orleans, and other riverboat outlets to beef markets. Cattle were driven eastward to these outlets from coastal areas, especially from around Victoria, Texas. Herds went west out of Texas along what became known as the Goodnight-Loving Trail to Colorado and New Mexico. These were fledgling days for the cowboy culture in Texas.

After the Civil War, the situation began to change with access to a major beef market through railheads in Kansas. The urge to meet this need grew from a paucity of money and goods but a surplus of cattle in Texas. One cowman there reportedly put his proposition to the men who had somehow survived the ravages of the Civil War: "We have two ways to go—north or broke." The Texans trailed north with their herds, and the cowboys, the drovers, tended to drift, to pick up work in season on various ranches and to feel no loyalty to a particular ranch.

The need for beef in northern markets led to the famous trail drives of cattle to the railheads in Kansas. Men such as Jesse Chisholm, Richard King, Charles Goodnight, Oliver Loving, Shanghai Pierce, and others established themselves as leaders in the industry. Routes such as the Chisholm Trail and, later, the Western Trail served as avenues from South Texas that put beef on dining tables in the East and gold into otherwise empty pockets in Texas. The importance of the cowboy grew as it was necessary for drovers to take the cattle from home ranges to the railroad corrals in Kansas.

As many as five million Longhorns went "up the trail," driven north by an estimated thirty-five thousand men between 1866 and the mid-1880s. Black cowboys, although much of the literature ignores them, made up a significant percentage of those who engaged in this cattle working during the period following the Civil War and into the present. Mexican vaqueros from South Texas were often part of the crews as well, though vaqueros often did not mix in well in crews where an Anglo was in charge.

The "typical" trail drive from Texas to Kansas, the most common (but certainly not the only route) of those moving cattle to market, began in the South Texas diamond described by Webb, where cattle were plentiful. The herds ran often up to 2,500 head of steers from two to ten years of age if going to market, mixed sexes if going to breeding ranges in the Northern Plains, including Montana, Wyoming, and Dakota Territory. A dozen or so men with a cook, wrangler, trail boss, and often a *segundo*, or second in command, made up the crew. Each animal in the herd was given a common brand, called a road brand, to identify all of the stock in case the herd became mixed with other cattle along the way, a fairly common occurrence as a result of stampede. The drive usually started in the spring when the grass was greening up. Green grass was important because the cattle were often poor coming out of the winter. The effort culminated weeks later as the herd slowly moved northward, grazing and gaining weight as it went. The men were with the cattle constantly, with little chance for sleep because of the need for the men to watch the herd in shifts, called "guard," to keep it settled and safe from possible attack by Indians or rustlers during the night. The days, of course, were spent keeping the herd spread out, grazing, but moving all the time to cover as much ground as possible.

The men's lives centered on the herd and the chuck wagon, their home away from home. The cook, typically recalled as mean-tempered but greatly appreciated, fed the men usually only two meals a day, breakfast at daylight and supper at dark after the herd was settled down. During the day, the wagon was on the move to the next bed ground specified by the trail boss. On the treeless plains, the tongue of the wagon was always pointed at the North Star each night so that the cowboys could keep the herd aimed toward its destination.

Meals varied little—beans, bacon, beef, bread, and coffee—with perhaps some comestibles traded for along the way. The bread, usually sourdough from the "sponge" carried in the chuck wagon, was a staple item, the smell of which leaves yearnings in the mind and stomach of a hungry cowboy.

Night guard was a drain on the men's energy but was a necessary activity. The men sang or whistled much of the time to keep awake as well as to let the cattle know of their presence so as not to startle the herd into wild stampede, a fearful event that happened often enough as it was. Causes could be an unfamiliar sound, a thunderstorm, or no ap-

A crew of cowboys in West Texas. *Swenson Ranch photo.*

parent reason at all. When "a run" did occur, the stampeding herd had to be turned or days of travel might be lost. Therefore, the object of the men was to ride to the lead, turn the leaders, and cause the herd to mill, or run in a circle. Best of all was for the herd to run north, toward the final destination, if at all possible. A wild ride in total darkness was dangerous and accounted for the deaths of many a trail hand.

When the herd reached the end of the trail, the railroad corral or the intended range, the cattle were sold or spread out to graze and the crew paid off and released. The wild time in town grew to legendary proportion as the men blew off steam and blew in their pay in the saloons, brothels, and clothing stores of the railheads. After being quiet around the herd, the Texans liked to make lots of noise. Often the men were broke in a matter of hours or days from the spree, which often included gambling in the saloons of Dodge City, Abilene, and other cattle towns.

The men returned home under various circumstances, sometimes as a group, often not, and the next spring many found an outfit going up the trail again and repeated the adventure. This heyday lasted only a relatively short period of time, from the mid-1860s to the 1880s, until railroad networks spread across cattle country and made the drives unnecessary. During this time, a legend was born, one that persists to this day, of the man on horseback herding cattle northward. Some of the adventures of these men are recorded in Marvin Hunter's *Trail Drivers of Texas*, in Teddy "Blue" Abbott's *We Pointed Them North*, and in novels like Andy Adams's *Log of a Cowboy*, Emerson Hough's *North of 36*, Benjamin Capps's *The Trail to Ogallala*, and Larry McMurtry's *Lonesome Dove*.

The trail drives spread the cowboy's presence and influence across the plains northward and east of the Rocky Mountains. As Texans trailed herds of beef cattle and, later, breeding stock to the northern ranges, some stayed to work in these new areas. Most soon returned to the warmer climates of Texas. An old cowboy song, "The Texas Cowboy," says, "Montana is too cold for me / And the winters are too long" (ll. 5–6) and "I nearly freeze to death, my boys / Whenever there's a storm" (ll. 11–12.) The speaker closes the song by saying, "You'll never get consumption / By sleeping on the ground" in Texas (ll. 59–60). Some

The reason for cowboys in the early days of the cattle kingdom—Longhorns. *Sonja Irwin Clayton photo.*

Cowboys holding a bunch of Hereford cows and calves around a tank, ca. 1920s. *Swenson Ranch photo.*

cowboys stayed to found ranches on the rich grasses of the Northern Plains, a pattern represented to an appreciative audience in recent years by Larry McMurtry in his novel and acclaimed television miniseries *Lonesome Dove.*

The climatic and economic factors that have caused the cowboy's life to change have been many and diverse. A major change was wrought during what is sometimes called the "die up" of 1886–1888. Unusually droughty summers and intensely cold winters killed huge numbers of cattle on all of the cattle ranges across the West. In some instances a heavy fall of snow would be followed by a brief thaw, followed by a long-standing freeze that deprived cattle of access to forage. No one in those days kept feed to care for all of their cattle, and the cattle starved and froze to death, leaving the ranges putrid when spring came. It was a disaster for the cattle business that ended open-range practices.

Ranching changed radically. Ranchers who came back in the business fenced their ranges to control the breeding of their herds, upgraded the quality of their herds with imported breeds such as Hereford and Durhams, and arranged to feed their cattle during bad weather. This parallels the greater care given cattle discussed by Jordan.

The traditions developed during trail driving continued as the men spent long weeks, even months, each year, doing the work on these early ranches. In the cow camps the men slept in their bedrolls, as they did when on the trail. The traditional bedroll was made of an eighteen-ounce tarpaulin, eight feet wide and eighteen feet long, folded to protect the sleeper. There was no mattress at all in this bedroll, and cover consisted of quilts and, in colder weather, a blanket or two. The tarp offered ample protection from the wind and even from the rain. A four-sided canvas tepee afforded additional protection in bad weather. These bedrolls and tepees were carried during the day in the chuck wagon. On ranches that had larger crews, the beds rode in a separate wagon known as the hoodlum wagon, often driven by a young would-be cowboy who got his start that way.

The men had to be ready when the wrangler brought the horses in, in the half-light of early morning. The men attached their lariats in one large circle and surrounded the horse herd. Designated ropers would

A crew of cowboys roping and dragging calves on the Swenson Ranch. *Swenson Ranch* photo.

A crew of cowboys finished with a freshly branded calf. Note the hats and shotgun chaps. *Swenson Ranch photo.*

then enter the remuda to rope out those horses which the men, indicating the horses by name, had chosen to ride that day. Once a horse was roped, the roper took the animal to the cowboy who called out its name, bridled it, and led it away to saddle up for the day's work.

The men drifted the herd of cattle to areas with suitable grazing, and in those days possession and ownership of the land amounted to about the same status. Later, as ranchers laid legal claim to tracts of land

and the more important element, water, ranching became more settled. The ranch headquarters became a series of buildings instead of a wagon, and bunkhouses and cookhouses replaced the cow camp and the chuck wagon for at least part of the year.

The pattern of ownership of ranches varied. Large corporations and foreign investors put money into ranching, and huge operations grew up in the West. The XIT and Matador ranches are good examples. Many other large operations were privately owned—such as the 6666, the Pitchfork, the Spade, and the King ranches. Many others were much smaller family spreads where a man and his wife simply raised livestock and their families. In Texas the majority of the land was privately owned, and the owners later fenced their land to control it. In many other states, much of the grazing land is still owned by the government and leased to ranchers.

Some ranchers kept a full complement of hands only during the busy working season—the warm months. During the winter little help

A branding-iron heater with numerous branding irons being heated. The mesquite wood on the rear of the old truck is for firing the heater. Note the wooden fence in the background. *Swenson Ranch photo.*

Chuck time around the wagon. Note the bedroll to the left of the picture. *Swenson Ranch photo.*

Two bedrolls showing signs of wear and in their natural setting, beside the chuck wagon. *Lawrence Clayton photo.*

Cowboy tepees designed to shelter two men from bad weather. The setting is the South Texas Ranching Festival in Kingsville, Texas, in February.

was required because feeding stock in the winter was not a common practice. The few hands who did work primarily spent their time riding through areas to turn back cattle drifting before winter storms. Lonely line shacks were erected in isolated regions to afford shelter for these men, and the crude structures also were used by travelers who chanced upon them and needed temporary shelter. Cowboys might spend part of their time in the winter skinning what was called "poverty hides," skins from cattle that had starved to death during the winter. They might also hunt wolves and take those pelts to make extra money during the winter season when cowboy work was slack.

Once spring arrived, a major chore was gathering cattle that had been driven far south by the winter storms and driving them back to the home range. Then the roundups for branding came, bringing a season of great activity requiring more help. In the 1920s men rode in to the ranch at the time this work normally took place, worked through the roundups, and drifted on, perhaps to return for the same work year after year.

A timeless scene—horseman penning cattle. This is on the Nail Ranch near Albany in 1985. *Sonja Irwin Clayton photo.*

The annual routine culminated in the fall with the gathering of cattle for market. This pattern differed noticeably from that of the vaquero, who tended to remain at one ranch over a period of many years.

The day of driving cattle is over. Now trucks do that job. The practice of hauling cattle grew steadily after World War II with the advent of various forms of mechanization and improved roads. On the day selected, the men round up the animals, separate those to be sold from the others, and load the animals on huge cattle vans. By noon, the job is completed. In the afternoon the cows are pregnancy tested, the culls sold, and the bred cows returned to the pasture to begin the cycle anew. This hauling technique has allowed the shipping of younger cattle that could not have withstood the rigors of trail drives. The physical demand on the animals is also lessened.

Cattle are easier to work today than in years past. Most ranches are fenced and cross fenced, and camps in which one man and his family live are strategically placed around large ranches. The camps usually sit at the point where four pastures join and have a set of pens, a feed house, barns, and a horse pasture. The pens are sometimes made of pipe welded to form strong barriers for the cattle but may also be of two-inch planks or net wire. Some ranchers have constructed pens of the heavy metal

Cowboys loading cattle into a cattle car for shipment to market, ca. 1930. *Swenson Ranch photo.*

A restored cattle car on the Chimney Creek Ranch. *Lawrence Clayton photo.*

The modern way to get cattle to market—the cattle van. Note the construction of the loading chute with steel pipe and sheet iron. *Sonja Irwin Clayton photo.*

panels used as guardrails on highways and welded these to pipe posts. Determining factors are materials readily available and money available for the project. Also common are cutting alleys, working chutes, and the like to make the work easier—and to make it more efficient by requiring fewer cowboys to do the work.

Ranges vary in mountainous areas such as Wyoming and Colorado, where ranchers graze their cattle in mountain meadows during the summer. This arrangement may require men to live in cow camps near the cattle or travel to and from the herds periodically to check on their condition. Trail drives, often on paved roadways, are required for herds to reach mountain pastures in spring and to return to the lower-level pastures before the snow flies. In most areas, cattle may be moved from pasture to pasture, especially as they are sorted for marketing.

Where camps are common, the men in each camp have responsibility for the animals in the pastures near the residence and perhaps other duties as well around the ranch. Relatively few bachelor bunkhouse cowboys exist any more, and the often-crude structures that housed them, spartan at best, have fallen into disrepair, are used as feed-storage facilities, or have been modernized to shelter hunters who pay handsomely to hunt deer and other game on the ranch.

Economics is today's watchword. Herds are carefully monitored for productivity and efficiency. Cows are palpated to assure pregnancy or culled from the herd to avoid the pasturing of unproductive females. Bulls are tested for fertility. The trusty Longhorns, which fell out of favor after the disasters of 1886–1888, have seen a resurgence of interest for breeding heifers of the beefier breeds—Hereford and Angus, for example. This practice is sound because the Longhorn breed's characteristic of having slender-frame offspring allows heifers to calve earlier than they might if bred to a bull of the beefier breeds known for heavier, bulkier births. The Spade Ranches in Texas are even using Jersey bulls, known for their slim torsos, to breed the heifers at a young age. The animals are then able to calve on their own. Since a cow's productive life is ten to twelve years, it is a bonus for the rancher to see that she has the

A variety of fencing with the old net wire on wooden posts in the foreground, steel pipe in the background. *Sonja Irwin Clayton photo.*

Modern welded-steel fencing, Nail Ranch, Albany, Texas. *Sonja Irwin Clayton photo.*

first calf as early as possible. If too early, the heifer cannot birth the calf. Unless she has help, she will die. A distinct preference for Longhorns that are not spotted has developed because buyers who detect the Longhorn characteristics refuse to pay top price for these calves. The slender conformation of the animals is a negative factor in the feedlot. The dark color hides this identity but not the slender build.

Economics has also led to reduction in the labor force. The pickup and the stock trailer have become important to the life of the modern cowboy and allow relatively few men to do the work once performed by larger crews. Horses are hauled to the area in which they are to work, thereby cutting down on time spent riding across country to gather the horses from their pastures. Cattle are hauled not only to market, but to desired locations on the ranch, and strays can thus easily and quickly be returned to the correct pasture.

On most ranches, the men feed cattle in the winter from automatic feeders mounted on the backs of trucks or, even today, from a wagon pulled by a team of horses or mules. In extreme cold, trucks are hard to start; teams of horses are more reliable. There are no more "poverty hides" because winter feeding and careful culling of old or diseased animals have virtually eliminated winter losses of cattle.

The methods employed for gathering cattle in a pasture have their roots in the old days. One method is known as the wheel maneuver, and another as the line drive. For the wheel maneuver, one cowboy is sent around the outer edge of the pasture and others establish a line of contact with this outside man with a line anchored in the center of the pasture. The foreman usually rides near the center to observe the conduct of the drive and give arm signals if necessary. The riders sweep the cattle before them toward the corrals. This pattern works well, particularly in large pastures if there are not enough cowboys to form a line all the way across. The line maneuver requires that the cowboys haul their horses to the back of the pasture and unload them there. Then the men mount up and spread out in a line across the pasture and move the stock ahead of them. Although many large pastures still exist in cowboy country, the big circles of twenty or more miles are rare.

The Quarter Horse has become the mainstay in the work of gath-

Terry Moberly uses a hoolihan loop to catch one of the remuda in the headquarters corral on Lambshead Ranch, Shackelford County, Texas. *Sonja Irwin Clayton photo.*

Part of the remuda tied up to the trailer while the cowboys work in the pens. *Lawrence Clayton photo.*

ering cattle, although some Thoroughbred crosses will be found. Some use of Arabians also has been tried, particularly on the Renderbrook Spade Ranch in West Texas. These animals have the stamina to cover great distances but sometimes lack the innate cow sense necessary for a good working horse for a cowboy. The supply of horses has become excellent, especially with the current interest in cutting horses, which has provided some outstanding ranch horses from those rejected from cutting horse training. Most cutting horse prospects are smaller than the horse some cowboys prefer for ranch work. Ted Gray, who worked with cattle all his life in the Davis Mountains of Texas, commented on the unsuitability of small horses for much of cowboy work: "Those little horses can trot in the shade all day and not cover the ground I need to cover to get my work done." Some ranches still keep herds of brood mares, but many prefer to buy horses or trade for them. Some cowboys find they can buy horses from people who live in town and use the animals infrequently and "spoil" them. The men then work that streak out of the horse and have an outstanding ranch horse cheaper than they can raise, break, and train their own animals.

The ranches that still have mare bands need a trainer to work with the untrained horses. Someone designated for the job works with the animals until they will accept the saddle. Now horses are broken to ride by methods of gentling to accept the rider. Ray Hunt, a well-known horseman, has pioneered and developed these techniques, and the horse is not allowed to learn to pitch, certainly a welcome change from earlier practices. After gentling, the animals are distributed to the cowboys, who ride each of the new horses in rotation. Sometimes ranches sell off part of the remuda. A good example is a sale in October 1997, at which the 6666, Pitchfork, and Beggs ranches sold sixty ranch horses to appreciative buyers.

Most cowboys in modern times complain that the training of their horses is not the same as that found before 1960. With the advent of

Two cowboys, ca. 1930. Note the hats, manila lariats, split leather reins, and saddles with swelled forks. The one on the left has a "bronc" swell. *Swenson Ranch photo.*

George Peacock on the Nail Ranch, 1985. *Sonja Irwin Clayton photo.*

trailers and the elimination of the screwworm menace, the amount of work a horse gets is greatly diminished. When the men had to ride eight, ten, or more miles to the pasture to work, it gave them time to train their horses. Morris Ledbetter, an Albany rancher, said that "the quality of a horse has a lot to do with how many wet saddle blankets a cowboy takes off of it." Now the horses are hauled, and the long rides to pasture are no more. With the elimination of the screwworm, the men no longer spend time prowling the cattle herds, looking for infested animals, then roping and doctoring them. Most of the animals are worked in pens while the horses stand idly by. Frank Graham, who has worked in the South Texas brush country around Hebbronville for many years, says that the last good horses they had were trained during an unusual outbreak of ear ticks in that area in the 1970s. The screwworm, which had been virtually eliminated, made a remarkable comeback on the bloody ears of the cattle. Frank says that "for a year we kept our horses saddled all the time and rode a lot of long hours roping calves in the brush and doctoring them. That's the kind of experience that a horse has to have in order to be a good horse."

When the wrangler gathers horses from a fenced horse pasture for the day's work, he may bring all of the horses in at night or early in the morning to the horse corral at the headquarters. In the outlying camps, each man wrangles his own. Some horses stand to be caught. Others usually dart off from the cowboy at least once or twice to be sure, it seems, that he is the horse that the cowboy wants. Then typically the horse stands to be caught, bridled, and saddled for the day's work. If the horses are roped, the hoolihan—a flattened loop that settles around the horse's head—is often the loop of choice.

The work intended for that day determines which of the horses the man will select, since some horses are better on wide sweeps and others in the pens branding calves. The wrangler must feed the horses and ensure that the animals are through eating by the time the men show up at the saddle house to saddle up for the day. The crew usually loads the horses into trailers and pulls out to the pasture to be worked in order to be in position to begin the work when enough daylight shows to allow the men to ride off.

Horses in a trailer headed to work. *Sonja Irwin Clayton photo.*

George Peacock first went to the Nail Ranch in the 1960s as wrangler. The ranch kept a large black Thoroughbred horse as a night horse; that is, one kept in the corral at night to bring in the remuda the next morning. Peacock remembers that the horse loved his work. Peacock would saddle the horse, open the corral gate, mount up, and ride into pitch darkness. All he had to do was hang on as the horse left at a dead run to the back side of the pasture where he would round up the remuda and bring it to the house. It was an interesting game that the horse played with the remuda. Peacock also remembers that the horse might suddenly dart to one side at a dead run. Peacock knew that one of the horses was trying to break away and that the night horse was bringing it back. Humor in cowboy life can be found even in this work. When one of the men asked Peacock how he knew he had them all, Peacock responded with his dry humor: "I just count the hoof beats there in the dark and divide by four and that tells me how many horses I've got."

Because the market for slaughter horses to export to Europe for food has been so lucrative in the 1990s, the price of all horses has escalated sharply to the point that from two thousand to six thousand dollars is not uncommon for a horse trained enough to work ably. Well-trained, gentle horses can bring far more. On most ranches cowboys ride and train young horses as has been done since the beginning of this kind of work. On the Brown Ranch in Throckmorton County of Northwest Texas, the cowboys train young horses and receive part of the selling price if the horse is sold to an outside buyer.

Branding is one of the aspects of working cattle in which changes in technique have increased efficiency. Once the cattle are gathered and the calves separated from the cows during the branding season, the animals are "worked." The calves are separated from the cows either by pushing the cows through a gate and cutting the calves back or by running all the animals down a cutting alley with gates that open to various pens. Men standing overhead maneuver the gates in such a way that the animals are separated into pens for working. Some of the new devices used by modern cowboys are metal traps, called working tables or calf cradles. One of the men pulls the trap shut on a calf and then lays the metal framework, calf secured inside, on its side. The calf is then worked without the threshing and fighting often seen in other methods. This drive toward efficiency in working the cattle tends to be more characteristic of the cowboy than of the vaquero and the buckaroo. Ramirez notes that the patience characteristic of the vaquero was picked up by the buckaroo, but not by the cowboy (p.264).

Use of the old roping and dragging method reveals the true cowboy. In fact, some consider skill in using the rope well the best indicator of a cowboy's ability. The cowboy rides into the herd and uses his thirty-foot lariat to snare a calf at close range. He may tie his rope hard and fast or he may dally his lariat. No long catches are typical here, as they are in the buckaroo culture. The small calf may be caught by the head and dragged to the crew waiting to work it. If the calf is larger, then the roper snares the heels to drag the animal to the crew. As the rider passes by the men on the ground, one man grabs the rope and another the tail of the calf. The two pull in opposite directions and throw the animal to the ground. The crew then releases the rope immediately so that the roper can return to the herd to catch another calf.

The use of the lariat is far older than the cowboy. One of the vaquero traditions adopted by Texas cowboys was the use of the lazo. In their ways of handling livestock, Texans preferred a different kind of rope, one made from twisted grass or manila or other natural fibers and thirty to thirty-five feet long, not sixty or more as the vaquero's rawhide riata usually was. These stronger ropes and sturdier saddles led to the practice of tying the lasso "hard and fast" to the saddle horn, not of wrapping or dallying the rope around the horn as the vaqueros did so as to give slack to the plunging animal and thereby spare the riata, which could break if too much strain were applied by an animal.

For cowboys, a single roper, not a team, catches each animal by the head or heels, not both, and drags it to a crew waiting to work it. Team roping, in which one roper catches the head and a second the heels, is mostly a sport reserved for the arena or for doctoring an animal too large, strong, or wild to throw down otherwise. Some cowboys dally when roping and dragging, but many tie off to avoid the risk of losing a finger or a thumb when the rope tightens around the saddle horn.

Tying the rope "hard and fast" to the saddle horn is done by half hitching the rope around the horn or by using a honda, an oblong ring of metal or even plaited rawhide through which the rope passes to form a small loop that is snugged around the horn. This device allows the rope to be loosened and easily removed from the horn.

An entangled cowboy can be dragged to death by a spooked horse or hurt by the entangling rope itself. In one recently recounted incident, a young cowboy had his arm caught in the loop of a rope and, if not for the quick action of his partner, who rode in and cut the rope, would have been more seriously hurt. As it was, the loop of rope around his bicep severed most of the muscle, which had to be reattached surgically.

Two ropers engaged in the arena sport of heading and heeling. *Lawrence Clayton photo.*

George Peacock, a West Texas cowboy and ranch foreman, says of the rope: "It is a tool a cowboy needs, but it is like a gun—it's always loaded and can hurt you."

Anyone who dresses up like a cowboy, mounts an appropriately outfitted horse, and rides out to do cattle work is still not a cowboy. Those who really understand this work do it with the ease and expertise expected of a professional. No motion is wasted as they do their work quickly and efficiently. Only by seeing a man work can one tell if that person really deserves to be called a cowboy. As George Peacock and I rode off on a roundup on the Alexander Ranch near Abilene one morning, I said, "George, we have lots of cowboys today." George wisely responded, "We have lots of riders. By noon we'll know how many cowboys we have." He was right.

Many things about range life have changed over the years, but cowboys still exist. Cattle have to be herded and shipped, and, despite the picture presented in the movies, life on a ranch is less romantic than it seems in the Grade-B western movies. Many of the cowboys are married, and the pickup has replaced the horse for transportation home at night or off to town. Some things have remained the same, but the food is less boring, and the life is less lonely now that so many cowboys have wives and television sets and pickups. Cowboys today eat a more diversified diet than cowboys in the early days of ranching. Like his predecessor the vaquero, the early cowboy existed on a poor diet limited to what was available and would keep without refrigeration. This situa-

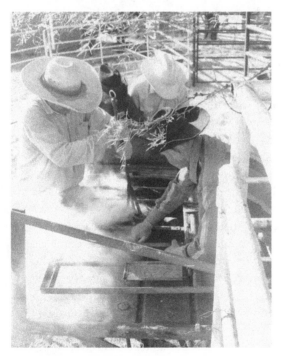

A four-man crew working a calf in a working table. *Sonja Irwin Clayton photo.*

The working table in its upright position. *Sonja Irwin Clayton photo.*

tion restricted him to beans, cured bacon, bread from either sourdough starter or baking powder, and whatever fresh meat was available. Sometimes the meat was wild game but frequently it was beef, though some ranchers became particular about who killed calves on the ranch and for what reasons.

Variations in the early cowboy's meals were few and far between. Molasses was the universal sweetener because it was much cheaper than sugar. Dried apples, raisins, and prunes, though available in short supply, sometimes provided variety in diet, and when canned goods became available, corn, tomatoes, and peaches found a friendly reception. Fresh vegetables, eggs, and milk were rare and were purchased from farmers, when possible, on trail drives. An old joke about the Texas range is that it had more cows and less milk than anywhere else in the world. Charlie Cone, a West Texas cowboy, recalls the old chuck wagon diet and also remembers the effect of World War I on the bread. Too young to serve, he stayed with his cowboy life but missed the biscuits due to wartime rationing of flour. He adjusted to the cornbread instead, even for breakfast.

Coffee was the standard drink, and lots of it. Arbuckle was the name of the company that provided roasted beans that would retain freshness until ground. Each wagon had a coffee grinder mounted on the side or on the grub box to do the grinding. The pot was kept over the coals of the fire in order that the beverage would be ready for anyone who needed a cup.

The cook (*cocinero* or *coosie*) who could take these few ingredients and turn them into a tasty meal was a valued member of the crew and drew higher wages than the regular cowboys, whose wages ranged up to thirty dollars a month until well after the turn of the century. The coosie's domain—chuck box, campfire, coffee pot, dutch ovens, and pots—was his to rule alone, and he was either loved or despised, depending upon his ability and temperament. Besides being cook, he was doctor, nurse, and pharmacist, frequently performing these functions under adverse conditions at best, whether he was in a cow camp, on the trail, or back in the cookshack at the ranch headquarters. Most of these cooks were notorious for wanting simply to be left alone and did not like

A lariat half-hitched hard and fast to a saddle horn. *Sonja Irwin Clayton photo.*

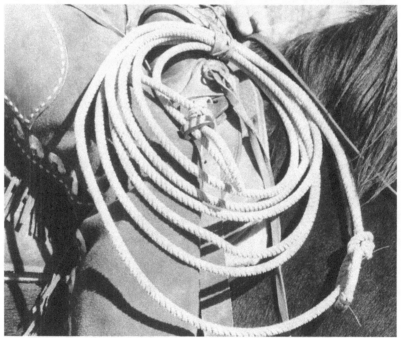

A variety of hondas for securing hard and fast. *Sonja Irwin Clayton photos.*

A mule-drawn chuck wagon, c. 1920s. *Swenson Ranch photo.*

loafers hanging around the wagon picking at the food. A good reason was that men walking around on dry ground raised dust, an unwanted ingredient in the cook's food. One tradition says that the cooks regularly dumped their dishwater beneath the wagon to keep men from lying in what was often the only shade available on the treeless plains.

The diet of today's cowboys resembles that of the rest of the population, with refrigeration making possible fresh vegetables, ice, and the like. The men still favor fresh beef, beans, potatoes, fresh bread, and sometimes a dessert for the noon meal. Iced tea is a favorite at noon in hot weather, but coffee is still the standard breakfast drink and may be consumed throughout the day when opportunity exists. For his lunch when he is working, the cowboy does not like to eat ham, fish, or other salty meats that cause a burning thirst during an afternoon away from the water keg. Feral hogs taken from the ranch may provide pork for breakfast or barbecue on special occasions.

Some ranches still have cooks, but the cranky old "coosie" may have changed into the wife of the foreman or that of one of the cowboys. Sue Peacock, whose husband, George, is manager of the Nail Ranch, is one of the best cooks in the area. Lambshead Ranch keeps a cookhouse to serve meals to the cowboys, ranch family members, and guests. Bill Cauble, a widely known chuck wagon cook, is often the chef for these meals. The cook may prepare the meals for the crew only on days when the men are working the cattle. On some ranches today, the men may be expected to fend for themselves for all of their meals. The men drive in their pickups to their houses, where the wife has the meal ready or has left it to be warmed in the microwave oven, if she has a job in town.

Clothing has changed over the years, but today's cowboys still retain many of the traditional garments of the early cowboys. In fact, clothing is the most obvious part of the cowboy's image. Anyone can "see by your outfit that you are a cowboy," as the dying cowboy in the old folk song "The Cowboy's Lament" plaintively states. This typical "outfit" for the cowboy developed over a period of time. Like the vaqueros along the border, the first Texas cowboys were poverty stricken. On their roundups, forays on which the men roped and branded unclaimed cattle, Texas cowboys wore whatever kinds of nondescript clothing they could obtain or make from available materials. Pants, shirts, and moccasins as well as hats and caps made of leather served the purpose of some. Homespun shirts were common (Dary, p. 85, and Abbott, p. 7). Thomas Horton described the head covering as "a dollar wool hat." He also cites "stogy" boots—rough, cumbersome footwear, likely with tall tops resembling the stogy, or cigar—and a homemade overcoat (p. 142) that served as protection from cold and rain and doubled as a covering at night as the men wandered far from home and stayed wherever night caught them.

As the trail drives began, largely after the Civil War, some change in appearance occurred. Many of the drovers wore parts of military uniforms and hats. Before many trail herds had made the drive to Kansas, however, distinct patterns of clothing made for the task began to appear, and the outfit of the Texas cowboy soon began to emerge because it fitted the work. Trail drivers bought what they could in Kansas as well as items along the way up and back. The clothing was not uniform, and especially was it not clean or often in good repair because the chance to bathe and change clothes regularly was uncommon, even if the men had extra clothes to change into. Marsh cites one of the rules of the cow camp on the LX Ranch in Texas: "If you pull off any old clothes that you don't want, burn them, as it doesn't look good to leave a camp ground so filthy" (n.p.).

By 1870, hats of beaver felt became the standard head covering for cowboys. The men, according to Rollins, left the crown of this hat "at its full height, but applied three or four dents running vertically at the top of the crown, a style later to become known as the Montana Poke" (p. 104). Other techniques of shaping the hat followed, but the tall crown and rolled brim were common by the turn of the century. The name of John B. Stetson, the most popular manufacturer, came to be the dominant one, frequently being applied to a hat regardless of the source. For their hats, cowboys preferred leather hatbands, sometimes of rattle-snake skin. Ornamentation of nails or silver conchos, or in rare cases gold or jewels, decorated the leather bands. Whatever their construction, these bands were more than merely ornamental; they were intended to control the size of the hat to make it fit the cowboy's head more securely, especially in the wind. A "bonnet string," a leather thong descending from the inner edge of the brim, running behind the wearer's ears, and pushed under the base of the skull, kept the hat in place when the wind was high or the ride fast. It differed from the string that passed under the chin on the sombrero, and from the "stampede string" of the bucka-roos. When not needed, the "bonnet string" was tucked up inside the cowboy's hat (Rollins, p. 104). For some years after the cowboys on the border no longer wore sombreros, that Spanish term was used in a slang sense to refer to the cowboy's hat (Rollins, p. 105) and is still recognized in that way.

Indeed the cowboy's hat has undergone many transitions in ap-pearance, the shape being one of the ways of identifying the home re-gion of the wearer. Today's younger cowboys are shaping the brims of their hats differently from the generation of cowboys before them. The crowns have fairly traditional crushes, but the brims are not rounded up on the sides as the older cowboys prefer. Instead, the younger cow-boys roll the edges up slightly on the sides and slant them down in the front and back. Although some older hat wearers also prefer this style, it seems to predominate among cowboys age twenty-five and below.

Also common among the younger cowboys are vent holes in either contrasting or compatible colors on the hats. Quite common in black hats, for instance, are red vent holes. This system allows ventilation to the wearer's head, and in hot weather the felt hat is tolerable. The bon-net strings are quite rare in modern cowboy hats. Buster McLaury, a fine cowboy and writer-poet, says of these strings—they are "something to hang a limb in" (Dec. 1994, p. 41).

The neckerchief preferred by the cowboy is approximately thirty-six inches square and will likely be of silk, though smaller pieces of bandanna cotton have long been a favorite among cowboys. In fact, the inexpensive cotton bandanna, costing ten cents each in the 1850s, has been preferred historically because early-day shopkeepers kept these in stock and the cowboys had little other choice. The neckerchief may sport a slide, often of plaited rawhide, or a wooden ornament with a hole through it to hold the ends. More than likely the ends will be tied, usually in a square knot. When the rider is herding cattle, the neckerchief may be loosely secured to form a mask pulled in place over the mouth and nose for protection from the dust. In cold weather, the neckerchief may be tied snugly around the neck to provide protection against the cold wind. The neckerchief has many other uses: a blindfold to calm an outraged cow, a makeshift rope, a towel, a napkin, a bandage, a handkerchief, or just an ornament (Horgan, p. 13).

The early cowboy's shirt was made of cotton flannel or wool and was usually collarless. Cowboys preferred colors other than red, since that shade was traditionally worn by miners (Rollins, p. 109). The shirts always have long sleeves for protection from the brush and the rays of the sun. The typical cowboy shirt today is cut with a yoke, perhaps of contrasting color or design, in front and in back and has a collar. Sturdy blue denim shirts are popular, but all kinds of shirts of various descriptions, often discarded dress shirts, may be seen. When a cowboy is conscious of his appearance, however, he will wear the "typical" cowboy shirt, usually with pearl snap buttons and in a bright color, contrasting stripes, or sometimes a floral pattern. Pieced contrasting colors and contrasting patterns of cloth, especially with bright colors, have characterized a new generation of Western shirts in the 1990s, apparently triggered by those worn in performances by Garth Brooks and other popular country and western singers. Yellow is not a suitable color, especially for today's rodeo cowboys, to whom it symbolizes cowardice.

The early cowboys wore pants of various sorts, though a kind of striped wool pants from Oregon City found great favor. Charlie Cone recalls that in the early decades of this century in Eastern New Mexico and West Texas, the men often wore khaki pants year round but put long underwear and perhaps another pair of pants on in cold weather. And this was under their chaps. Today's cowboy will be found in blue cotton denim jeans bearing the brand of Levi or Wrangler, brands that compete for the "cowboy image." These are usually tight-fitting and may sport a bandanna handkerchief protruding from one of the back pockets. Often a round can of Skoal or other "smokeless tobacco" will rest in one of these back pockets and leave its imprint, viewed by some as a mark of maturity if not virility despite medical warnings against the use of to-bacco. Since cigarette smoking around barns and dry grass poses a threat of fires that could sweep out of control, some ranchers limit or forbid smoking.

A man may or may not wear a belt to hold up his pants while work-ing. Some men shun a belt because it may hang on the saddle horn of a bucking horse and cause the rider to get hung up and hurt if jarred loose from the saddle. Hand-tooled belts have been common for years, espe-cially with the wearer's name gracing the back. This style lost favor in the 1970s and 1980s, and the tooling of oak leaves, basket weave, or other patterns covers the entire belt. A style using a pass-through buckle of silver with tips and loops has seen extensive use.

Still widespread is the use of a trophy buckle; that is, a large flat buckle with a stud on the back inserted through a hole in the leather to secure tension on the belt. These are often prizes at ropings and ranch rodeos and are silver with gold, brass, or copper embossing and word-ing indicating the occasion for the trophy. Figures include men or even horses in various activities such as horse riding, barrel racing, roping, and the like. Suspenders are rarely used by cowboys, though occasion-ally one may be seen wearing suspenders advertising a popular brand of beer.

When warmer clothing is needed in the winter, a vest becomes a standard part of the cowboy outfit. This sleeveless garment allows free movement of the cowboy's arms while still providing insulation from the cold. One of the principal uses is afforded by the vest pockets, which serve to hold the cowboy's "makings." Today that is less commonly Bull Durham than ready-rolled cigarettes. In cold weather a down-filled vest is popular, but the cowboy's light leather vest is part of his outfit when he goes to town, even in summer. Coats may be down-filled models in cold weather or denim jackets usually cut at the waist. A coat extending to the hips and made of brown cotton duck lined with wool has lately proved more durable in the brush than the nylon down-filled jacket, which is easily torn by thorns. These sturdy canvas coats may or may not be lined with wool or artificial fleece. Long coats or dusters are rare and are almost never seen when the men are working, especially on the southern ranges, where long underwear is not always necessary. Yellow rain slickers, either waist or full length, have long been standard wear, replacing the old "fish," or raincoat.

Although many Texas cowboys rode on the open plains, some rode in heavy brush, from which they needed protection. Texas cowboys who rode the brush of South Texas were commonly known as "brush poppers," and they owed more to the vaquero than did the open-range cowboys. Frank Graham has worked for over thirty years in the heavy brush of South Texas. He says that in order to catch cattle, several men ride through the brush barking like dogs to make the cattle move out of cover. Then the chase is on. One or more of the men get in front of the animal needing to be caught and rope it when it breaks into a clearing. The man has to act quickly and throw the lariat with unerring accuracy in this setting, or the animal will escape again. When these riders come out of the brush, they and their horses may be scratched and bloody, and tree limbs may be caught around the horns and front swells of their saddles. These limbs the men have "popped" off while running through the brush; hence the name.

The vaquero had early worked out a system whereby cattle could be rounded up and otherwise handled in the thick, thorny brush. This methodology included being protected by heavy leather chaps and an unlined jacket, often called a brush jacket, made of a heavy cotton duck material. Lee Clayton, who ranched in Live Oak County in the 1940s and 1950s, rode with all of the protection he could and still emerged scratched and bleeding from the brush, as did his horse.

The boots the cowboy wears while riding are special to him. He will likely have a pair of dress boots, perhaps with a low heel and a rounded toe, and a pair of rough work boots he wears when he feeds stock or does menial chores. The riding boots are usually handmade with a high underslung heel, so that the foot will be less likely to slip through the stirrup, and a more pointed toe (not the sharply pointed one) to slip into the stirrup easily. The heel may protrude slightly in the rear or on the side to form a ridge that keeps the spur from sliding down over the heel and being lost. The tops, often with a vee in front and back, come to the bottom of the knee. The cowboy often tucks his pants legs into the tops of the boots, and the brightly colored and ornately stitched and decorated tops are thus displayed to public view. Black bottoms and red tops are frequent color combinations, but variation from this combination is common, such as yellow or green tops and brown bottoms. In the past decade some cowboys have begun wearing "packers," a lace-up style of boot common among buckaroos. A lace-up, flat-heeled boot has shown up in recent years, a combination of the packer and the flat-heeled, low-top boot called a "roper." Cowboys usually find these unsuitable for work. One of the best-known boot makers in Texas is James Leddy of Abilene, a man whose family has been making boots for de-

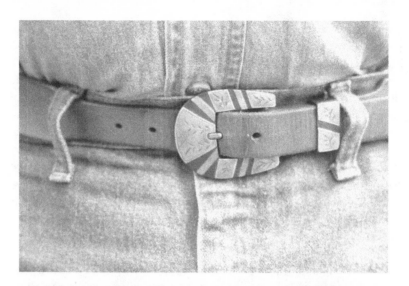

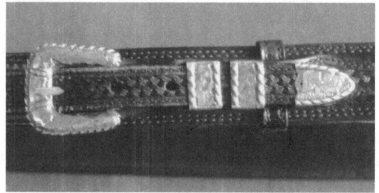

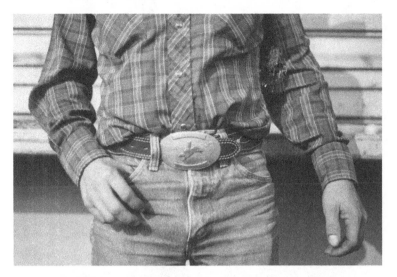

A series of belt buckles in styles found among cowboys. *Sonja Irwin Clayton photos.*

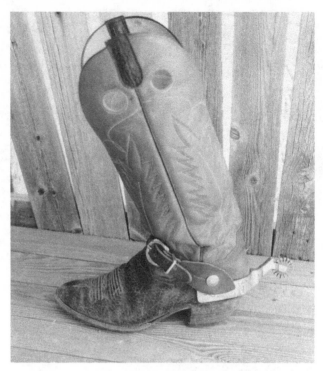

"Manly footwear"—a typical cowboy boot with spur attached. *Lawrence Clayton photo.*

cades. He is one of many who supply a demand from working cowboys but even more so from a clientele of lawyers, physicians, businessmen, and truckdrivers.

The history of the cowboy boot is interesting and the original source debatable. Some early-day boot makers located their shops along the cattle trails north to serve the demand of drovers headed to Kansas. The tops of these boots were often decorated with Texas stars and other such designs. Tom C. McInerney had a shop with sometimes up to twenty makers in Abilene, Kansas, at trail's end (Dary, p. 202). Later shops, especially those associated with the names Justin and Hyer, worked out a way for the men to measure their own feet and request custom-fitted footwear by mail order. These early-day boots often cost as much as a month's wages, usually around thirty dollars. Today's cowboy may pay as much as seven to eight hundred fifty dollars for a pair of boots suited to his taste. Although the inflation in price is enormous, the ratio has changed little. A good pair of working boots cost a month's wages in the 1920s, and they still do. The wages of the cowboy have fluctuated just about to that extent.

In addition to protecting his feet, the boot is where the cowboy straps on his handmade spurs, one of his prized possessions. Anyone who shows up for work in spurs made in Korea or some other foreign place is sure to be suspected of being a greenhorn, or novice. The spur that found earliest acceptance on the range was the Spanish-influenced Mexican spur characterized by large, spoke-like rowels. Some of these spurs were ornamented and engraved in floral or geometric patterns. The spurs sometimes carried a small metal piece, later called a jingle-bob, that sounded against the multispoked rowel. These models evolved into a spur with a smaller rowel. One commercially mass-produced model was the OK spur, a somewhat modest style available from merchants, which sold in large numbers before handmade spurs became preferred. Famous makers include Joe Bianchi, J. R. McChesney, the Kelly brothers (especially P. M. Kelly), Oscar Crockett, and a number of regional and local workers. Jerry Cates of Amarillo, Billy Klapper of Pampa, Gerald Stockard of Bowie, Tommy Spraberry of Anson, and Bob Williams of Albany are examples of these artisans. Stockard, Spraberry, and Williams, like many others, are also cowboys, and they make spurs on order only and then only when spare time is available for that activity. Some cowboys still measure their wealth by their bit and spur collections.

Earlier cowboy spurs were typically fashioned from a single piece of steel cut and hammered into the shape of the finished product and then polished to a smooth finish. Today the cowboy's spurs may well be of two parts, the band and the shank, which are welded together. They may have stationary or swinging buttons to which the leather straps attach. The spurs are not overly ornate. The brand of the ranch or the owner's name or initials in either brass or silver are frequently mounted on the band of the spurs, and the shank sports bars or other decorations, most if not all on the outside to be visible to everyone and to be away from the horse sweat, which can corrode the decoration enough to cause it to drop off. Some stainless steel is used, but more common is steel that forms a patina of rust that contrasts with the decorative figures. The short-shank, small-roweled spur is preferred. Chap guards on the shanks are common but far from universal. Jingle-bobs are even less often worn; riding in brush can tear these off anyway. The noise that they make alerts cattle and wild game that a human is around and is, therefore, undesirable to some cowboys. The spur straps, called "leathers," range from plain to ornately tooled. A growing trend is to have on the leathers

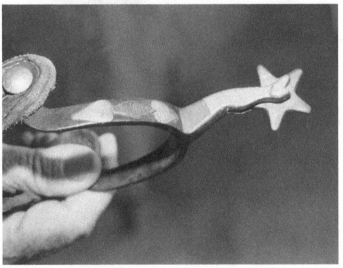

A montage of cowboy spurs. Note that two have the gal-leg design. *Sonja Irwin Clayton photos.*

handmade, ornate buckles sporting the wearer's brand or initials in silver or brass.

Handmade spurs are often given as prizes at ranch rodeos and for special gift occasions. Cowboys may own several pairs of spurs, often worth hundreds of dollars a pair, but these expensive ones are worn on special occasions, such as parades, and less often for work. Contemporary designs have left behind the gooseneck and gal-leg in favor of a plainer shank.

Leather leggings, or "chaps," are one mark of the cowboy. Made from a moderately soft, supple leather, these coverings are essential for protecting the cowboy's legs from brush and, in winter, from cold. In areas where the thorny brush is more threatening, the leather is thicker. The straight-leg shotgun chaps are most common. These are closed on the back, usually by full-length zippers, so that the cowboy does not have to run his boot through the tube-like leg. Often the boot has traces of manure or other "foreign matter" that is best not spread on the inside of the leggings. The chaps may or may not sport fringe. The fuller cut batwing chaps are also seen occasionally, and more recently the shorter "chinks," or "summer chaps," borrowed from the buckaroos have gained popularity in some areas.

The clothing is certainly part of the image. As the old song indicates, a cowboy is easy to spot by his "outfit," each part of which has historic precedent and continues to have distinct functions in order to survive in use.

The author dons his shotgun chaps. Note the zippers on the back to close them. *Sonja Irwin Clayton photo.*

The tack of the cowboy is another distinctive feature of the mounted herder. The saddle, the centerpiece of his working gear, is a true mark of the type. It developed over decades into a tool that fits the work.

The first stockmen to come into Texas from the East came with hornless Eastern-style saddles, but these were soon found quite unsatisfactory for the rugged wear and tear required for working cattle and riding wild mustangs. These early Texans quickly adopted the Mexican saddle with its wooden tree covered with rawhide to provide strength. The single-rigged saddles—with one girth coming down from the rigging around the saddle horn—also featured a large horn convenient for use in roping and rider safety. When commercially tanned leather became available from tanneries in Indianola, New Braunfels, and even later in Waco, Dallas, and San Antonio, the Texans added leather coverings to these saddles. Trees were lengthened to make the saddles more comfortable and easier on the horse's back, and wool fleece underlinings were added. As the needs apparent in trail driving became a motivating force for saddle makers, the production of suitable Western stock saddles became widespread. Andy Adams in his famous *Log of a Cowboy* said that the early-day cowboys' saddles covered their mounts "from withers to hips, weighed thirty to forty pounds, and were bedecked with the latest in the way of trimmings and trappings" (p. 14). These saddles were made to sit in for long hours of riding. Perhaps the best-known of the early Texas saddle makers was S. D. Myres, who reached the peak of his fame from his Sweetwater, Texas, shop before later moving on to El Paso. Myres's saddles are widely known as the standard of quality in Texas, though saddles from shops in Pueblo and Denver, Colorado, and Miles City, Montana, and from other well-known makers found extensive acceptance on the range.

Saddles underwent a transition in the 1950s in response to the rodeo calf roper's need to get out of the saddle quickly to tie the calf. This need prompted the rolled cantle and shallow seat. In short, it forced the creation of a saddle made to get out of easily rather then to stick in tightly. The influence has not completely disappeared.

Today's cowboy saddle is a double-rigged, rimfire model; that is, one with the front girth passing down directly below the saddle horn and the second girth dropping down from below the cantle to secure the saddle when the cowboy ties a plunging animal to the saddle horn with the lariat. The front girth, or girt as it is usually called, is fashioned from mohair. Leather or, less often, nylon latigos on each side provide the means to cinch up the saddle. The back girth, called a "flank girt" is of heavy leather and is snug but not tightened, unless the rider expects a heavy pull while roping. These double-rigged saddles are common in cowboy country, and few variations are found. A cowboy riding a three-quarter- or seven-eighths-rigged saddle (which has the front girth moved back a short distance behind the swell in the saddle) probably grew up or worked for a time somewhere else, likely west of the Rockies. The saddles have swelled forks, sometimes exaggerated to form what is called a "bronc" saddle that offers a protrusion at the sides to help the cowboy hold his seat in the saddle by locking his legs under the swell. Joe Keefe, of O'Connor Ranches near Victoria, says the high swells protect the rider from being knocked out of the saddle by the brush. The cantles may be straight or rolled, with the latter being preferred in most areas in later years. The horns, forks, and cantles may be bound in tough rawhide to protect them from the rubbing of the lariat when the cowboys are roping cattle.

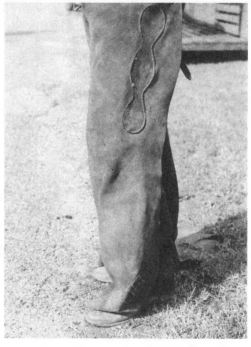

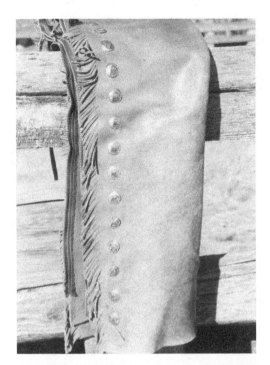

Several examples of cowboy chaps. Note that one saddle has a carrying bag made of a boot top cut off and laced across the bottom. *Sonja Irwin Clayton photos.*

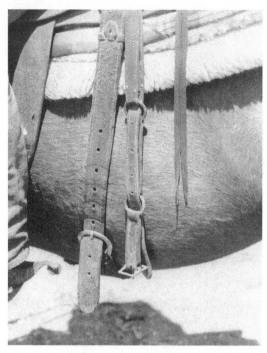

Something of a rarity in cowboy country, a pair of hobbles secured to the rear cinch ring.

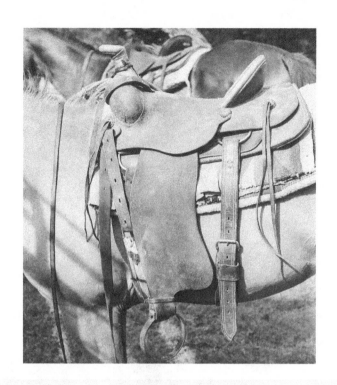

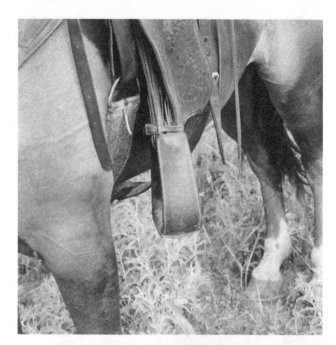

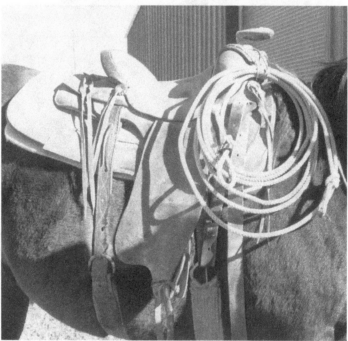

Details of cowboy saddles. Note that one of the horns is wrapped with rubber for dally roping, cowboy style. *Sonja Irwin Clayton photos.*

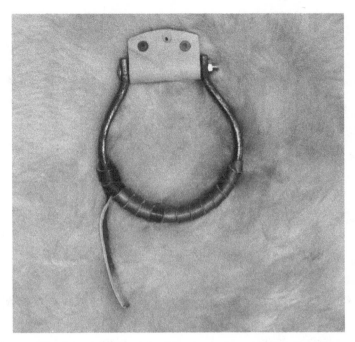

A plain metal oxbow stirrup with leather wrapped around the bottom. *Lawrence Clayton photo.*

Stirrups made of metal-bound wood ranging from two to three or even four inches in width and covered with leather are found along with metal "oxbows"—semicircular on the bottom portion—fashioned usually from blued steel or plain steel that is allowed to form a rust patina. The oxbows are sometimes called "widow makers" because the cowboy's foot fits into the oxbow up to the heel and is, therefore, more difficult to extract if he should be bucked off the horse. This situation increases the likelihood of getting hung up and dragged. Hence the label. These metal stirrups may be decorated with the owner's initials or with the brand of the ranch for which he rides. Stirrup hobbles, a leather strap passing under the horse's stomach to keep the stirrups from flapping when the horse pitches, are rare, and, because they do not allow the stirrups to swing freely, are considered by some men to be dangerous.

In those areas where thorny brush is a problem, the cowboy equips his stirrups with tapaderos to protect his feet from the brush. When present, these are typically simple types with no ornamentation and without flaps. These are essential in areas with thorny brush because, if a thorn is driven into the rider's instep, it is all but impossible to re-

An oxbow stirrup decorated with a ranch brand. *Sonja Irwin Clayton photo.*

move the thorn without removing the boot, and it is all but impossible to remove the boot without removing the thorn first. Also the brush can knock the rider's foot from the stirrup, and the thorny brush will quickly wear the toes out of the cowboy's boot. In addition, a limb accidentally run through a stirrup jerks the horse and rider to a sudden stop, or damages the saddle, both situations that can cause serious injury. On open plains or in mesquite flats where the thorns are on trees, not on low-growing brush, "taps" are uncommon and unnecessary. They do help keep a rider's feet warm in cold weather but are uncomfortable in hot weather.

Some but certainly not all of the saddles for cowboys are made with the rough side of the leather out, for working saddles frequently do not sport much tooling. Some of the skirts and the edges of the sweat leathers may be tooled, but little such ornamentation will be found on the parts that the cowboy's body contacts—saddle seat and sweat leathers—because it irritates the skin. Padded seats, despite a degree of comfort, are risky because they wear through quickly, absorb rain too readily, and hold moisture, which irritates the rider's buttocks.

The undersides of the saddles are still lined with fleece, and the skirts are usually full. Many cowboys, in addition, ride with a breast harness or collar made of either heavy braided mohair or stitched leather to increase the number of layers from one to at least two and thereby provide strength. These keep the saddle from slipping backward when the rider is dragging calves at branding time or riding up a steep slope. The saddle horns of recent times are more commonly four to five inches tall with a large cap and are covered with leather. Wrapping these large horns with rubber cut from tire inner tubes (although the tubes are not so readily available as they once were) is a common practice. The rubber not only protects the horn but also offers a degree of friction to provide more secure managing of the slack in the rope. Cowboys do not give slack until the horn smokes, as does the vaquero. The larger horn meets the needs of the arena team ropers, especially the younger ones, who have taken up the dally style and changed the practice of tying hard and fast. The older, shorter style of horn made of German silver is not common on new saddles, nor is the post horn of the buckaroo.

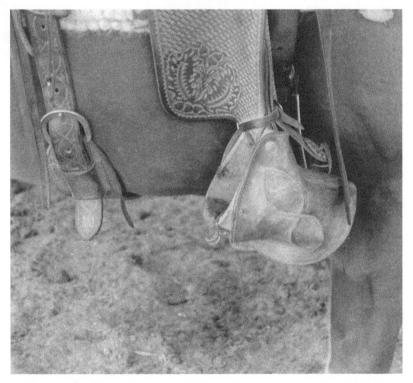

The most common type of cowboy tapadero. This one is made of rawhide and came from Arizona. *Lawrence Clayton photo.*

View of bridles in a cowboy tack room. *Lawrence Clayton photo.*

The blankets to pad the horse's back against the saddle are often of Indian design (called "Navajos" because of the early use of blankets woven by these Indians), though a hair or wool pad is used next to the back of the horse, and the Indian-style blanket is used as decoration as well as extra padding to avoid galling the horse's back. The saddle pad, however, is gaining great currency because of the benefits to the horse, and the "cool back" pad, common in the northern regions, is now gaining popularity across the southern portions of the cowboy West.

Bridles have at least three parts—headstall, reins, and bits. The headstall is cut from heavy, oiled harness leather and may be simply a strap going over the top of the horse's head without even a brow band and throat latch, and especially not a nose band. More elaborate models are found, but simplicity is a key factor. Some sport simply a slit through which the horse's ear passes. The polished leather, silver-mounted headstalls are for arena riders and show stock, not for cowboys, to whom cost and durability are important factors. Fancy buckles with silver initials or brands or just geometric designs may well be on the cowboy's headstall. Bosals are rare because most ranch horses, even young ones, are ridden with bits, not with hackamores. In fact, young horses being broken usually are controlled with at least a snaffle bit if not a bar bit within the first two or three months of riding. This method differs from both vaquero and buckaroo methods.

Two single or "split" reins are used almost exclusively. These reins, one-half inch or so in width and ranging up to eight feet or more in length, are cut from strong but supple leather to make them more pliable than heavier leather would be. Rawhide or horsehair reins are found only upon extremely rare occasions in cowboy country; no craftsmen live there to do the work because there is no market. When found, these items will usually come from Mexico or South Texas. Some plaited nylon cord is gaining favor, especially in damp climates, because it is strong, inexpensive, and long lasting despite wear and climatic conditions. Most cowboys, however, demand leather. When a cowboy dis-

Side bars on a pair of bits showing ranch brands. *Sonja Irwin Clayton photo.*

Three styles of hackamore. The first two have rawhide bosals. The first has twisted horsehair reins, the second plaited nylon. The third is a mechanical hackamore. *Lawrence Clayton photos.*

mounts, he takes the reins down and ties the horse to a fence or tree limb. A few train their horses to be "ground tied," that is, to stand with the reins hanging to the ground.

Tie downs, straps running from a bosal to the breast collar and on to a small D-ring on the front girth, hold the horse's head down, a helpful step for a roper. These are used primarily in the roping arena and corral work, not the pasture. The reason is clear—if the horse stumbles for any reason when running, it must be able to get its head up in order to recover its balance. If the head is tied down, this recovery is far more difficult, and the horse is more likely to fall head first with the hindquarters and tail coming over like a huge flyswatter. Serious injury or death is a possible, even probable, result.

Bits may be handmade, although many factory-made bits are seen. The bits are usually the shallow-port style. Some cowboys continue to

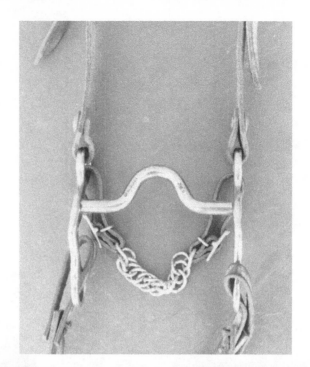

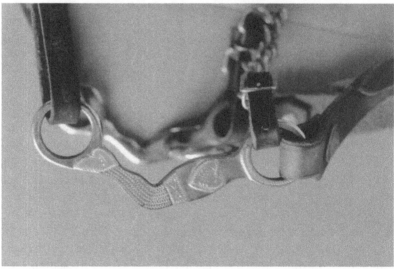

Two views of a shallow port bit with a gal-leg design on the side bar. *Lawrence Clayton photos.*

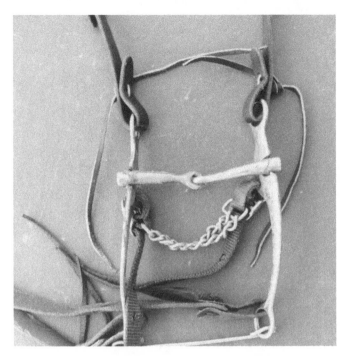

A snaffle bit with side bars rather than rings. *Lawrence Clayton photo.*

ride with a form of snaffle bit, one hinged in the middle of the bar running through the horse's mouth. One determining factor is the personal preference of the cowboy; a second is the preference of the horse. Some of these bits are adorned with the brand or initials of the owner or with small silver bars to provide decoration and personalization. Most cowboys know the makers of bits and spurs and also collect the items as valuable investments. Such names as Trammell, Klapper, and Bayers are highly respected, if not revered. Stainless steel is common, though blued steel is also used. Aluminum, popular at one time, is no longer used. As on spurs, the rust patina that forms on the blued metal with exposure to the weather makes an attractive background for any ornamentation.

Gloves made of cowhide, pigskin, or, less often, elk hide, pliable but still durable, have long been standard wear. Few use a glove with a gauntlet, and the use of leather cuff protectors is also rare. The gloves are very important for protection from brush and rope burns. For roping, a man may choose a soft, thin wool glove that offers protection from the heat generated by the ropes sliding through the hand but still allows a

A rawhide bosal rigged to a regular headstall and split leather reins. *Lawrence Clayton photo.*

good "feel" for the rope. For working with cattle, the men prefer a thin glove because it is important to feel the branding iron, rope, or other tool being used. The men wear no gloves when holding calves at branding time because the grip is less secure with a glove. If the leg held by the cowboy slips loose, someone could be seriously injured by flailing legs and sharp hooves. When repairing or building barbed wire fences, however, the cowboys wear a heavier kind of glove, even a thick welder's glove. Handling barbed wire devastates the soft riding glove.

Another traditional item of gear for a cowboy, at least in the popular image, is the pistol. Horton says that the early cowboys carried two six shooters at their waist, and each of the holsters was tied down with a buckskin thong. The low-slung position of the pistol on the thigh relieved the weight from his waist. Abbott notes that later cowboys who carried more than one pistol did so with one as a "hideout gun down under their arm" (p.25). The weapons were not turned against other men nearly so much as popular fiction and film would have us believe but were, instead, for use against varmints and various threats—human ones among them—to the ranch property and livestock. The pistol could be any one of several large calibers, but the forty-five and forty-four caliber single-action models by Colt, once they were available, found great preference among the cowboys. The lever-action repeating rifle by Winchester in the 1873 or the later 1894 model became widely accepted by these men and was usually carried in a leather scabbard attached to the saddle. The butt of the rifle might point to the rear or to the front, depending on personal preference and whether the cowboy would want to get his rifle without dismounting. The style of carrying with the stock to the rear generally made the rifle accessible only from the ground.

Modern cowboys rarely carry weapons on horseback. To combat predators, the men usually carry bolt-action rifles with telescopic sights. These are carried in a rack mounted either across the rear window or over the driver's head in the pickup truck, not on horseback.

Like the clothing, the cowboy's tack serves a utilitarian purpose. What did not serve well gave way to new ideas or technology. Like many relics of the past, the discarded items sometimes became art objects, much as did the armor of Medieval knights. No matter how highly prized, however, decoration and skill in manufacturing still do not diminish the demand that the item serve the user, not the reverse.

The specialized gear of the cowboy, the way he dresses, and how he performs the tasks unique to ranch work distinguish him from the buckaroo and the vaquero. To the familiar ear, there is also some specialized terminology in cowboy lingo. He chooses his horse from the *remuda* or *horse herd*, not the *cavvy* or *cavvyard*. He carries a *lariat* or *lariat rope*, not a *riata*, *lazzo*, or *laso rope*. The cowboy works for a *foreman*, not a *cow boss*, or *mayordomo*, or *buckaroo boss*, and the horses are brought in by a *wrangler*, not a *wrangle boy*, *wrango*, or *remudero*. The *hoodlum wagon* hauls his *soogan;* a *bed wagon* or *buckaroo wagon* does not haul his *bedroll.* The list is long and intriguing, as a look at Ramon Adams's *Western Words* reveals. Many of the terms show signs of their origin in Spanish from the vaquero tradition, though many are so anglicized that the original source is not readily apparent.

The life of the cowboy is visible to the public in various ways. Two of the best museums that highlight this way of life show a somewhat different focus on the term *cowboy*. The first, the National Cowboy Hall of Fame in Oklahoma City, celebrates the life of the North American herders, especially the cowboy tradition. Ranchers and cowboys get a fair share of the attention in displays, programs, and artwork, especially paintings and bronze sculpture, that depicts this way of life.

The Cowboy Hall of Fame has honored many individuals who have contributed to the western way of life. One category of members is Western Performers, and it includes such familiar names as Gary Cooper, Joel McCrea, Walter Brennan, James Stewart, John Wayne, Randolph Scott, Glenn Ford, Ben Johnson, William Boyd (Hopalong Cassidy), Tim McCoy, Buck Jones, Roy Rogers, Dale Evans, Gene Autry, and a host of others.

In the category Great Westerners are found Charles Goodnight, Oliver Loving, Richard King, Mifflin Kenedy, Daniel Waggoner, Charles Schreiner, John H. Slaughter, Burk Burnett, George T. Reynolds, Robert J. Kleberg, and Watkins R. Matthews (all ranchers), as well as Esbeio Francísco Kino of Arizona (the pioneer missionary). Also included are writers such as J. Evetts Haley, J. Frank Dobie, Will James, and Tom Lea. Members come from all over the cattle-producing West—California, Idaho, Nevada, Utah, New Mexico, Oklahoma, Texas, Montana, Nebraska, Colorado, South Dakota, North Dakota, Arizona, and Kansas.

The Hall of Fame's magazine, *Persimmon Hill*, in excellent articles and accompanying photographs, highlights the western way of life for a wide public. It is safe to say that the Cowboy Hall of Fame is indeed a remarkable celebration of the western way of life.

Although the Cowboy Hall of Fame also honors rodeo performers, the second museum, the Pro-Rodeo Hall of Fame and Museum of the American Cowboy in Colorado Springs, Colorado, has as its central focus the professional rodeo athlete or performer. The displays, exhibits, and multimedia presentations—as well as live animals there for viewing—communicate the essence of rodeo and highlight the champions in the events that make up the professional sport.

In addition to *Persimmon Hill*, there are several fine magazines that interpret the western life. *Western Horseman* and *Cowboy Magazine*, for example, both carry articles on ranch life. *Horseman Magazine* focuses more on rodeoing than ranching but nonetheless deals with the image of the cowboy.

Excellent collections in various museums house memorabilia and documents of the cowboy way of life. Few, however, rival that housed in the Panhandle-Plains Museum on the campus of West Texas A&M University in Canyon, where an excellent archive of information is also available. A second major resource is the Southwest Collection at Texas Tech University in Lubbock. A third entity in that same region is the American Quarter Horse Heritage Center and Museum located in Amarillo.

Photographs of western life are widely displayed in advertisements and in books. Advertisers have found that using western motifs to market non-Western items—cosmetics, cigarettes, restaurants, and even church revivals—is effective, and the use is enormous. The Marlboro cigarette ads are the best known. Among the best published photographic studies are the early work of Erwin Smith in *Life on the Texas Range* (1952) and Ray Rector's *Cowboy Life on the Texas Plains* (1982). The photographs in these two collections were made in the 1920s and 1930s. Numerous archival collections hold rich treasures of western photographs. One of the most notable is that of Frank Reeves housed at the University of Texas in Austin. The more recent collection by Martin Schreiber in *Last of a Breed* (1982) reflects the modern life of the cowboy. The photographs by Sonja Irwin Clayton in *Cowboys: Contemporary Ranch Life along the Clear Fork of the Brazos River* show the details of the actual work of the modern cowboy. Some of her photographs appear along with numerous others in John Erickson's *The Catch Rope*, a fine study of cowboy roping. All of these are in black and white. David Stoeklein's excellent color plates in Saunders's *The Texas Cowboys* (1997) convey more than just the images. An excellent and long-overdue study of an important facet of cowboy life is Sarah Massey's *Black Cowboys of Texas*. All, however, do focus on the cowboy. One that combines cowboys and buckaroos without noting the differences, except in the color photographs themselves, of course, is Barney Nelson's *Voices and Visions of the American West* (1986).

Music is still part of the cowboy's life, but it has changed over the years. A collateral development with early trail-driving techniques was the emergence of a body of songs known generically as "cowboy songs." Some of the songs were original compositions, but many were adaptations of British ballads brought to the area by immigrants and changed to fit the western life and landscape. The old favorite "The Cowboys Lament," also known as "Streets of Laredo" because of the use of that phrase in the first line, is an adaptation of a British ballad. Cowboy songs, actually poetry sung to a large extent to traditional melodies, were a variation of traditional work songs, though the rhythms of the lines themselves did not serve the same purpose that those did in the chain gang songs, for example. The work-related orientation of the songs came from the fact that men sometimes sang them when herding cattle, particularly when on night guard. Anyone familiar with working livestock, particularly mature animals that have lived on the open range away from human kind, is aware that suddenly startling one of these animals produces a predictable result—a mad dash to escape the perceived threat. Since cattle have herd instincts, the tendency is for all of the animals to run. On the old trail drives, the result of this instinctive behavior was the much-feared and often-mentioned stampede. A song or low whistle, especially a continuous one, keeps the cattle aware of a human presence and lessens the chance that the animals will be startled into the mad dash over unknown terrain in the dark of night. One of the best-informed treatments of this phase of trail life, albeit fiction, is Benjamin Capps's meticulously researched *The Trail to Ogallala*.

Another work purpose of the songs was to alleviate loneliness. Singing is soothing to the spirit, and familiar words are certainly a comfort, especially when set to a tune. The life of a cowboy—particularly when riding night herd, baching in a line camp, or traveling alone across country—was an isolated existence. The cowboy style of music lent itself to this setting because it was sung usually by a single voice without instrumental accompaniment or, when available, to the accompaniment of a single fiddle or guitar. Carrying an instrument of any kind other than a mouth organ, with the rough handling it would receive in this kind of life, was certainly a threat to the musical instrument.

Although the cowboy did sing around the campfire or in saloons or elsewhere, there was most often not an audience to which he could perform. This condition and the ties of these men to the Anglo-Irish folk song traditions of their forebears probably account for the presence among Texas cowboys of a much stronger song than poetry tradition. The poetry tradition made immensely popular by the buckaroos has only recently been picked up by cowboys. Modern cowboy poets in Texas were previously unknown, if present at all. The cowboy poet phenomenon almost certainly emerged as a result of the buckaroo influence, rather than being an outgrowth of the folk music tradition. The traditional music of the folk, including the cowboys, all but disappeared with the onslaught of radio in the 1920s and 1930s, and Country and Western music replaced "cowboy" music. Early declamation societies did stimulate some poetry reflecting life on the range. For example, "The Last Longhorn" and "The Cowboy's Christmas Ball," both given as songs in the Lomaxes' *Cowboy Songs and Other Frontier Ballads*, began as poems (see Pound and Tinsley).

Today's cowboy music with such singers as Red Steagall, Don Edwards, and Michael Martin Murphey differs noticeably from typical Country and Western music. "Cowboy" music deals with the life of the cowboy. Country and Western deals with the lives of people who—although perhaps having a certain amount of the cowboy mentality—are stuck in town and dealing with the problems of urban life. The cowboy does not sing at his work, but the radio in the pickup, where he spends a lot of time, usually is set on a station known to play Country and Western music, and the tape deck, if present, will feature a well-known artist in this tradition.

This attempt to depict the cowboy is necessarily general, and exceptions can be found to many of the statements made here. There is no doubt, however, that the cowboy is a reality, both in the past and in the present, and he is an individual proud of his heritage and his contribution to it. A man does this work because he wants to do it more than anything else. Frank Graham, a South Texas ranch foreman and die-hard adherent of this life, said, "Men who don't like this kind of life and work move on to town jobs. This has to be something you love."

The men have not changed with time because they have always been proud of their work and enjoyed, even reveled, in it. As John Erickson notes, "The modern cowboy, like his old-time counterpart, chooses to show an uncanny knack for transforming what he wears into plumage. Watching cowboys strut at spring roundup is one of the rewards of being in this business" (*The Modern Cowboy*, p. 29). The cowboy came to represent the West to many people, and the continuing interest in cowboy clothing and horses is proof that the attraction of the image has not flagged.

SOME REAL COWBOYS

Many aspects of the life of the cowboy can be found in books, but there is still no substitute for the words and actions of real cowboys, as the interviews which follow will, I hope, demonstrate.

CHARLIE CONE

Charlie Cone was born in Texas in 1905 and moved with his family to homesteaded land in New Mexico. They farmed and ranched and raised most of their own food because the nearest store was in Tatum, some twenty-five miles away. The next town was Roswell, some fifty miles from the homestead on very poor roads. Cone learned his cowboying ways from riding the milk-pen calves and the horses and mules used to plow the land. He began working during the summers on nearby ranches

Charlie Cone as a young man with his wife, Delia. *Cone family photo.*

and went to school in the winter. At age seventeen he went to work as a cowboy full time. He spent more than two decades in this work before getting married and settling into work in town.

Charlie's range was New Mexico and far West Texas. His life on the wagon was usually with a crew of eighteen to twenty men whose home for most of the year was a chuck wagon and a soogan. One of the ranches where Charlie worked was over a hundred square miles of rolling grassland, rocks, and brush. The food was mostly beef, beans, potatoes, sourdough bread, and coffee. The beef came from a mottled-faced or spotted calf, one whose markings would keep it from bringing top price at market time. The calf was driven to the wagon, slaughtered, skinned, and quartered. Then the legs on each quarter were inserted between spokes on the wagon wheels so that the carcass could drain out all of the blood. There were no trees on these plains to hang beef from. If at the headquarters, the men hung the carcass from the windmill tower. Following the slaughter, the cook prepared a famous cowboy dish, son-of-a-gun stew, into which went the marrow gut, the heart, the liver, and other parts of the animal. It was spicy with pepper. Cone said it included "everything you might not otherwise eat." He remembered it well: "It was great; I wish I had some right now."

The meat required special handling. After the meat had cooled overnight, it was wrapped in a piece of tarpaulin and put in the bed of the wagon with the bedrolls piled on top to insulate the meat from the heat of the day. If at the headquarters, the men stored the meat by hanging it on the north side of the house where the sun would not shine on it. In this way the meat would keep for several days until the men ate it all. Because the nights are cool in this area most of the year, there was no need to dry the meat to preserve it.

The bread was cooked in dutch ovens. The horse wrangler, whose job was to bring in the remuda so that the men could catch the horses for work each day, also helped the cook with chores around the camp.

When Cone worked on the Slaughter Ranch in far West Texas, the crew branded six thousand calves a year. All of this was done with the crew mounted on horseback and living off the wagon. The calves were roped and dragged to the branding fire by men tying their lariats hard and fast to the saddle horns. Usually two crews worked on the ground, and each had one roper. The ground crew consisted of a flanker, whose job it was to throw the calf down, and another man to hold the rear legs. Another man branded the calf while other members of the crew would vaccinate, mark the ears, and castrate the bulls.

In winter, the men were scattered around the ranch in camps, each with a small house for the man staying there. The man was given a stretch of range to see after, which included feeding the cattle on that part of the ranch. The camp was resupplied once a month, the only time the cowboy in the camp saw another human being. The cowboys in those days were nearly all bachelors and had no money to go anywhere. Part of the cowboy's routine was to check the fences, usually only on the exterior boundaries of the ranch in those days, and to drive the cattle back to the home range if they strayed.

One of the cowboys' chores in warm months was to "prowl" the range to look for trouble with the stock and to doctor screwworms that plagued the cattle. If the men did not find and doctor each animal with the infestation, the infected animals would die. Not until years later did modern science devised a method of sterilizing the flies and eliminating the threat to livestock and wild game.

Cone did not drive cattle up the trail, but he did help move a herd of 2,200 cows between Tatum and Hobbs, a drive that included a crew of thirty cowboys and lasted several days. The men had the challenge of temporarily letting down the fences on the ranches they drove across. A crew preceded the herd to let the wire down, and another followed behind to re-erect the fence.

The horses ridden by the men were just horses, the Quarter Horse not yet being developed. Cone remembers that the ranch bought the mounts as unbroken horses from a rancher who raised nothing but horses. Only geldings were broken to ride. Mares were never mixed in with the geldings because around a mare, a gelding forgets all he ever knew about his work. Cone recalls that these horses were tough and mean and would kick, bite, or do anything else to hurt a man or one another. The variation in colors ran from gray, sorrel, black, and roan to a large numbers of bays. Not until later did ranchers determine that it cost no more to feed a good horse than it does a bad one, and, with the Quarter Horse's arrival on the scene, the quality of ranch horses improved.

To break horses, Cone, like most other bronc busters, made his own hackamores from grass rope, a fiber that has prickly, hair-like projections that over time can irritate the horse's head and make him sensitive to the pressure brought to bear by the rider. This device, consisting of only a bosal and a head stall, served as the only form of bridle until the horse was ready for the bit in its mouth, usually in a few weeks. The reins were a single looped one, not the two-rein set up preferred by cowboys on the bridles of working horses. In addition, a piece of rope eight feet long was attached to the bosal so that the cowboy, if he was bucked off, could hang on to the rope and thereby keep his mount. This saved him an embarrassing walk back to the ranch headquarters or the wagon.

The ranches did not feed their horses. The animals had to survive on what they could get from the range. That is one of the reasons that the men kept a string of several horses, so that an animal could regain its strength from grazing after being deprived of food for the day on which it worked. Usually the men had enough horses in the string that a horse had to work only one day a week. Cowboys who stayed at the ranch during the winter were each given two horses to ride, and these were fed regularly.

Catching the horses was not a problem when the men were on the range. The wrangler looked after the herd at night, but at daylight he was helping the cook with breakfast. Then two men dubbed "rustlers" brought the herd in at daylight. The cowboys usually got up when they heard the horses coming in. The men hooked their lariats together to form a makeshift pen, and as the horses came into the enclosure, the men closed the loop. No horse that had been broken ever tried to run through the rope, because once a horse learns the lesson of the rope, that lesson is permanent.

The clothing of the men was not particularly distinctive. Cone recalls that the boots, handmade by a man in Carlsbad, New Mexico, had medium-height heels and tops eleven inches high. They had boxed, not pointed or round, toes. The pants at this time were usually khaki and the shirts cotton. In the winter heavy underwear was necessary, often with two pairs of pants in addition to batwing chaps, which provided a measure of warmth as well. The hats were John B. Stetsons, white or brown, with brims rolled up on the sides.

The gear was typical of cowboys. The double-rigged saddles usually cost about seventy-five dollars each and a pair of boots nearly thirty dollars. This stretched the men's thirty-dollars monthly wages, but that was the gear they had to have. The spurs that Cone first observed had large rowels, but later rowels were smaller. The lariats were thirty feet long and fashioned from a roll of rope carried in the wagon.

The saddles were rimfires with swelled forks, often extending past the rider's knees. The horns were often small silver ones. Some of these were wrapped with leather, but heavy use of the lariat usually cut the leather off the horns in a short time. The stirrups were oxbows wrapped in cowhide. The stirrups also sported tapaderos in those areas that had thorny brush, such as that around Odessa, Texas.

Although Charlie Cone's experiences provide a fine touchstone for the daily life of the cowboy in the early decades of this century, other men shed additional light on this way of life in the same period.

G. D. LONDON

G. D. London was a cowboy and rancher all his life. Born in 1910, London was an accomplished horseman. He began breaking horses to cowboy work when he was just a boy. His technique was widely used. He and his brother roped the horse and snubbed it to a strong post in order to put a hackamore on it. These hackamores London fashioned from "nickel rope," small grass rope. He fashioned a headstall and a bosal with a lead rope attached to it. The boys tied the lead rope to a stone large enough to provide some weight but not enough to allow the animal to hurt itself while pulling it around. Then they left the horse for the night. The next morning they pulled the horse's head around for a time and then took the animal to a round pen for the next step, saddling. To saddle the horse, the boys snubbed it to a post and tied a rope around its neck. Then they got a second rope through the loop and around the horse's back foot,

G. D. London on Sonny Boy, about 1934. London is dressed for the July 4 rodeo at Stamford, Texas: hence the tie and watch chain. Note the extended swell on the fork of the saddle, the double rigging, the small silver horn, and the short lariat tied hard and fast to the horn, as well as the two split leather reins that reach within a foot of the ground. The rope around the horse's neck ensures that the horse faces the animal roped.

thus lifting the back foot off the ground and preventing any serious cutting up by the animal. Then they saddled it, and one of them mounted up. Loosening the rope so that the back foot was free was a test not only of courage but of the youngster's riding ability. The horse was ridden in successively larger pens until the time came to ride it out into a large pasture and began the training for cow work.

London recalls when the upgrading of horses in his area of Throckmorton County began. An area rancher bought a fine Yellow Wolf stallion from the Waggoner Ranch to breed his mares, many of which were Spanish or mustang bred. A government breeding station at nearby Seymour also made available to farmers and ranchers two jacks, two Percheron, and two Thoroughbred stallions to breed mules, draft horses, and riding stock. The government's motives were not altogether altruistic. Their main objective was to breed satisfactory cavalry remounts.

London saw the gear and tack change as well. He recalls a good many slick-fork saddles in use when he was a boy, most made by Tunstall of Miles City, Montana, and R. T. Frazier of Pueblo, Colorado. He saw only spurs with short shanks and small rowels. He also witnessed the introduction of shotgun chaps, which were initially disliked because they were sewn down the sides and the cowboy smeared whatever was on his boots down the inside of the legs every time he put them on. The advent of zippers to close the back made this style of chaps more popular. In true cowboy fashion, London recalls tying his lariat hard and fast.

London also saw the methods of marketing cattle change. He recalls seeing cattle hauled in trucks to regional markets such as Fort Worth, a method that replaced hauling the stock on the train. Then auction rings began to spring up. He called the early ones "shell games" in which a few buyers manipulated the markets and often cheated ranchers out of a fair price for the stock. As competition increased, however, these "rings," as ranchers called them, became legitimate markets for small ranchers who did not have enough cattle to hire trucks to haul cattle to regional markets or to feedlots. The role of the cowboy as drover ended by degrees but was gone by the 1930s.

BARNEY BALDESCHWILER

Barney Baldeschwiler, born in 1912, grew up and worked as a cowboy in South Texas all his life. Unlike Cone, he continued to work as a cowboy after he married, and he has fond recollections of the children riding their horses to school each day.

Like Cone, he was too late for trail driving, but there were short drives to the railroad corral. The shipping point was Hebbronville, about twenty-five miles from the ranch on which he worked. The trip took two days. The crew took a chuck wagon and a remuda of horses and drove the cattle slowly to the shipping pens. Baldeschwiler recalls, "We'd take several hundred head at a time. I remember seeing big herds of cattle waiting their turns in the railroad shipping pens." He also recalled in those days a tick inspector checking the cattle to see that all fever ticks were killed, an effort that resulted in the eradication of the menace. He also remembers when the drives gave way to shipping by truck. The first trucks were small, only twenty feet long, and could haul about twenty calves. Soon, however, larger trucks that could haul forty were built.

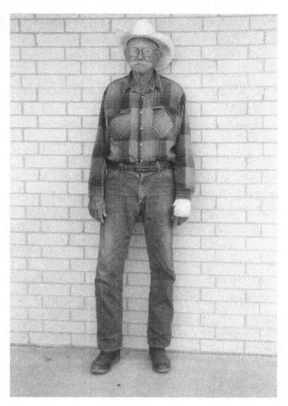

Barney Baldeschwiler, a South Texas cowboy. *Lawrence Clayton photo.*

Now, of course, cattle vans haul eighty or more, depending upon the size of the cattle.

Baldeschwiler cowboyed in a region that also had vaqueros. The interesting part of this overlap of cultures is that each man knew what he was, cowboy or vaquero. Although Baldeschwiler learned a lot from talking with and watching vaqueros, he was always a cowboy. He kept his rimfire saddle, tied his thirty-foot manila (later nylon) lariat hard and fast, and kept his typical cowboy accouterments, such as shallow port bits and small-rowel spurs. His favorite spurs were made by Joe Bianchi in Victoria, Texas. Nevertheless, he admired the fine work of the *vaqueros, vaqueros completos,* the complete cattle handlers and horsemen.

The horse was important to the culture of these men, and methods of breaking them were somewhat different from those in other areas. The man would put the horse in a round pen and rope it by the forefoot and throw the animal down. Then he would put a hackamore on it and teach the young animal to respond to this device by pulling the horse's head around some. When the horse began to respond to this treatment, the man would tie up a front foot, usually with a rawhide rope that would not burn the horse, and saddle the animal. After letting the horse get used to the saddle, he would mount up. The ride was usually a wild one, but it was the common way to break a horse to ride in those days.

The horses got a lot of work. The separating of calves from cows for working or market was done outside the pens. Some of the men would hold the "cut" while others rode into the herd to cut the desired animals out. This kind of work regimen produced horses much better trained than ranch horses are these days.

Among Baldeschwiler's recollections are catching horses from the herd when he was with a crew on the wagon on the Kennedy Ranch. The remuda consisted of 125 horses, and the designated ropers had to be able to skylight each one against the first signs of dawn, recognize it, and then rope it. Then the roper led it to the cowboy, who bridled it and saddled it for the day's work. On this particular ranch, the crew rotated the remuda every six months, so the ropers had to know 250 horses by name and be able to identify them in the early morning half-light. The ropers got a lot of practice otherwise, as well. In the hot humid area of South Texas, the men often changed horses four or five times a day as the horses tired and the men needed fresh mounts. The men also changed horses when one was needed for specialized work, such as cutting or roping. Two wranglers kept the remuda nearby.

Although Baldeschwiler kept to his cowboy ways in this area, he also picked up crafts from the vaqueros. He learned to make rawhide and horsehair ropes and used them to some extent. One of the uses of the horsehair rope was to spread around his bedroll at night. Tradition had it that a rattlesnake would not cross a horsehair rope. He also used the hair ropes for lead ropes because they were "springy" and as hitched girths for his saddle as well. The horsehair that he twisted for the ropes came from the ranch band of 125 Percheron mares used to breed mules. The men kept the manes roached, or cut short, and thereby secured the needed hair. He also braided rawhide to make bridle reins and ropes as well as quirts.

His chaps were full cut and closed on the back with buttons, much like those of the vaquero. In this hot country, this style was cooler than the shotgun chaps, which were fully closed in the back.

One specialty learned by the cowboys of this region was removing wild cattle from the heavy undergrowth. To do this the men had to rope

A herd of buffalo on the Long X Ranch at Kent, Texas. These are descended from those that Jimbo Reynolds and Glenn Leech helped build the pen for. *Lawrence Clayton photo.*

the animals in the brush and often tied them to a gentle animal to drive them out. Roping under these conditions called for a small loop, a short rope, a good horse, and lots of nerve. The men did a lot of roping because of the need to inspect the cattle for screwworms.

JIMBO REYNOLDS

Jimbo Reynolds cowboyed in both Texas and Wyoming, and his recollections of working on the Long X Ranch in far West Texas provide some interesting glimpses of this life.

The horses that the men rode he described as not particularly well-bred but nonetheless conditioned to the work. Reynolds said that the men thought nothing about loping a horse ten or fifteen miles on a roundup. He said, "We rode some big circles in those days, and the horses got used to that kind of work. Horses these days could not hold up to that kind of work without a lot of conditioning."

Getting the cattle to market involved gathering the animals from all over the ranch and driving the steers to be sold to one of the few fenced pastures on the ranch. Then the herd was driven to the railroad corrals at Kent. Several ages of cattle could be shipped by rail, and that differs from the trail drive days in which only mature animals could be driven to market. One technique to swell the herds of cattle was to spay heifers so that they too could be driven to market. Because they were not needed for the breeding herd, there was no other real use for them.

Reynolds recalls that once in the 1930s the ranch had so many mares in the band that they made a deal with a Mexican rancher to trade a number of the females for an equal number of geldings. The ranch ran twenty stallions and between three hundred and four hundred mares. The Mexicans drove the herd of geldings to the ranch, which is not too far from the border, picked up the mares, and drove them back into Mexico. He remembers that the work with these unbroken horses was wild and dangerous.

Several of the men who broke horses on the Long X were of Mexican descent. One, José Guerrera, came there as a boy and bet all of his belongings, a pair of gloves and fifteen dollars, that he could ride one of the worst outlaws on the ranch. He failed, but the foreman liked the young man's spirit and gave him a job. He remained with the ranch until his death.

GLENN LEECH

Reynolds's friend Glenn Leech also shared recollections of this early period. When the men got ready to go out on the roundups, they had to shoe their string of ten horses each. Since the crew carried ten or more cowboys, the remuda would include more than a hundred horses. Many of these horses were ridden for only part of the year and had to be rebroken to ride each spring, something that added drama and excitement to the cowboy's life. This tradition differs noticeably from that of the vaquero, who prided himself in training his horses. The cowboy had little time for, or interest in, the vaquero's type of skilled, patient horse training.

The chuck wagon was resupplied periodically by someone who drove a car or truck from the headquarters to the wagon as needed. Food for the men consisted more of fresh beef than anything else. Like the

Glenn Leech on a fine Quarter Horse. Note the stacked-rock fence in the background. *Leech Family photo.*

crew Cone served with, the men slaughtered a mottled-faced heifer calf for this meat. The wagon was pulled by six mules and had attached to it a small hoodlum wagon for carrying the bedrolls. The men slept in their soogans and, on nights that rain threatened, erected small, peaked, rectangular tents called tepees, which accommodated two men each.

Roundups were accomplished by a wide-ranging net of cowboys who rode a large circle in the area designated for the day's work. This hard riding lasted usually until noon. As the herd was finally pushed together, half of the men rode to the wagon to eat. Filled with beef, bread, and coffee, these men returned to the herd so that the other men could go eat. Once the men had all eaten, roping and dragging the calves to the branding fire began.

One of the first jobs Leech remembers doing was helping to construct a sturdy pen to corral the herd of buffalo that ranged on the ranch. Mexican hands cut the timbers in the mountains and pulled them to the site of the pen. Leech helped erect the timbers. When the job was completed, it was roundup time. He then began shoeing his horses and went to live on the wagon for several months.

GEORGE PEACOCK

George Peacock is a third-generation cowboy who has seen his occupation come into the modern period with pickups, trailers, trucks, and reasonably comfortable housing on the ranch. Peacock vividly remembers his first days as a cowboy, after high school graduation in 1953. He lived in a bunkhouse so drafty that, in the winter, snow came in through the cracks. The men, all bachelors, covered their beds with pieces of tarpaulin to keep warm and dry in their blankets. The cowboys cooked their own meals and, for lunch, carried tin cans of peaches, sausages, and the like and ate wherever noon caught them.

When the men drove cattle to the railroad for shipping, the route was down a county road fenced on each side. The fencing was not always good, so often the crew placed a rider in the pastures on each side of the

George Peacock, Nail Ranch, Albany Texas. *Sonja Irwin Clayton photo.*

Benny Peacock, Green Ranch, Albany, Texas. *Sonja Irwin Clayton photo.*

road to turn back cattle that tried to escape from the herd. One of the unique demands of this area was that the cattle had to cross a river on the bridge in order to reach the railroad corrals. To accomplish this feat, the lead riders roped a calf each and dragged it across the bridge with the mothers of the calves following. Seeing these animals leading the way, the rest of the herd followed along across the bridge. Now the movement of cattle is accomplished by huge cattle vans.

Peacock now uses pickups and trailers to haul horses on the ranch. His interest is in efficiency in working the cattle, with the fastest way the preferred one.

BENNY PEACOCK

Benny Peacock, George's younger brother, has been a cowboy all of his life as well. Among his many recollections is his first experience breaking horses on the Waggoner Ranch in North Texas in the late 1960s. The geldings to be broken, usually two years of age, were collected at the bronc pens so that a crew of several men could begin to saddle and ride them. Once the men had "put a few saddles" on each horse so that it tolerated the rider and knew the basics of being ridden, the bronc riders, mostly young men, drove the herd to where the wagon was located. The wagon boss divided the new horses among the cowboys, and each man then became responsible for training his new horses for the work. He remembers these horses, many descendants of the famous Waggoner Quarter Horse Poco Bueno, as being particularly "hot" or spirited. Any cowboy who did not watch the horse he was riding might end up on the ground.

The Waggoner was among the first ranches to use a helicopter in roundups. Peacock remembers that when the machine flew over, especially if the pilot hovered the craft near some of the green-broke horses, a "wreck" might occur because the horse would surely pitch.

Peacock, like many of his kind, drifted about a great deal as a young man. With his belongings, especially his saddle, his bedroll, and his collection of bits and spurs, he roamed from job to job until he mar-

Sonny Edgar, Bluff Creek Ranch, Albany, Texas. *Sonja Irwin Clayton photo.*

Jack Pate, who cowboyed around Albany as well as in the mountains of New Mexico. *Sonja Irwin Clayton photo.*

ried and settled down to a less nomadic existence. Like many of his friends, he regrets that he was born a hundred years too late to have been part of the open-range period.

SONNY EDGAR

Sonny Edgar's recollections of living off the wagon on the S. E. Waggoner Ranch in the 1950s differ somewhat from Cone's memories of earlier decades. Although the routine was little changed in work and sleep, the modern influences were beginning to be felt. He remembers that if one of the cowboys wanted to go back to the headquarters with the supply truck, he could do so. The man who chose to return, however, got relatively little sleep that night, because he had to get up early enough to return to the wagon well before daylight. The men who stayed at the wagon usually went to bed when it got dark and did not get up until they heard the wrangler bringing in the remuda. In those days living conditions had already improved—the men slept on cots that got them off the ground and away from crawling creatures, especially snakes, during the night. It was common practice for cowboys to string a circle of rope around their beds at night to keep the snakes away.

These men represent the best of cowboy life. Cone and Reynolds have died since the time of their interviews, but the others are still active in the work. They are cowboys to the core.

Dwight Hill, a buckaroo living in Idaho, at the World Finals of Ranch Rodeo in Amarillo, November 1999. Note the flat-topped hat with straight brim, cloth vest, and slick-fork saddle with post horn. The sixty-foot nylon lariat is secured to the horn and can be used as a handle for the rider to grip. He has finely braided rawhide reins, slobber chains on ornately decorated bits with high port, and a roller on the port. A quirt hangs in front of his right leg. The mecate hangs down outside his right leg. Between his horse's front legs is a long shoo-fly. Since this horse is shorter than many he rides, Dwight has left off his twenty-eight inch tapaderos. His stirrups are about four inches wide and bound in engraved silver. His bits and spurs are decorated with playing-card emblems. *Lawrence Clayton photo.*

The Buckaroo

JIM HOY

What is the difference between a cowboy and a buckaroo? Ask that question of anyone from the Rocky Mountains eastward and the response will undoubtedly reflect some variant of "I didn't know there was a difference." Even among members of the ranching community itself, particularly in the Southwest or the Great Plains, many if not most would probably say that the term *buckaroo* is just a fancy word that people who don't know any better use to refer to a cowboy. To most members of the general populace, if they have a mental image at all, a buckaroo is a flashily dressed cowboy, perhaps a wrangler from a dude ranch (big hat, silk neckerchief, fancy shirt), whose exaggerated appearance reflects the supposed origin of his name—someone who rides horses that sometimes buck. Or, the term is often used by rodeo or radio announcers when referring to children, as when members of the cowboy singing trio Riders in the Sky extol the "cowboy way" to all the "little buckaroos and buckarettes" in their audience. The "-aroo" suffix used in this context implies something juvenile or novice, just as an apprentice stockman (i.e., cowboy) in Australia is called a jackaroo (or, if female, a jillaroo). A buckaroo, in the popular mind, is either simply a cowboy or else a flamboyant cowboy whose vanity has been enhanced by an onomatopoeic name.

But in the high, cold desert country that lies northwest beyond the Rockies, people know the difference between a cowboy and a buckaroo. The Great Basin, as the rugged expanse of sagebrush-covered rangeland that encompasses northern Nevada, northeastern California, southeastern Oregon, southwestern Idaho, and northwestern Utah is commonly (if imprecisely) called, is the home of both the historical and the contemporary buckaroo, a distinctive mounted herder who, like the cowboy of the Southwest and Great Plains, traces his ultimate origin to the vaquero of Old Mexico but by a different route, through California.

The term *buckaroo* itself, in fact, is an anglicization of *vaquero*, the American pronunciation of a Hispanic word, as the earliest spellings (*bakhara, buckhara, buckayro*) suggest. Although the buckaroo, as a distinct type, evolved from the cattle industry of the Great Basin, which began serious development in the 1860s and became fully established over the next two decades, interestingly, the first recorded usage of the term was from Hispanic Texas a generation or so earlier. In 1829, according to the *Oxford English Dictionary*, W. B. Dewees noted that work on the ranches of Texas was performed by "peons and bakharas or herdsmen." By 1890 the term *buckhara* was being used in California to designate a cowboy or drover of cattle. The link to Spanish is made explicit in a 1910 work, *Vigilante Girl*, "I can talk what they call 'buckayro' Spanish," while the modern spelling, *buckaroo*, seems to have emerged in the following decade. Leslie Stewart, owner (and grandson of the founder) of the 96 Ranch near Paradise Valley, Nevada, who was born in 1922, recalls (in an oral history on file in the Humboldt County Library in Winnemucca, Nevada) that as a young boy he heard the term *vaquero* used more often than he heard *buckaroo*. He also remembers that the Circle A Ranch employed Mexican vaqueros for the roundup crew. Mike Hanley, whose great-grandfather began the ranch near Jordan Valley that Mike now runs, told me that the early-day ranches of southeastern Oregon also employed Mexican vaqueros. In fact, until the breakup of the big Nevada ranches in the 1920s, about half of the herding workforce was Hispanic. Carl Hammond, owner of the Hot Springs Ranch near Golconda, Nevada, and founder of the Buckaroo Hall of Fame and Heritage Museum, notes that even in 1996 an old-timer who was buckarooing in the 1920s or 1930s would refer to a former companion as a "good baquero." Ernest Morris (in his book *El Vaquero*) associates the term *vaquero* in California with Hispanics, the term *buckaroo* with Anglos, the two titles (and nationalities) melding through pronunciation (and sun tans) into "*baqueros.*"

Another indication of the Spanish influence on Great Basin ranching is that during the nineteenth century the foreman was commonly called the "major domo." A more tangential, if fascinating, instance of Hispanic influence in buckaroo country was provided at the turn of the century by Galo Mendieta, a Spanish Basque. He left home at age twelve and spent some dozen years working as a gaucho on an Argentinian cattle ranch before going on to San Francisco and thence to the Great Basin, where he buckarooed for Miller and Lux and was buckaroo boss for Abel and Kurtner. He was, his son Tony recalled (in an oral history interview on file at the Humboldt County Library), the only buckaroo who would occasionally use a bolo instead of a riata.

Today the terms *cowboy* and *buckaroo* are both used in the Great Basin, but not always interchangeably as often happens in other parts of the country. Rather, the former term is generally applied to an all-around ranch hand, while the latter is reserved for those hands who prefer, even insist, on limiting themselves to that work on a ranch that is done primarily from the back of a horse. A cowboy, to paraphrase Gary Bengochea, general manager of the Garvey Ranches in northern

Nevada, is capable of handling any job on the ranch, from breaking horses to tending cattle to irrigating hay to overhauling a four-wheel-drive pickup, while a buckaroo is good only for working cattle from horseback.

Others I talked to in my research visits to buckaroo country during the fall of 1995, the summer of 1997, and the spring of 1999 responded in similar vein to my question: What is the difference between a cowboy and a buckaroo? A cowboy, I was told, (1) was an all-around ranch hand who could do any job asked of him, (2) was a rodeo competitor, (3) drove a truck, (4) line danced and hung around drugstores. Buckaroos, on the other hand, were cattle tenders who worked horseback and didn't want to (or would not, or, according to their detractors, could not) do much of anything else around a ranch.

In addition to that question, I would also ask working cowhands if they called themselves buckaroos or cowboys. Some, like Pete Marvel of Paradise Valley, Nevada, who were attempting to make a go of relatively small (by Great Basin standards) family cow-calf operations, thought of themselves as cowboys. Others, such as Rod McQuery, who was reared in Nevada's Ruby Mountain country southeast of Elko, thought of themselves as buckaroos. Chuck Hall, who ranches with his father Tom near Bruneau, Idaho, makes and uses buckaroo gear but calls himself a cowboy because he "feels limited" to horseback work if he calls himself a buckaroo. Then there was Mark Galyen, who told me when I talked to him in Jordan Valley, Oregon, that he used to be a cowboy, when he was rodeoing, but that he had reverted to being a buckaroo since he had begun working on ranches. In any case, the term *buckaroo*, like *cowboy*, can be, and is, used as a noun, a verb, and an adjective, as in: "When I was a young buckaroo I used to buckaroo for Miller and Lux with a buckaroo wagon."

THE VISIBLE BUCKAROO

It used to be that you could tell where a cowboy came from by the crease in his hat, the type of boots and chaps he wore, or the kind of saddle he used, but in the past few decades homogenization of styles—the result of rodeo, cowboy poetry gatherings, and television—has erased many of these regional distinctions. Chinks, for instance, the just-below-the-knee-length chaps that New Mexico cowboy storyteller and humorist Curt Brummett refers to as "chapettes," once were confined strictly to buckaroo country. Today, however, they are widely worn throughout range country, from Montana to Texas to Arizona. Still, enough regional variation exists to allow for some observations about the general appearance of a buckaroo.

Buckaroos not only think of themselves as different from cowboys, they have also developed a distinctive style of clothing and gear. As with the cowboy, their basic accouterments and equipment reflect the requirements of their work, i.e., handling cattle and horses in a certain manner in a certain physical environment. However, some of the external flourishes and designs in their clothing and gear have changed over the years, as various fads and fashions have dictated.

Perhaps the most realistic description of a set of working buckaroos in the later twentieth century has been given by Mackey Hedges, a working buckaroo himself, in his novel *Last Buckaroo*. In the following excerpt, the two protagonists, Tap McCoy and Dean McCuen, have just arrived at the Flying D cow camp in southern Oregon, and Tap describes the scene:

> The men led their horses down by the pen that surrounded the water trough. After they'd unsaddled, they led the horses into the corral and turned 'em loose to drink. Each of them was dressed differently and yet alike. By that I mean they all had on the same type of clothes, even if they showed different amounts of wear and were different styles. They all had on western hats, some with stampede strings and some without. The hats were all different colors and shapes, yet they all had about the same size crowns and brims. Each man wore a silk scarf around his neck; a few were rolled and tied tight while others flapped in the breeze. Each wore chinks for chaps. Some of 'em were fancy and some plain; some were just about worn out and others looked new. All of 'em wore western boots that were so scuffed and dirty, they really did look alike. A couple of the boys had on spurs with wide bands, and others wore narrow ones. Some had big rowels and others small, but all of 'em were the ol' California vaquero-style, silver inlayed with long drop shanks.
>
> The one thing that sticks out most in my mind about those kids was the amount of horse jewelry they were packin'. There was more silver in that camp than the United States mint had in its vault. They had silver conchos at the corners of their headstalls and on their chaps. Their saddles had silver horn caps and cantle plates. They all had big hair tassels hangin' from their

Early-day buckaroo holding a bottle of whiskey. Note the neckerchief, suspenders, long riata, silver-mounted headstall, spade bit, and rawhide reins and romal with slobber chains. *Owyhee County Historical Society photo.*

cinches, and a couple had little silver bells on 'em, too. Only one man had a nylon rope on his saddle; that was Roy, the kid, from California. All the rest had rawhide riatas. The twins and Red had big, long taps on their stirrups like Dean wore.

The whole bunch may have been a little crazy like ol' Frenchy said, but they damn sure looked like what buckaroos were supposed to look like.

As Hedges suggests, there is room for quite a bit of individual variation among buckaroos, yet the general appearance leaves no doubt as to the type. Hedges himself wears felt hats (straws are not common among buckaroos) that have open five-and-a-half-inch crowns and four-and-a-half-inch, flat, raw-edged brims. That size is popular in buckaroo country, he told me, although many will dent the front of the crown and put a slight roll in the brim, which is sometimes bound. Buckaroos actually wear several different makes (Stetson and Resistol are preferred) and styles of hats, including a low-crowned, flat-topped, small snap-brim model that looks almost Argentinian. The old-style Spanish hat, also with a flat crown but with a wider, straight brim and a fancy throat string, has recently made a comeback among buckaroos, as has the fedora.

Buckaroos, like other cowboys (particularly rodeo cowboys), are faddish in terms of hats. In earlier years buckaroo hats were of derby or fedora style. Carl Hammond believes that the big Tom Mix–style hats came in during the 1930s as a result of rodeo and movies. Mackey Hedges recalls that when he first started buckarooing back in the 1960s, no one wore black hats. One day, however, the foreman of the outfit he was working for came back from town with a black hat, which he had bought not for the color but because it was the only one he could find that felt right to him. Hedges said that within six months everyone on the ranch was wearing a black hat, and within a year so was nearly every buckaroo in northern Nevada.

Another hat tale: one of my research trips to buckaroo country happened to coincide with the opening of an art show at the Western Folklife Center in Elko, Nevada, a show that featured the work (ranging from sculpture and painting to rawhide braiding and horsehair weaving to bit and spur making) of area artists, both men and women, most of them with a connection, sometimes direct, to the cattle business. The hats of those in attendance that evening varied from the tall-crowned and bound-brimmed to the flat-crowned and snap-brimmed and most everything in between. One in particular, however, struck me as being out of place. It was a black felt with a crown crease and brim roll that would have looked right at home in West Texas. Later, when I got a chance to meet the wearer, Don Farmer, one of the artists, I learned that although he was indeed a native of northern Nevada, he had rodeoed heavily in his younger years. He had, indeed, been the Rookie Saddle Bronc Rider of the Year a couple of decades earlier. And thus he considered himself more cowboy than pure buckaroo, an element of self-image made explicit in his choice of hat style.

On the bottom end of the mounted buckaroo one finds a variety of footwear, ranging from boots of various makes to the lace-up packer boot, which has become more popular in the past decade or so. For ground work around a line camp or in a pen, a buckaroo will often wear a low-heeled boot or a pair of laced work shoes. Some even carry their alternate footwear with them, strapped to the saddle, if they know that they will be doing ground work, thus being able both to work in greater comfort and safety and to save unwanted wear and tear on their good riding boots. Traditionally, the favorite boot of the buckaroo has

Three styles of buckaroo hats. Above is Mackey Hedges (Jim Hoy photo); on the facing page are Bill Wood, a buckaroo and buckaroo poet now living in Newell, South Dakota (Lawrence Clayton photo), and Newt Dodge (Jim Hoy photo).

been a custom-made Blucher or Paul Bond or, in earlier years before the company closed, a Hyer. Today many buckaroos wear the tall-topped, high-heeled boot, called the buckaroo model, developed and made popular by Hyer's successor, the Olathe Boot Company. This boot is bought off the shelves by working buckaroos, as are the similar models marketed by Justin and Tony Lama. What one does not ordinarily find in

Newt Dodge, UC Ranch, McDermitt, Nevada, 1999. Note the flat crown on his hat, horsehair reins, and neckerchief. *Jim Hoy photo.*

a buckaroo's stirrups are ropers or any other kind of low-topped, flat-heeled boots. Nor will you find lizard, emu, or snakeskin; buckaroos like French wax calf, kangaroo, or some other serviceable, attractive leather for both dress and work. In fact, their dress boots become their work boots after they have been worn a while. In general the buckaroo prefers a tall, scalloped boot top ranging in height from fourteen to seventeen inches, a two-inch undershot heel with spur ridge, and a medium rounded toe. And the buckaroo often wears his pants on the outside of his boots.

Around his neck, today's buckaroo will have a wild rag (some call it a tough rag), a thirty- to thirty-six-inch square neckerchief, preferably of silk although a slick synthetic material is acceptable (and only about half as expensive). A solid color, particularly black, seems most popular, although some wild rags will have a design woven into the fabric. What is not found around a contemporary buckaroo's neck is a cotton bandanna: "Silk for show, cotton for blow," is their adage. Early-day buckaroos, however, often could afford only one silk wild rag, which they saved for special occasions, wearing a cotton bandana or even a section of old feed sack for everyday use. A major advantage of silk is that moisture does not stick to it, which is a particularly desirable feature when the scarf is pulled up over the nose to ward off either dust or cold. Sometimes the wild rag is worn with a square knot so that it hangs loosely around the neck, the tied end in either the front or the back. Or the buckaroo might tie it four-in-hand style, like a regular necktie, and adjust it around his neck with the ends hanging down in front. Sometimes a slide, often made of ornate silver or intricately braided rawhide, is used. One of the most popular ways of wearing the wild rag is doubled, with the front of the scarf under the chin and the ends circled around the neck and tied in front.

In terms of clothing, contemporary buckaroos wear long-sleeved shirts, often of cotton but not necessarily of "western" styling. Some individuals like plaids, others solid colors. Their preferred pants are blue denim jeans, usually Levis or Wranglers. Although many bucka-

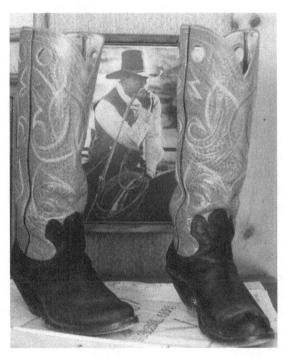

A pair of Paul Bond boots. *Jim Hoy photo.*

Waddy Mitchell, widely known buckaroo and talented poet, with the mustache, the hat with contrasting ribbon, and the neckerchief. *Lawrence Clayton photo.*

roos wear suspenders, some do wear belts, usually of leather or of webbing. Silver buckles are typical, or buckaroos who have rodeoed will use their trophy buckles. Many buckaroos wear vests, down-filled in winter, but of leather or, more commonly, of cloth (such as a vest from a dress suit, with a wool front and a silk back) in the summer. Popular jackets include the blue denim Levi jumper, lined or unlined, and the Carhart brown-duck canvas coat, with down-filled or lined coats for winter use. Some will also wear an old jacket from a wool dress suit. A buckaroo will wear a wool cap with ear flaps when the winter gets really cold (temperatures up to sixty degrees below zero Fahrenheit have been recorded in the Great Basin), but he would rather wrap his wild rag around his head, scarf fashion. Some may even prefer to have ear flaps sewn inside their Stetsons, as Candy Hedges has done for Mackey. Buckaroos will wear mittens or warm cotton gloves in winter. They also sometimes use the knit roping glove when dragging calves to the branding fire, while those men wielding the branding irons will often wear light buckskin or goatskin gloves. To ward off precipitation, when it does happen to fall in this arid environment (which averages ten inches or less of rain per year), buckaroos have over the years employed a variety of rainwear. Their choices over the years have included the old "fish brand" oiled canvas slicker, a black three-quarter-length rubberized coat, and the yellow plastic slicker, although this one has not been so widely adopted because of the belief that its color will spook a horse more easily than a dark-colored coat. In recent years the caped Australian stockman's storm coat has become the slicker of preference.

Probably the single item of apparel most often associated with the buckaroo is chinks, the distinctive style of chaps that come just below the knee and are usually decorated with silver conchos and leather fringes. Chinks, as much as any other part of his attire or equipment, reflect the environmental influence in the development of the appearance of the buckaroo. In the past, buckaroos often wore "woolies," the full-length chaps made of angora goatskin (or sometimes bearskin or some other fur), for warmth in the winter, as did (and do) the cowboys of Alberta and Montana. Shotgun chaps can still be found on Great Basin ranches, while old photographs reveal the common use of both shotgun and batwing chaps in the past. Nevertheless, chinks are the chap of choice among today's buckaroos. Buckaroos did not have the mesquite thorns of Texas or the giant cactus of Arizona to ward off, nor the blackjack oaks and hedge trees of Oklahoma or Kansas to contend with, all of which respond best to full-length, heavy leather leggings, even in the heat of summer. Moreover, batwings and shotguns are more cumbersome when walking or when mounting. Another disadvantage of batwing chaps is suggested by George Smiraldo, an Elko, Nevada, buckaroo who noted that riding down a steep canyon path in a swirling wind with the batwings whipping around could sure spook a green horse and cause a bad wreck. Chinks, by descending below the knee, protect the buckaroo's upper leg when riding, while at the same time his tall-topped boots provide protection for his lower leg. Chinks are cooler than full-length chaps and allow for better mobility.

According to Jo Mora, chinks originated in Old California, among the early vaqueros who came up from Mexico, where they had equipped their saddles with *armas* for protection in the big-cactus country. Armas were big slabs of leather that hung from the sides of the saddle bow and reached down to cover the rider's feet and back to cover his thighs, sort of like the molded plastic shell that one sometimes sees on the front of a motorcycle. In California, as later in Nevada, however, there was no big cactus and thus no need to add this heavy, and hot, apparatus to the load borne by the horse. Instead, the California vaquero discarded armas

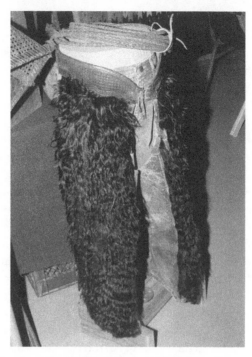

A pair of woolies, long chaps with the hair—either goat or bear—out. A rawhide riata sits atop the display stand. *Lawrence Clayton photo.*

in favor of *armitas*, originally a kind of leather apron made of two rectangles of buckskin attached to a belt and strapped to the waist. These leggings, the forerunner of the modern buckaroo's silver-conchoed chinks, extended just below the knee and were tied around the upper leg with a couple of straps. Sometimes these armitas were decorated with fringes cut into the bottom (as were a pair I saw in the museum of the old mission at San Juan Bautista, California), sometimes not (as a pair pictured in a 1904 catalog of the Visalia Stock Saddle Company of San Francisco).

Les Stewart of Paradise Valley's old-line 96 Ranch offers a more prosaic theory as to the origin of chinks, as quoted by Marshall and Ahlborn in *Buckaroos in Paradise:*

> Chinks probably originated when a buckaroo's old [batwing or shotgun] chaps became well worn and frayed and in an attempt to salvage something and save the cost of new ones, he trimmed them down until "chinks" were all that remained. Then the idea

caught on and the style became popular. I think their origin is as unromantic as that, purely a practical evolution.

Carl Hammond agrees with Stewart, stating that "All chinks were was batwings cut off three-fourths of the way down." Early buckaroos wore batwing chaps, Hammond says, but because the predominant sagebrush "didn't really offer any damage" from thorns or spikes, buckaroos just cut down their old chaps into chinks, a style that became popular, he believes, in the 1920s. Undoubtedly many a pair of chinks was made by cutting off an old pair of batwings or shotguns, but Mora's theory seems more probable as to ultimate origin. As to the etymology of the term, Marshall and Ahlborn speculate that it came either from *chingo* (Spanish for leather stirrup covers) or *chingadera* (cut off or blunted). The latter makes more sense to me. Because of the generally shorter stature of Orientals, folk etymology associates the term *chinks* with the biased name given to the Chinese, many of whom worked on ranches in buckaroo country, primarily as cooks or gardeners.

I have not been able to learn precisely when chinks became widely used, for many of the Great Basin range country photographs I saw show that shotgun and batwing chaps were popular well into the 1920s. Marshall and Ahlborn suggest that chinks came into popularity sometime between 1930 and 1950, an opinion shared by Griff Durham, who has studied the history of the Visalia Stock Saddle Company. The first use of the term *chinks* in print that Durham has found comes from a 1914 catalog from the Goldberg Staunton saddle company of Winnemucca, Nevada. Armitas, Durham told me, are first pictured in an 1896 Visalia Saddlery catalog, where they are termed "cowboy aprons." Chinks, heavily fringed and mid-calf length, first appear in a Visalia catalog in 1947. Waltzy Elliott, however, who was born in 1905, recalls that when he was "just a little fella" a Mexican cow boss named Clay Rambo "took me under his wing. . . . I got me a little saddle and he put chinks on me and I rode right with him as a little man." When I was in Elko, I saw a pair of hundred-year-old chinks owned by George Smiraldo and even snapped a photo of Stanley Griswold, then ninety-five years old, wearing them. However widespread the use of chinks may or may not have been in the early history of buckarooing, they are certainly ubiquitous among buckaroos today and, as noted earlier, are becoming popular with cowboys in all parts of the American West.

The contemporary buckaroo has tended to exaggerate the distinctive stylistic differences between himself and other cowboys, whereas old time buckaroos tended to be less flashy in appearance. Mike Hanley told me that the most skilled buckaroo he ever knew was an old-timer who wore oxford shoes and bib overalls, while Carl Hammond said that early buckaroos often wore jeans, brogan shoes, batwing or shotgun chaps, and fedora hats. Hammond also noted that in earlier years buckaroos wore cotton scarves, or even flour sacks, around their necks while out on the range, reserving their one fancy (and expensive) silk wild rag for dances, rodeos, or other public celebrations. The increasing emphasis on silver ornamentation, he believes, began to grow around mid-century. Hanley, in his book *Tales of the I.O.N. Country* (the initials refer to Idaho, Oregon, and Nevada), calls those hands who seem obsessed with their appearance "buckaroo revivalists" and records this exchange at the 1982 Big Loop rodeo in Jordan Valley, Oregon:

> The revivalists sported much silver, custom made saddles, stirrups and one was wearing knee high laced packer boots. My neighbor Laz Mendieta commented, "Look at those sons-of-a-bitches." I replied, "They dress like a cross between a French Canadian half-breed and an old time California Vaquero." "I don't know about that," he said, "But I'll bet there's not a day's work in the bunch."

BUCKAROO GEAR

Excepting chinks, the common thread linking the less flamboyant early-day buckaroo with his more flashy modern counterpart is more truly found in gear and work methods than in attire. After chinks, the most visibly distinctive piece of equipment used by the buckaroo is his slick-fork, single-cinch, high-back, round-skirted saddle. The earliest saddles of the plains cowboys, back in the era of the big Texas-to-Kansas trail drives, were also slick forked and high backed, but they were double rigged and square skirted, and by the turn of the century, innovations such as wider swells and a Cheyenne roll on the cantle had become well established. During the first part of the twentieth century the "bear trap" saddle with its extremely high back, form-fitting swells, and ox-bow stirrups was the favorite of bronc riders. Going to the other extreme, by mid-century the low-backed roping saddle, with heavy, wide roping stirrups and minimal swells, had come into vogue, while a standard association tree was mandated for rodeo bronc riders. Horns varied all the way from straight-up bare nickel or stainless steel to low, leather-

A typical buckaroo saddle with post horn, high cantle, and twenty-eight-inch tapaderos. This one has a rear cinch ring. *Jim Hoy photo.*

covered pelican or dinner-plate types; skirts were generally square. By the end of the century, Great Plains and Southwest cowboys had finally settled on a happy medium, with a double or seven-eighths rig saddle exhibiting modified association swells, a dally-roping horn, square skirts, and a medium-high cantle with or without a Cheyenne roll.

In buckaroo country, however, this free-swinging pendulum of saddle evolution did not occur: saddles stayed high backed, A-forked, round skirted, and single cinched in the old-time California style. Setting the standard was David E. Walker, who began making saddles in San Francisco as early as 1877 and later moved to Visalia. Today the Visalia Stock Saddle Company is still in business, with headquarters in Fresno. Visalia pioneered many of the innovations (such as Sam Stagg rigging and square skirts) that later were attributed to plains saddlers such as Frazier, Gallatin, and Meanea. The major changes between Walker's Visalia saddle popular on early Nevada ranges and, say, a Tipton or Capriola saddle of today is that the modern saddle is more heavily built

Another buckaroo saddle, this one with single rigging and four-inch bell stirrups. *Jim Hoy photo.*

(on a Wade tree to handle a nylon rope) and has the tall, wide post horn, whereas the earlier saddle had a tall, narrow, tapered horn. The disadvantage of attempting to ride a "cranky" horse (the buckaroo's term for an ornery horse that is inclined to buck) in a slick-fork saddle can be overcome by attaching bucking rolls (often crudely referred to as "squaw tits") to the swell of the saddle. In lieu of bucking rolls (first patented in 1901), a buckaroo might tie his slicker across the pommel of his saddle in order to gain more purchase for his thighs.

A wide-topped post horn is not the easiest thing to grab and hold onto when your horse is pitching, but a tightly coiled lariat is, especially when fastened to the saddle in typical buckaroo fashion. A plains cowboy usually attaches his rope (invariably, these days, made of nylon or poly and some thirty or so feet in length) to his saddle with a medium-weight leather-thong rope holder. One end of the holder is fastened (usually by a screw) low down onto the right swell of his saddle, the length is looped a couple of times around the coiled rope, and the split end is then slipped over his saddle horn, which itself is often wrapped with inner-tube rubber. The cowboy's rope hangs loosely along his knee, the saddle, and the horse's neck and shoulder as he rides along and can be quickly and easily unhooked and put into action. One end of the buckaroo's heavy leather rope holder, by contrast, is firmly screwed into the upper part of the right fork, and the length of the holder is wrapped tightly several times around the tightly coiled rope; the holder is then wrapped once or twice around the saddle horn (which is usually wrapped with leather) and, finally, fastened into a buckle that is firmly screwed into the upper left fork of the saddle, a style sometimes referred to as an "Oregon crossover." The rope (often a rawhide riata, or else a small-diameter, hard-twist nylon, usually sixty to eighty feet long), secured in this fashion, rests snugly against the buckaroo's upper leg. If the buckaroo's rope is not as quickly and easily accessible as that of the cowboy, it nevertheless serves as an excellent, and solid, handle should the bucka-

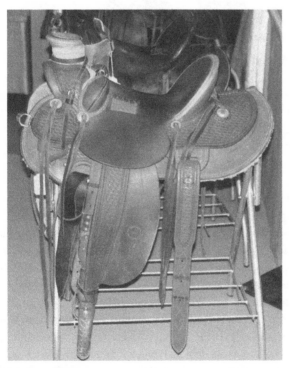

A third buckaroo saddle, this one with double rigging and with leather-covered oxbow stirrups. *Lawrence Clayton photo.*

The post horn and secured lariat of the buckaroo style. *Jim Hoy photo.*

roo's horse begin to pitch. Further, it has the advantage of keeping the rope off the horse's neck and thus away from the sweat that might damage a rawhide lariat. If a buckaroo has time, and he usually does, he will unfasten his rope and rewind it into bigger coils before chasing after a critter.

Some buckaroos prefer oxbow stirrups, while others like the bell-shaped Visalia stirrup, sometimes covered with leather, sometimes bound with brass or Monel (a nickel alloy), and sometimes bound with etched silver. Many hands will, in fact, have more than one pair of stirrups, including a set of deep ones with flat bottoms for use with overshoes in winter. In summer the rider might switch to the bell stirrup or perhaps to the oxbow if a long ride is in store. Mackey Hedges told me that buckaroos usually trot and post when heading out from camp to the roundup grounds (sometimes a distance of twenty or more miles away). Ernest Morris, on the other hand, asserts that California buckaroos seldom post when trotting. When Hedges once complained of back pain, his foreman suggested that he try riding oxbows so that he could put his foot fully into the stirrups and take the stress with his full body, not just

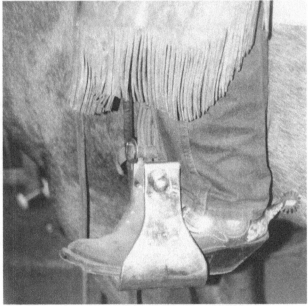

Two styles of stirrups, approximately two-inches wide, silver bound with engraving, and four-inch bell bound in metal. *Lawrence Clayton photos.*

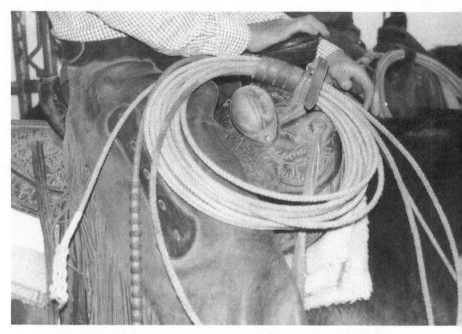

Details of a buckaroo's tack. Note the large horn, secured lariat, bucking roll, romal, and fringed chink chaps. *Lawrence Clayton photo.*

the front part of his foot. On the other hand, Charley Amos, cattle manager of the Nevada First Corporation near Paradise Valley, Nevada, finds that a flat-bottomed stirrup does not hurt his foot the way an oxbow can. Tom Hall agrees, saying "which way do you stand on a two-by-four—edgewise or flatwise?"

Many buckaroos ride with tapaderos, not the squatty bulldog type often seen in south Texas brush country, but the eagle-bill variety with long, fancy, carved leather pieces hanging as much as two feet or more below the bottom of the stirrup. These flowing leather pieces are not only decorative but utilitarian: a good rider can reach out with a foot and slap the nose of an ornery or inattentive horse with these tapadero "tails," or he can slap a cow or calf in the face while "parting" cattle. Tapaderos can also be dangerous; a short-legged horse can trip if it steps on long-tailed taps. Some buckaroos do use the bulldog or monkey-face tapaderos, lined with sheep wool, for warmth in winter riding.

The single-cinch saddle rigging, which usually ranges from three-quarters to center-fire, was developed, according to Jo Mora, because the original double-rigged saddle of the vaquero was not suited to the hilly terrain of Alta California. The center-fire rig with small round skirts would not tip up when a roped cow pulled against the horn, which itself was made strong in order to withstand this pressure. Today, according to Mike Hanley, some buckaroos will also use a breast collar, particularly if dragging calves, but most prefer not to. Buckaroo-style breast collars are usually fastened high, closer to the saddle horn than the cowboy-style, which usually attach to the D-rings of the front cinch. Buckaroo saddles are often decorated with silver: silver conchos on the cantle, silver stirrup bolts, a silver plate with the buckaroo's brand embossed in gold on top of the post horn.

Roping methods are another trait that typically has distinguished the buckaroo from the cowboy. The Great Plains cowboy generally ties on hard and fast, or used to until the advent of team roping on the plains around 1960 (a major result of which has been an increase in dally roping in the pasture, especially among younger hands). The Southwest cowboy has historically been more inclined to dally than to tie on. Both Great

A single-rigged saddle with stirrup leathers raised to show design. Note the Navajo blanket and hobbles attached to the rear of the saddle. *Jim Hoy photo.*

An ornate horn cap with ranch brand. *Jim Hoy photo.*

Plains and Southwest cowboys wrap their saddle horns with rubber so that their nylon ropes will not slip an inch once they make a single dally. In contrast, a buckaroo wraps his horn with a strip of mule hide leather so that he can "play" the rope, letting his dallies slide when the cow lunges, taking up slack when she stops. The purpose of this method is to prevent his riata from breaking, even though nowadays he might well be using one made of nylon instead of rawhide. While the nylon would not break if the buckaroo were to tie hard and fast and jerk a steer down, still he prefers the traditional method of give and take, which is much easier on both the steer and his horse's back. Some buckaroos, such as Jack Frusetta, would braid the first thirty feet of a riata five-eighths of an inch in diameter for better throwing, then taper down to three-eighths of an inch for the last forty feet for ease in working the dallies.

No one style of saddle pad seems to predominate in buckaroo country, although good Navajo blankets are prized, as they are throughout the West. Foam pads, wool pads, hair pads, and other types of coolback pads are often used under a Navajo. Seventeen- or nineteen-strand mohair cinches are normally used to hold down a center-fire saddle, although twenty-one-strand horsehair cinches are occasionally found. Some buckaroos will tie a decorative bob of woven horsehair or a small bell to the bottom of their cinch, thus providing a little music to break the monotony of hours alone in the saddle. Music is also provided by the large-roweled California drop-shank spurs favored by buckaroos, sometimes augmented by chains under the heel or by jingle-bobs attached at the end of the spur shank. Spurs are often made of steel that rusts to a brownish color so that the ornate silver overlay or inlay with which they are embellished shows up nicely when polished. Most buckaroos, however, do not seem to spend much time polishing the silver on their saddles, spurs, or bits, preferring, in what seems to me a strange sort of understatement, not to appear too ostentatious. They know, and their fellow buckaroos know, that the silver is there, so it does not need to be shined up.

The bit most preferred by the buckaroo is an ornate Garcia high-port spade and roller with short, straight shanks (held apart by a slobber bar), made in the Santa Barbara, Las Cruces, or Half-breed style. The base metal of the bit is steel decorated with silver. The roller gives the horse

A decorated horn cap with playing-card emblems and female figure. *Lawrence Clayton photo.*

A pair of dropped-shank Garcia spurs. *Jim Hoy photo.*

something to play with, while the three metals of the bit (steel, silver, and copper) keep its mouth moist, a wet-mouthed horse being regarded as a sign of an easy (or "sweet") mouthed animal, one that reins smoothly and easily. This type of bit, adapted from the California vaquero, looks cruel (and would be, if it were yanked) but actually isn't, because pressure is rarely if ever applied to it. By the time a buckaroo puts a bit into his horse's mouth, he has already ridden him extensively, sometimes for a number of years, first with a snaffle bit (also ornately decorated with silver), next with a rawhide hackamore, then with a combination of a smaller hackamore and a bit. Bridle chains (usually termed slobber chains), which both protect the rawhide reins from saliva and provide weight to hold the reins down and thus encourage a loose rein, are used to connect the shank of the bit to the reins.

The hackamore used by the buckaroo is not the mechanical device often found on the plains, but rather a braided rawhide nosepiece, called a bosal, made in various diameters and held onto the horse's head with a slim leather strap. The headstall used with a bit, on the other hand, is heavier and is often decorated with braided or woven horsehair or silver conchos. Brow bands and throat latches are not uncommon on buckaroo

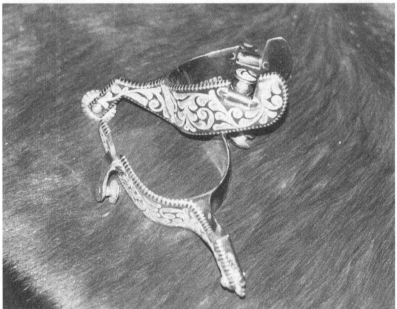

Two pairs of ornate buckaroo spurs. *Lawrence Clayton photos.*

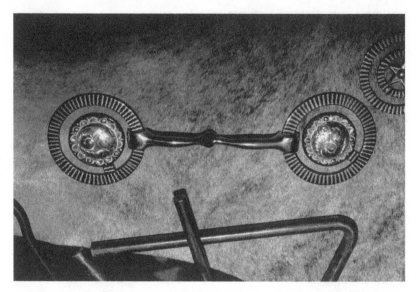

An ornate snaffle bit. *Lawrence Clayton photo.*

bridles, while a decorative knot of horsehair or rawhide is often a part of the chin strap or throat latch. A *tapa-ojos*, a heavy leather blind lowered over the eyes of a green-broke horse when mounting, sometimes functions as a brow band on a buckaroo's hackamore.

One of the biggest differences between cowboy and buckaroo riding equipment is in the type of bridle reins used. A typical cowboy bridle on the plains would have a pair of split reins attached to a long-shanked grazer bit. Buckaroos, on the other hand, when using a bit, prefer a single rein of braided rawhide with a quirt (called a romal) fastened onto the rein by a rawhide button, the entire apparatus sometimes being referred to as a romal, sometimes simply as reins. The actual romal can be detached when the buckaroo is roping. When I visited the Range Riders Museum in Miles City, Montana, during the fall of 1995, I saw several rawhide rein-and-romal sets in excellent repair on display. When I asked manager Bob Barthelmess, a former president of the Montana Stockgrowers Association, about them, he said that the reason they were there and in such good condition is because the Montana ranchers or cowboys who had donated them to the museum had never used them, but instead had brought them back from a visit to Nevada, attracted, as I was, by their artistry if not their utility. In fact, Barthelmess told me, his father would have "whipped him good" if he had ever caught his son riding with his reins tied together, believing that getting caught in the reins if you happened to be thrown from a horse was an excellent way of being dragged and injured. Buckaroos, on the other hand, rarely use split reins. The typical buckaroo way of holding reins is with the hand extended in a loose fist facing away from the rider, thumb up and pointing at the rider's chin, with each rein between separate fingers.

If a buckaroo is using a snaffle bit or a hackamore on a young horse, he will use a *mecate* (anglicized to McCarty or McCardy) for reins. The mecate is a twenty-two-foot length of rope, preferably horsehair although nylon or soft cotton is acceptable. Mane hair makes the best mecate ropes, with tail hair acceptable. Hair ropes made of cow tails, however, are extremely coarse and prickly. The mecate is tied in a single loop to the base of the bosal or the rings of the snaffle to form the reins, with some eight or ten feet remaining, which is looped and carried in the buckaroo's belt as he rides. This length of rope, the end of which usually

A high port or spade bit with decorative side bar in the shape of a human torso. *Lawrence Clayton photo.*

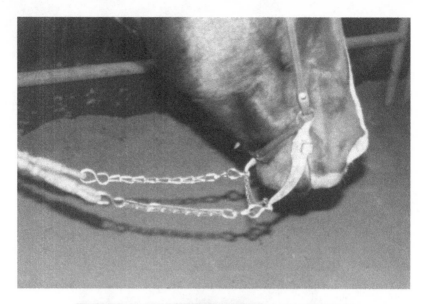

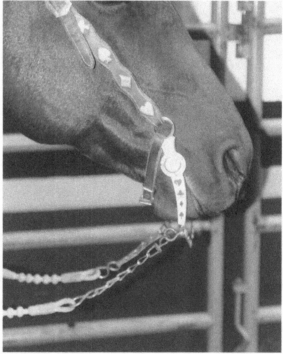

Two varieties of slobber chains with rawhide reins. Note the playing-card emblems on the second set of bits and silver-mounted bridle. *Lawrence Clayton photos.*

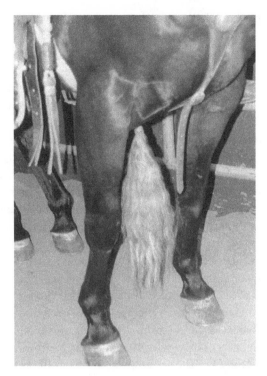

A long shoo-fly attached to the front girth. *Lawrence Clayton photo.*

has a leather popper attached to it, comes in handy for use as a quirt, as a lead rope, or as a means of keeping hold of the horse should the rider happen to be thrown. On ranches where daily rides of dozens of miles from a house or a road are not uncommon, a buckaroo likes to minimize his chances of being stranded afoot. George Smiraldo, for instance, recalls once kneeling to get a drink at a stream, and when he arose his horse jumped "like he'd seen a ghost" and dragged George thoroughly through the rocks and sagebrush before quieting down. If he had lost hold of his mecate, he would have been facing a walk of some twenty miles.

At the Western Folklife Center art opening referred to above, I had noticed a Don Farmer painting called *Bridle Horses* that showed three mounted horsemen, probably behind the chutes at a rodeo or fair, with ornate bits in their horses' mouths. When I first saw the picture, I simply thought that it referred to the fancy mouthware. Later in the evening I met Farmer and got to talking with him, and he explained just what a bridle horse was, how it was trained, and how one holds the various types of reins used by buckaroos, particularly the double rein, commonly called a "two-rein," which actually puts four reins in the rider's hand. As a young horse matures, Farmer told me, and is ready to be transferred from a hackamore to a bridle, the trainer will use both a hackamore (in this case a bosal of smaller diameter) and a bit simultaneously. A mecate, for reins, is attached to the bosal, braided rawhide reins with romal to the shanks of the bit (or sometimes a bit without reins will be hung in the horse's mouth for a time to get him used to the feel). At first the rider holds the mecate reins closer, the romal reins looser, then gradually lets the mecate out and takes up the romal reins as the horse responds more to leg and neck cues and needs less pressure on his head. At one point in the training process, the mecate and the romal reins will be even in length, while toward the end of training the romal reins will be held more tightly and the mecate more loosely. Finally, the bosal will come off and the buckaroo will have his most highly prized equine possession, a bridle horse, which he will ride with a spade bit, rawhide reins, and romal.

Methods of keeping a horse in its place also vary among cowboys and buckaroos. Many horses on the plains have been taught, with varying degrees of success, to be "ground tied" out in the open, that is, to stay near the spot where the rider dismounts and throws his split reins to the ground. Horses in the Great Basin are more likely to be hobbled or staked out with the bridle removed. In a corral a cowboy will tie his horse to a rail or a post with the split reins, whereas a buckaroo is more likely to hook his single rein over the saddle horn; tying to the fence could break the expensive rawhide reins and hurt the horse's mouth if it pulled back. A buckaroo, especially on a bridle horse, will never jerk the horse's head with the reins, nor will he toss the reins on the ground where his horse could step on them, either action being capable of rendering severe injury to the horse's mouth. George Smiraldo told me of a method some horse breakers use to accustom a horse to hobbles. They will, in a sandy patch, tie the hobbles solidly to a ground anchor so that when the horse tries to leave it will be thrown to the sand. A couple of lessons and the horse will not try to run with hobbles on, and a buckaroo is thus not so likely to be stranded miles from nowhere.

Both in clothing and in gear, the buckaroo presents a colorful exterior, one that distinguishes him at a glance from either the vaquero or the cowboy. Pride in appearance and adherence to tradition are traits to be valued in cowhands of any type, although some occasionally go to the extreme of becoming "shadow riders." That is, they will look at their own shadows as they ride. (I remember my late uncle Marshall, a top pasture and arena cowhand, once telling of how he was almost thrown one early morning when the colt he was breaking was pitching and he was admiring his ride in the shadow rather than watching as the horse ducked into an open gate instead of bucking on down the lane.) Shadow riders can be found throughout the West (Charles M. Russell describes one from Montana, nicknamed Pretty Shadow, in his collection of tales, *Trails Plowed Under*), but they are undoubtedly more prevalent in buckaroo country than anywhere else. Again to quote from Mackey Hedges's novel:

> Nearly all buckaroos spend a lot of money and time on their gear, but Deak was a real "Shadow Rider." He carried a seventy-foot rawhide riata, wore silver spurs and ol'-style black Angora chaps, and packed a big six-gun with ivory grips. He musta had six or eight silver-mounted bits with fancy headstalls. He rode a saddle similar to Dean's, only newer. It had a silver horn cap, cantle plate, and conchos. He was pretty to look at and a pleasure to work with, but I had to be careful on sunny days 'cause you could go blind from the light reflectin' off all that horse jewelry.

As Hedges notes later in the book, the high point of a shadow rider's day comes if he happens to ride by a pickup window or a pond where he can see his reflection.

THE INNER ESSENCE OF THE BUCKAROO

There is no question that a buckaroo's appearance differs from that of a cowboy, in sometimes small but significant ways, while his equipment and cattle-tending methods also have their distinguishing features. But is there a fundamental difference between the buckaroo and the cowboy, some sort of theoretical distinction that demarcates one from the other? If, based on my observations and ponderings, I were to speculate on the two most salient inner qualities of a true buckaroo, I would say that they are time and aesthetics. The latter quality is more readily apparent, for a buckaroo situated in the midst of a bunch of cowboys could be easily spotted by the silver inlay on his spurs and bridle bit, the silver conchos on his chinks, and the bright silk wild rag around his neck. His sense of aesthetics runs deeper than mere appearance, however, and merges with his concept of time. The buckaroo would rather do something right and pretty, whether it's saddling a horse, roping a cow, or branding a calf, no matter how long it takes, than to do it quickly and efficiently. Getting the job done and done right does not mean as much to the buckaroo as does getting the job done and done right *in the right way.* And that's according to his sense of what the right way is, which means, for instance, throwing the appropriate kind of loop in a particular set of circumstances when roping. None of this catch-as-catch-can business for the true buckaroo.

The buckaroo concept of time was made explicit in a conversation my wife and I had with Rod McQuery and his wife, Wyoming-ranch-raised cowgirl Sue Wallis. We were sipping a beer in the barroom of the Western Folklife Center in Elko, talking about the differences between cowboys and buckaroos, when Sue volunteered an example. She and Rod and a number of other neighbors (in the Great Basin a neighbor might live a hundred miles away) had recently helped a neighbor brand some calves. "We spent all day," she said, "just to brand fifty calves. At home we'd have been done in less than an hour."

"Oh, it was more like a hundred and fifty," Rod said, but that did not negate Sue's point. Nobody ever got in a hurry, she continued, and when the wind blew the flames from the branding fire into the big pile of sagebrush that the rancher's kids had dragged up for fuel, setting the dry wood ablaze in a matter of minutes, no one got excited or angry. They just dragged up more sagebrush. Where Wyoming plains cowboys might have used a more efficient propane burner to heat the branding irons, and maybe a set of pens with a squeeze chute to handle the cattle, such modern conveniences don't square with the buckaroo's sense of aesthetics. And even if the Wyoming hands had roped and dragged the calves to the fire, they would still have polished off a hundred and fifty calves in a couple of hours at most, for the two or three best ropers would have provided a steady stream of calves to at least three ground crews for working and branding.

When Mackey Hedges was managing a ranch near Dillon, Montana, he invited some of his old buckaroo friends up at branding time. The calves were sorted out into two equal bunches, with both the Montana cowboys and the Nevada buckaroos roping and dragging calves to the fire. The cowboys, Mackey told me, finished an hour and a half sooner than the buckaroos, but whereas the former were riding in and dragging out at a rapid and steady pace, the latter were taking fancy shots with their ropes, throwing from forty or fifty feet away, and giving everyone, not just the best ropers, a turn at roping the calves. The main criterion in a buckaroo calf branding is that one use correct form without

A scene of buckaroos working cattle. They have kept the animal, roped by both head and heels in the buckaroo fashion, on the ropes while working it. *Jim Hoy photo.*

undue regard for how much time passes. Correct form for a buckaroo mandates a long rope (sixty to eighty feet of nylon or rawhide riata) and a big loop (up to fifteen feet and more) as opposed to the thirty- or thirty-five foot nylon with a four- to six-foot loop used in cowboy country.

The contrast between cowboy efficiency and buckaroo aesthetics was perhaps best summed up by a West Texas rancher who once told cowboy poet and singer Andy Wilkinson, "Hell, I can gather two pastures while a buckaroo is still dressing his horse!"

The question is, why should time and aesthetics have become so important to buckaroo style? Geography provides one part of the answer, evolution the other. The buckaroo traces his origin back to the California vaquero, the mounted herder that developed in looking after the large cattle herds maintained by the early missions in Spanish California at the time of the American Revolution. Some of these early herders were recruited and trained from the native populations, but others, particularly those responsible for bringing to California both the equipment and work methods of the vaquero, were immigrants from Old Mexico. These immigrants, according to Jo Mora, were proud of their Spanish blood and were loath to do any kind of work except from horseback. They were artists with a riata and artisans with leather and

Mackey Hedges tosses a hoolihan loop at a horse. *Jim Hoy photo.*

silver. They were, in other words, perhaps more akin to the charro tradition than strictly to the vaquero, perceiving themselves more as masters than as laborers, more as Spanish than as the Mexican-Indian cross they actually were. Thus, just as a modern charro contest emphasizes form and style over speed and time (just the opposite of rodeo, as developed by the plains cowboy of the Southwest), so the buckaroo likewise emphasizes artistry rather than efficiency in his work.

Geography has played an important role in the development of the buckaroo's concept of time. A cowboy on a Nebraska or Oklahoma ranch, for instance, is handling more cattle on fewer acres with more fence to contend with, and he may be working under the watchful eye of the ranch owner, who, like any manager, equates wasted time with wasted money. But Great Basin ranches have tended to be huge, rivaled in size only by the legendary spreads of the Southwest, with cross fencing a relatively recent phenomenon. Pastures of a hundred thousand acres are still to be found in buckaroo country, country that is relatively treeless (as opposed to ranches in mountainous regions) and not heavily afflicted with spiny mesquite or cactus (as in the Southwest). The terrain is rough, but generally not impassable. A buckaroo, then, when he sees a cow that needs roping, does not have to worry about the cow holing up in the brush or hiding out in a rocky canyon, for he can keep his eye on her until he gets to her. In fact, she might be half an hour away when he first sees her, for you can see for miles in that big country. The bucka-roo has plenty of time, and lots of space, to trail a cow before he tosses his rope. Moreover, he has to think ahead before he ropes; he has to ma-neuver the cow into the right position and location without putting too much pressure on her so that she doesn't get hot and fighty and perhaps die. Nor does he necessarily want to put his rope on a freshly jumped cow, which would fight harder than one that had been run a ways. Be-cause a sudden jerk by a nine-hundred-pound cow can easily snap a raw-hide riata, the buckaroo will instead play a cow on the end of his rope like a fisherman plays a ten-pound salmon on a two-pound-test line, in the words of Rod McQuery, giving some rope when she pulls away from him, taking in some slack when she lets up.

His horses, too, reflect the buckaroo's apparently lackadaisical ap-proach. Whereas a plains cowboy might well start a colt when it is two or three years old and have it cowing in excellent fashion by the time it is four or five years old, a buckaroo will often not even begin to break a horse until it is four or five and will not consider it fully trained until it is ten or twelve. Even then, a Texan might not think a Nevada horse that good in a sorting pen because buckaroos do not prize the same kind of cutting-horse action that plains cowboys do. Rather than putting a horse's nose on the tail of a ducking and dodging steer and bringing him right on out of a tightly held herd, a buckaroo will ride into a loosely held herd and slowly (again not caring about time) guide the steer to the edge of the herd, letting him pick his own way rather than trying to force him. Not as much fun, perhaps, if you like the feel of tensed muscles under the saddle and the ears of a good cow horse pointed at the steer you are taking from the herd, but easier on the cattle.

To theorize even further, if one considers the buckaroo an art-ist, then his primary medium is the horse. To put it another way, the buckaroo is more a horseman than a cowman. It might take him two or three times as long to develop his bridle horse as it does a cowboy to develop his cowhorse, but when the buckaroo finishes he will have a "sweet mouthed" mount, one that will respond to the slightest com-mand, whereas a cowboy might have a horse that will work cattle with few if any commands at all (maybe even without a bridle). But as a horse-man rather than a cowman, the buckaroo would prefer to give cues to

his horse while working cattle rather than to turn over the responsibility to the horse. In the words of Charley Amos, a buckaroo is a true
reinsman. As Jo Mora has observed, what's the point of riding a horse
that knows more than you do? Shouldn't the rider be in charge and the
horse responsive to his commands, rather than to its own innate sense of
cowing? Most cowboys I know feel just the opposite: they prize a horse
that will cow on its own, that can sense what a cow will do, perhaps even
before the cowboy himself has noticed her move. For an artist like the
buckaroo, however, the process of making art is more important than
the finished artwork itself; for the buckaroo, the process of developing a
sweet-mouthed horse, and the directing of such a horse in the working
of cattle, is more important than the finished task. The cowboy, on the
other hand, may well consider the good cowhorse he is riding as itself
the artist and himself as a facilitator, a co-worker. Thus the buckaroo's
pride and joy is his bridle horse that responds instantly to his slightest touch (Art), the cowboy's his cutting or roping horse that will work
without any direction at all (Nature).

In much the same way, the buckaroo's second most important
artistic medium is the riata. Catching a steer quickly and bedding him
down with a good trip would elate a cowboy, but would not be nearly as
satisfying to a buckaroo as making an especially long throw (or shot, as
they like to say), or using a particular type of throw in a particular circumstance—a figure eight around the neck and front legs (to catch and
throw a running steer), the underhand *piale* for heeling, the overhand
mangana for forefooting. Granville Martin recalled, in an interview on
file at the Buckaroo Hall of Fame, seeing a Nevada buckaroo rope a run-
away horse around the neck with his long riata, then, still at a dead run,
flick a half-hitch down the length of the rope and around its nose in
order to create a makeshift halter, then pop the rope between the running horse's front legs in order to jerk it down. I recall Rod McQuery
telling me of a good roper who had thrown an unusual open loop that
traveled low and vertical some thirty-five or forty feet over a fence to
catch a steer that was facing him and standing between two trees. It was
a loop the thrower may well have practiced for years before ever getting
a chance to use it, but, as Mackey Hedges has observed, that is exactly
what a buckaroo will do—practice for hours every day, not for speed
but to perfect all sorts of loops and fancy throws. Aesthetics, not strict
utility, is the hallmark of the buckaroo.

Another quality of the buckaroo, one shared with the cowboy,
only perhaps heightened in the former because of his even greater iso-

lation, is a sense of strong individualism. The less-pleasant flip side of this coin is that many (certainly not all) buckaroos (and cowboys) are not only lacking in social skills but can be downright antisocial. The collection of eccentric, misanthropic, violence-prone misfits that populate the buckaroo camp in the novel of Mackey Hedges (himself a most humane, helpful, friendly man) are, he told me, all based on life.

THE BUCKAROO AT WORK

As with cowboys throughout the West, the buckaroo has seen the nature of his work change as ranching has become more mechanized—from horseback cattle trailing to cattle trains to semi-trailer trucks, from riding to work to hauling horses in trucks to gooseneck stock trailers. Even so, Great Basin buckaroos are arguably less mechanized than cowboys elsewhere, with the possible exception of those big spreads of the Southwest that still field chuck wagons. The buckaroo wagon (their term for the chuck wagon) is pretty much a thing of the past, having been replaced by a four-wheel-drive truck to haul gear and food, but many of the large ranches in the Great Basin still send out a crew of buckaroos to handle the summer work.

Consider that the yearly cycle of work begins with spring branding at ranch headquarters, where the cows have been dropping calves while being wintered in fields (i.e., pastures) with good native grass, such as winterfat, or on hay if snow has covered the forage. After the calves have been roped, branded, castrated, and earmarked (they are often vaccinated for blackleg at weaning time), the cattle are driven to summer pasture on those federal grazing allotments held by that particular ranch. Because bulls often run with cow herds year round, calves continue to be born throughout the summer.

Once the cattle are placed, branding of more recently dropped calves continues throughout the summer. Because the summer range may cover over a million acres, buckaroos often must ride great distances daily. A typical day might begin well before morning light with the horse wrangler bringing in the cavvy (about five horses for each buckaroo) to be held behind an improvised corral made of lariat ropes. After breakfast the foreman (or a top roper he designates) will rope each buckaroo's mount, who will then feed it grain before saddling and bridling (a process that sometimes requires hobbling if the horse is cranky) and stepping aboard, ready to take out the kinks should the horse decide to buck, as many of them will. The crew will then set off at a good

Early-day buckaroos branding and castrating horses in southwest Idaho. Note the fence type. *Owyhee County Historical Society photo.*

clip, riding not at what Mackey Hedges calls a Texas jig, but instead at a stiff trot, posting as they ride. (Ernest Morris, as earlier noted, states that California buckaroos did not usually post.) Once they have arrived at the area to be worked, which in the old days may have been as much as fifty miles from the base camp and even today often is ten or fifteen miles away, the cow boss will make assignments for each buckaroo, who will then move to that area and begin pushing cattle toward a predesignated spot where the herd will be worked. This process, which would be called a roundup in Texas or a gather in Montana, is called in Nevada a *rodear* (or *rodeer*), from the Spanish term *rodeo,* which means to encircle or round up. Rodear is used both as a verb and a noun: the cattle are rodeared into a rodear, where the calves will be roped for branding, the dry cows sorted off, or some other task performed. The process of separating an animal from the herd would be called "cutting" by a cowboy, and the animals thus sorted out would be called the "cut," whereas a buckaroo would refer to the process as "parting," and would call the smaller group of animals drafted off and held separately from the main herd a "paratha." Sometimes there will be a set of pens at a rodear ground, but often the buckaroos will simply use a fence or one side of a canyon wall as a place to hold the cattle. In any case, the cattle will be held loosely, not bunched up tightly, so that the buckaroo can ride among them easily without stirring the herd.

The type of horse that a buckaroo likes to use for rodearing is called a "circle horse," typically a leggy, easy riding mount that can cover lots of ground quickly without tiring too soon. Today, as in much of the rest of the West, the American Quarter Horse is popular with buckaroos, but as a group they are more interested in horses of the right conformation for the country they have to cover than in bloodlines. Mackey Hedges estimates that when he first started buckarooing in the 1960s, probably half the horses in northern Nevada carried some Thoroughbred blood. Thoroughbreds crossed with Arabians are touted by Les Stewart, while others have valued a Morgan, a Percheron, or a Standardbred cross. The breed doesn't matter, Carl Hammond says, just so it's a long-legged, strong horse with plenty of stamina and ability.

Buckaroos hold the cattle in a rodear more loosely than cowboys holding a similar herd might, giving them plenty of room to move around. If the job for that particular day is to brand calves that have been

Paiute buckaroo Tex Northrup saddling up on the 96 Ranch in Paradise Valley, Nevada, mid-1970s. Note the fence type. *American Folklife Center, Library of Congress photo.*

Mackey Hedges and his son, Ben, working a young horse in a split rail corral. Note the fence type. *Jim Hoy photo.*

dropped since the herd was taken to summer pasture, then some of the hands will build a fire while others prepare the irons and sharpen pocket knives. Several ropers will move through the rodear, moving slowly so as not to spook the cattle, then maneuver a calf close to the edge of the loosely held herd before reaching out with their long riatas to snare a pair of heels, dally up, and drag the calf to the ground crew for working. When calves are small, they are heeled and dragged to the fire, but along about June, when the calves have grown larger, they are headed and heeled or sometimes forefooted and heeled. The ground crew sometimes transfers a head rope to the forelegs so that the ropers can hold the calf while it is worked. Rodears of this sort are usually fairly small, from fifty to a hundred and fifty head, because the cattle are thinly scattered over the vast acreage of their summer range.

In the afternoon, after the branding is completed, the buckaroos will trot back to their base camp, take care of their horses, clean up, have supper, and pass the time in various ways before unrolling their bedrolls. Each buckaroo has a range teepee to sleep in, a water-repellent canvas tent approximately eight feet square. His bed tarp is made of a piece of heavy canvas, about seven by seventeen feet, into which he rolls his quilts, blankets, pillow, and any extra clothes or personal effects he might have with him.

On days when a rodear is not called for, buckaroos might ride out singly or in small groups to look over the cattle, doctor sick ones, check water and salt supplies, and perform other chores. At shipping time, steers will be rounded up and driven to loading pens where semi-trailer pot-bellied cattle trucks will haul them to market or to feedlots. In earlier years, the drive would have been to a railroad shipping point, such as Winnemucca in Nevada, Murphy in Idaho, or Crane in Oregon. Today many cattle in the Great Basin are sold by electronic video auctions, with buyers bidding from thousands of miles away on cattle they have never seen except on a television screen.

As fall comes on, the buckaroo crew will begin to gather the cattle from the far reaches of the summer range and start heading them down

Mackey Hedges working with a young horse. Note the snaffle bit with nylon mecate reins. *Jim Hoy photo.*

toward the wintering grounds at ranch headquarters. There, hay crews will have been working during the summer, baling the winter's supply of hay or, in earlier days, loose-stacking it. After the cow herds have reached headquarters, buckaroos will help in weaning the calves and shipping them to market. Then some of the buckaroos might stay on for the winter ranch work, while others might take on some other type of job for the winter.

The time commitment required for buckarooing far exceeds that spent by any corporate workaholic, as is made evident in Mackey Hedges's description of an average year on the YP Ranch in Elko County, Nevada, circa the late 1960s:

> The year we moved to the YP, I left [ranch headquarters] in April and never got back until the Fourth of July. The wagon pulled out in April and we started branding the first part of May, and we branded clear up to the Fourth of July. Then they brought us home for four days, then we run out and branded until it got too hot and then we busted up and they put us in camps. Two guys would stay at Paiute and two guys at Stateline and two guys over on the Mountain. Anyway they busted us up until September, and when it cooled off in September then they'd bring us back together on the wagon again. That summer that I was out on the wagon, they'd bring me and the other married guys home like every ten days or so. They would bring us in when they got groceries for the wagon cook. They'd usually drop me off on Friday night and pick me up at two o'clock on Saturday morning. You got four days off for the Fourth of July. If you wanted any more time off, you quit. You got off four days for Fourth of July, you got off four days for Labor Day, you got off two days for Thanksgiving, you know, half a day and then Thanksgiving Day, and then Christmas they would split the crew and one part of the crew got Christmas and the other part got New Years and then you didn't get anymore time off until Fourth of July again. It didn't bother me when I was single, but when I got married, you start looking for smaller ranches.

Many Great Basin ranches are still large, especially in comparison to ranch sizes in other parts of the West, but mechanization has changed some of the work methods and routines. In 1998 Caleb "Newt" Dodge left the cowboy life of the Kansas Flint Hills to try the buckaroo life of

Nevada, taking a job under John Falen on the UC Ranch near McDermitt. The ranch covers some million acres and runs around eighteen hundred head of mother cows, but, whereas thirty years ago summer work on a ranch like the UC would have been done by a wagon crew, as described above by Mackey Hedges, today Newt and one other cowboy, each with a string of half a dozen horses, work out of a camp. Each day they load their mounts into a gooseneck trailer and drive out onto the range, where they will cover ten or fifteen miles while gathering cows with unworked calves, heading them toward a corral. After several days of this activity, gathering up to fifty head each day, they will be joined by several other buckaroos who will help with branding.

When spare time was available to the traditional buckaroo, he had a variety of ways in which to pass it, two of which involved music and poetry. Some buckaroos could play instruments, such as the fiddle or the accordion, which, along with singing, provided music around the camp. Others could recite the classic cowboy poems, while still others were poets themselves, a form of expression that has burgeoned in popularity throughout the West since the first big cowboy poetry gathering at Elko in 1985. It was, in fact, in buckaroo country that the tradition of reciting traditional, and writing original, poems about cowboy life had continued unbroken since the early days. The first public display of cowboy poetry occurred at the 1978 Pioneer Arts Folklife Festival in Elko, where Waddie Mitchell, Eldon Walker, Jack Walther, and Walt James performed. Each had learned his poetic craft while buckarooing in the Great Basin.

Concerning other pastimes, evenings in camp or at the ranch were a good time to repair tack and gear or to braid rawhide or horsehair or to work silver. Mackey Hedges recalls pitching horseshoes during the long evenings in a buckaroo camp, while reading has long been a favorite diversion of cowhands throughout the history of the West. Buckaroos, like cowboys and vaqueros, will practice their roping on almost any animate or inanimate object. Accounts of roping bears, antelope, and coyotes are plentiful in buckaroo country. So are tales of pranks, a favorite form of initiation among herders of all kinds: heeling someone else's horse while he is riding it, shoving a stick under its tail to make it buck, sneaking a pair of hobbles onto a horse while its rider is eating breakfast in the dark, or flipping the headgear off a horse then slapping it across the rump with a rope or quirt. And many buckaroos will relieve the boredom of a long ride by playing horseback games: various forms of tag, weed roping contests, follow the leader. Waltzy Elliott once roped an antelope, and, John Crow of Burns, Oregon, would, when he was younger, run down jackrabbits and earmark them, then turn them loose. The late Glenn Walcott won many bets by holding silver dollars between his boots and the stirrups while riding a bucking horse.

Many buckaroos, in fact, have been top rodeo saddle-bronc riders. In the first generation of professional rodeo (the first quarter of the twentieth century), buckaroos such as Pete Kershner, Glenn Walcott, and Ross Dollarhide were top competitors at the Pendleton Round Up and the Nampa Stampede, while Tom Minor nearly won Cheyenne in 1905 and did win Denver in both that year and 1906. In 1978, Joe Marvel of Battle Mountain, Nevada, whose father, Tom, was a well-known buckaroo boss in the area, won the Professional Rodeo Cowboy Association world championship in saddle-bronc riding.

More closely related to actual ranch work in the Great Basin are the Big Loop rodeo, held annually at Jordan Valley, Oregon, and the various ranch rodeos that have sprung up in recent years. The feature event at Jordan Valley is a horse dally-roping contest where two buckaroos must head and forefoot a wild horse, each using loops at least twenty feet in size. The regular team-roping contest at the Big Loop rodeo uses muley range heifers, not horned corriente steers, and ropers must dally on a slick saddle horn, not one wrapped with rubber. Carl Hammond, who has competed there, says that the long riata comes in handy on this fresh, spooky stock, for many of the non-buckaroo ropers using thirty-foot nylons will have the slack jerked out of their hands, whereas those ropers using the sixty-foot-plus riatas rarely have that trouble.

Throughout range country, ranch rodeos have become a popular sport (a grassroots reaction against the slick professionalism of regular rodeo). Great Basin "ranch hand rodeos" (as they are usually called) include events that typify actual ranch work in that area. In addition to horse roping, which does not occur in the Southwest or on the Great Plains, Great Basin ranch rodeos often have a calf-roping contest in which a single roper must catch and tie a calf, but must dally on a slick horn rather than tying hard and fast, thus mirroring the typical way that a buckaroo would operate by himself on the range. Chuck Hall told me of a calf-branding contest in which he had competed where, instead of having a single roper drag two calves to two flankers and a brander, as occurs in most ranch rodeos in the plains, two ropers headed and heeled two calves for branding by the two-buckaroo ground crew, then themselves dismounted and became the ground crew for the other two men. Another event, as described to me by Mark Galyen, features two horsemen riding double to the far end of the arena, where one jumps off and hands a rope tied to a stiff elk hide to his partner, who dallies up while the man on the ground jumps onto the hide. Then the mounted man takes off at a run, pulling both the hide and the man clinging to it back across the arena in a fashion similar to (but much faster than) the way a sick cow was sometimes dragged across the snow from the range to a hay corral in wintertime.

BUCKAROOING IN THE 1920S

Buckarooing in the 1990s, though more mechanized than it used to be, still relies more on horses and less on trailers than does similar ranch work in most other parts of the country. But 75 years ago, all work on the big ranches of the Great Basin was done with horses. At least that's how Waltzy Elliott remembers it. His father was a foreman, his mother a cook, for the far-flung Miller and Lux ranch holdings in northwest Nevada and southeast Oregon. Waltzy himself started buckarooing full-time at age fifteen and continued for ten years, until around 1930. The oral history he taped with Linda Dufurrena for the Humboldt County Library in Winnemucca, Nevada, is a storehouse of information about buckarooing during the first quarter of the last century.

Henry Miller and his partner Charles Lux, as reported in Mike Hanley's book *Owyhee Trails*, put together a cattle empire that spread over five states and contained millions of acres. Their million head of cattle made the S-Wrench brand one of the largest in the history of the American West. The major holdings of Miller and Lux were broken down into two divisions in Nevada (the Black Rock and the Quinn River) and some four in Oregon (Harper, Agency, Island, and White Horse). The cattle operation for the entire ranch was under the supervision of Charlie Miller, who reported directly to "old Henry Miller himself," as Elliott puts it. The ranch had numerous horse crews and cattle crews and haying crews on various of the divisions, as well as cooks, choreboys (who might well be not boys but old cowhands who were no longer able to handle the rough work of the ranch), gardeners, and other types of workers. The big company store, at the Quinn River headquarters, was where employees could buy clothing, gear, and tobacco without ever having to go into town.

One of Elliott's first jobs, when he was twelve years old, was driving the bed wagon for buckaroo crews when they were moved from one headquarters to another. Because at these times they were working out of one of the division ranches instead of out on the range with a buckaroo wagon, the buckaroos could eat at the headquarters cookshack. When Elliott was in his early teens, he helped with the massive Miller and Lux haying operation by driving teams of work horses on mowing machines. He had a knack for handling horses, which is why he sometimes got the job of matching up horses for teams. In other words, his job was to harness and drive all the scores of work horses in the weeks preceding hay season so that he could pair together horses of similar strength, speed, endurance, and spirit.

Elliott also helped break riding horses on the Wilson Ranch during the winter that he was thirteen years old. The horse breaker, Leslie Van Riper, who was working on a dozen young horses at a time, would go to the corral every morning and catch the gentlest of the colts for Elliott to ride. Then Van Riper would catch one of the wilder ones, take the buck out of him, open the corral gate, and the two of them would ride for about an hour. Then Elliott would saddle the one that Van Riper had just gotten off of, and the horse breaker would catch a fresh horse to ride. Thus every horse got two rides each day.

Elliott recalls that each buckaroo on the White Horse Division had a string of eight or ten horses, and that they were tough horses. A buckaroo could make a fifty-mile ride and then do range work without his horse giving out. An ordinary cowhand buckaroo was paid thirty dollars a month, plus board, but those, like Elliott, who could handle cranky horses would be paid sixty dollars a month for riding the rough string. One time, on one of the Oregon divisions, the cow boss, Bill Thompson, offered one of his horses to Elliott, a good but cranky horse named Paleface. Elliott saddled and mounted Paleface without a fuss, but as they were going down a canyon trail the horse suddenly ducked his head and started to buck blindly. "He made two jumps and he rammed his head into a tree," Elliott said. The collision surprised Paleface so much that he not only quit bucking then, he never again bucked with Elliott.

Walter McClure, a cousin of Elliott's who was buckarooing for Miller and Lux in the Island Division, had his horse start bucking with him near a cliff at the top of a canyon. McClure bailed off as the horse neared the edge, but the horse didn't even slow down. Instead he bucked over the rim and was killed in the fall. Bob Ward, on the other hand, got tired of having to put up with a particularly disagreeable horse and deliberately bucked him to the edge of a cliff, then jumped off and let the horse plunge to his death. The ranch owner was not particularly pleased, but Ward was such a good hand that he kept his job.

Del Harmon's experience, as related by Rick Steber in his book *Roundup*, was less fortunate. In 1941 a young colt suddenly started bucking and plunged headfirst over a steep canyon wall, trapping the seventeen-year-old Harmon beneath him. He lay there for twenty-three hours before an old sheepherder found him and managed to pull the dead horse off. Harmon recovered everything but his eyesight, a circumstance that did not stop him from subsequently earning his living as a horse trader. "I began using my hands to see a horse," Harmon said, "Fact is, I can actually tell the color of a horse and be right ninety-five times out of a hundred. Colors have a different texture." Harmon epitomizes the innate knowledge of horses possessed by many buckaroos.

The Great Basin is one of the few places in the West where wild horses still run, protected by federal statute since the early 1970s. They are not Spanish mustangs, however, but feral horses descended from farm and ranch animals that were turned loose. In Waltzy Elliott's day many of these horses were so inbred that they weighed only six or seven hundred pounds, and their manes and tails dragged the ground. Ranchers would sometimes turn out a good stud, hoping to get some decent colts from the wild mares. Often, however, the wild horses were good for nothing but chicken feed. Elliott recounts how wild horses were sometimes captured: a *partida* of some fifty or sixty head of tame horses would be driven to an area where wild horses ran, then the buckaroos would slip around behind the wild bunch and drive them toward the tame ones, hoping that the feral horses would mill with the ranch horses and could be driven with them into a set of pens. If the wild horses wouldn't stay with the tame ones, Elliott said, "Why the buckaroo boss stood there and shot every one of them as they went out." The only way to keep the quality of the wild horses up, even with a released stallion running with the mares, was to sort out and ship the "chicken feed" culls every year.

The main work of the buckaroo, however, was with cattle, and Elliott recalls that the cattle would be "graded" each fall when they were brought into the feed grounds so that the poorer cattle received hay to help them through the winter while the stronger ones could make it on their own. He remembers that the cattle at the time he was working were mainly Herefords and Durhams. Cattle in the Oregon divisions of Miller and Lux were shipped to Chicago out of the railroad yards at Crane, while those in the Nevada divisions were driven to Winnemucca to be shipped to California. A big ranch like Miller and Lux, Elliott said, often employed regular drovers to deliver cattle to the railroads, while the ranch buckaroos stayed on the range to sort the cattle to be shipped. Only when it was time to ship the final draft of range cattle did the ranch buckaroos get to drive cattle to the yards. Winnemucca, like most of the cowtowns in the West, provided plenty of opportunity for trail hands to let off steam. Mike Hanley, in *Tales of the I.O.N. Country*, quotes one old-time buckaroo who said that the "girls" would sometimes meet the herds when they were as much as three days from town, and another who recalled a time when the madams were having a price war in competing for buckaroo business: "Hell, we didn't mind," he said, "We had the demand and they sure as hell had the supply." Elliott recalls one Christmas in particular when he helped ship the last bunch of cattle to California from Winnemucca, where Miller and Lux maintained a large set of pens. The temperature that Christmas morning was thirty-two degrees below zero.

In the winter, after the final shipping, the buckaroos stayed at ranch headquarters, going out to do their cow work during the day but always being able to eat at the cookshack. Meals were served at 6 A.M., noon, and 6 P.M. If a buckaroo happened to be unable to get back into headquarters at noon, he normally had to wait until six to eat because he wasn't supposed to bother the cook in the middle of the afternoon. Sometimes, if a cook got too old to go out on a buckaroo wagon, he would be given the cooking chores at ranch headquarters, as happened with Jim Yow, a Chinese cook at the Soldier Meadows Ranch of Miller and Lux. Elliott recalled that, unlike many other cooks, Yow didn't mind feeding a cowhand during off hours, telling them: "You son of a bitch buckaloo, you come down, you eat a bite!" The buckaroo wagon itself was what would be called a chuck wagon by a plains cowboy. It was a box wagon with bows and a canvas cover, pulled by four horses, with a rear-mounted chuckbox to hold cooking equipment, flour, salt, and spices. The big dutch ovens were carried beneath the wagon, while the bed was used for hauling sleeping gear and tents for the buckaroos. An especially large crew might, however, require a separate bed wagon, such as Elliott drove when he first started working.

Ranches maintained large farming operations, particularly in the making of hay, but most of them also kept milk cows, chickens, and gardens in order help feed the twenty to thirty hands at headquarters, not to mention the buckaroo crews out on the range. Whereas buckaroo wagon cooks were always male, women, such as Elliott's mother, were sometimes employed to cook at a ranch. Elliott's father, Sam, would often cut the meat that his wife needed for the day, while she also had a chore-boy to peel potatoes, wash dishes, and do other such tasks. Lena Elliott would be up by four to have breakfast ready by six, then spend the entire morning preparing dinner. After a short nap she would then fix supper. She had to make, or supervise the making of, butter, bread, cakes, and pies, in addition to the main courses of meat and vegetables. Ranch gardens produced potatoes, carrots, lettuce, and other vegetables, while the orchard supplied apples or peaches in season. Most fruit, however, was shipped in: twenty-five-pound boxes of pears, peaches, and apricots on occasion, California prunes in hundred-pound sacks all the time.

Waltzy Elliott does not recall any poetry being recited around the buckaroo wagon, but he does remember that evenings were often spent washing saddle blankets and clothing, or in working with rawhide or horsehair. Several of the hands he worked with could play the harmonica, and one, Frank Lorenzana, played an accordion, so there was often some music around the camp at night. When back at headquarters, most of the buckaroos read the magazines and books that could be found on any ranch. When in town, the buckaroo would often blow his pay in the red-light district, or else on bootleg whiskey. Elliott recounted the time that he and his cousin, Walter McClure, happened onto a five-gallon keg of bootleg near Burns, Oregon, right at rodeo time. They both indulged freely in their windfall and signed up to ride bareback broncs. When it came time to ride, Walter had passed out behind the chutes, but Waltzy made a successful ride, his one and only venture into a rodeo arena.

Buckaroos would often spend their money not on wild times in town, however, but on good gear. The favorite saddle, Elliott recalls, was a slick-fork, center-fire rig built on the Visalia tree; it cost about three months wages and was made in San Francisco by Walker. Many of the buckaroos made their own rawhide reins and bridles but bought rawhide riatas made by prisoners at Carson City. They also bought riatas and gloves made by the Paiute or Shoshone Indians who lived in the Great Basin. Elliott preferred a relatively small hat, thinking the ten-gallon sombrero too gaudy. He did, however, like a silver-mounted bridle and silver on his saddle and headstall.

Stanley Griswold, like Elliott born in 1905, was a buckaroo in the 1920s and 1930s, working for the IL, the YP, and the Winecup ranches. He recalled his experiences for me as we sat and watched George Smiraldo and Lou Arano braid rawhide reins and romals in George's Elko workshop in late November, 1995. The buckaroos, Griswold said, lived in canvas tents while out with the wagon, either branding during the summer or delivering cattle in the fall. The horse herd would be brought in around the first of April and horses broke for either the saddle or to harness. There were usually about 125 horses in the cavvy, he said, with from 7 to 12 head in his string. Each buckaroo had to shoe his own horses, although the ranch supplied both the shoes and the equipment. (A round anvil, lighter and more portable than the regular kind, was often carried in the buckaroo wagon. Such an anvil, from the 96 Ranch, is on display at the Buckaroo Hall of Fame and Heritage Museum in Winnemucca, Nevada.) The buckaroos would leave in May and work until the Fourth of July, then go to town and get drunk. On a big roundup, a buckaroo wagon might service up to twenty men, counting reps from other outfits. The IL Ranch, Griswold said, normally had ten men to a wagon while he was working there. In the fall the IL used to drive eighteen hundred steers, split into two bunches, a distance of a hundred miles to railroad shipping pens, a trip that would last nine or ten days. The buckaroos who stayed on during the winter months lived in the bunkhouse.

No women, both Griswold and Elliott said, ever worked as buckaroos in their time, nor even today are there any women working on the range crews of big ranches. However, many cowgirls do perform buckaroo work side by side with their husbands, fathers, and brothers on Great Basin ranches. Both Carl Hammond and Mike Hanley agree that women began to do more actual ranch work during and after World War Two when labor was in short supply. Hammond, in fact, says that his wife, Helen, is better help around horses and cattle than any other hand he has ever hired. When I asked Hammond if any women had ever worked as buckaroos in earlier times, he said he knew of none, but that some could have if they had disguised themselves as men. That, in fact, is exactly what happened in the case of a "man" known as Little Joe Monahan of Ruby City, Idaho. Little Joe came into the Owyhee Mountains as a miner but left the diggings in the early 1880s to work as a buckaroo in Idaho and Oregon. Only after "his" death in late 1903 was it discovered that Little Joe was actually a woman.

Multiculturalism was common in the buckaroo section of the Great Basin, with early settlers (whose occupations included not only buckarooing, but, among others, mining, railroading, farming, ranching, and store-keeping) coming from Germany, France, Switzerland, the Basque provinces of both France and Spain, Mexico, Ireland, and England, as well as from other parts of the United States. Unlike the Great Plains, where perhaps from a fourth to a third of the cowboys on the

Texas-to-Kansas trail were African American, in the Great Basin only a few blacks became buckaroos. One, Lawrence Jackson, has been inducted into the Buckaroo Hall of Fame, and another, Bill Hearst, was considered one of the best buckaroos ever to ride in Owyhee County, Idaho. There was even an occasional Chinese buckaroo. Mike Hanley recalled one who, when asked to take over the cooking duties while out on the range, told the boss: "When I cookee, I cookee; when I buckaloo, I buckaloo. I quit." Many Native Americans—Paiutes, Shoshones, Bannocks—became buckaroos. Rick Steber, in his book *Roundup*, profiles Harry Clarkson, a Klamath Indian buckaroo. Two good Indian buckaroos Waltzy Elliott remembers were Moe and Jim Taham, and he also recalls a couple of Mexican buckaroos, Juan Redon and Clay Rambo, who worked for Miller and Lux. The earliest buckaroos, in fact, were primarily Hispanic, vaqueros who drove the first big herds into Nevada from California. Many of the early-day cattle workers in the Great Basin were Mexican. Fred Castro, a California vaquero, was buckaroo boss for Pick Anderson in Oregon, and most of his hands, as well as those of Pete French, who ranched near Steens Mountain, were vaqueros.

THE ORIGINAL BUCKAROO

Both the term *buckaroo* and the buckaroo himself ultimately derive from the vaquero of Spanish California, a herder that Jo Mora has termed the "Californio." The livestock industry in early California was started by the missions, the first of which, San Diego, was established in 1769. Within three years, four more missions had been established, reaching all the way up the coast to San Luis Obispo. A year later an inventory of livestock at the five missions revealed 205 cattle, 94 sheep, 67 goats, 152 pigs, 4 donkeys, 73 brood mares, 4 horse colts, 30 saddle horses, and 100 mules. By the turn of the century, thirteen additional missions had been started, and the missions had a total of 153,000 cattle. By 1834, and eight more missions, Spanish California boasted nearly 400,000 cattle and over 60,000 horses. To tend the herds, the priests trained vaqueros from the native Indian populations in the arts of horsemanship.

Soon after the establishment of the first missions, lay settlers, mainly from the Mexican provinces of Sinaloa and Sonora, came into Alta California, and many of them established ranches or became mounted ranch workers. These settlers, called "gente de razon," meaning people of reason to differentiate them from the native population, who, as barbarians, were considered to exist in a state of ignorance. The settlers brought with them the ranching equipment and work methods of Old Mexico, which they adapted to local conditions as appropriate. I have already noted how they moved the cinches on their saddles from directly under the horn back to a central position under the stirrup leather and how they abandoned the heavy leather armas in favor of armitas, the forerunner of chinks. The Californio wore long pants and a low-heeled boot onto which he strapped silver-mounted, drop-shanked spurs with big rowels that dragged the ground when he walked. He wore a broad-brimmed, low-crowned, black felt hat with fancy tassels, with a strap under the lower lip or chin. A large silk scarf around his neck, an open-necked shirt, a short jacket, a vest, and a serape completed his outfit.

The Californio placed an Indian blanket under his saddle and often carried a sword and scabbard on the saddle, under his left leg. He usually carried his rawhide riata tied to the right side of his saddle just behind the cantle. On a well-trained horse he would use a Santa Barbara spade bit with short straight shanks, the original design of which is attributed to Don José Francisco Ortega. The cheek plates were hand forged of iron and made to swivel with the ends of the mouth bar. The Las Cruces–style bit placed a silver concho where the cheek plate joined onto the bar. The headstall for these bits was usually a narrow band of leather decorated with silver. Braided rawhide reins with attached romal were used on bits, while the horsehair mecate was fastened onto rawhide hackamores or bosalillos (i.e., small bosals) as reins. Many horse breakers employed the "two rein" (i.e., the simultaneous use of both a hackamore and a bit) in training a horse.

The Californio tended to be free with his money in buying fancy equipment, and he took his time in training horses. The bronc rider was known as an amansador, and the riders often worked in pairs in going from ranch to ranch to break young horses. They would start a colt with a series of different hackamores, which would be employed until the horse was perfectly trained to turn, stop, and back. At that point they would put a spade bit in its mouth, but with no reins attached, and let the young horse get used to its feel for several weeks before the training with double rein was begun. The time and patience expended in this type of training was not necessarily the result of humane treatment, for horses were taught to respect a rope, usually by forefooting them in a breaking corral, a rough process that could result in injury.

Horses' tails were not cut or trimmed but were combed and washed, especially when the horse was to be ridden in a fiesta. A remnant of this tradition can be seen today in the buckaroo's tendency to tie a knot, often an attractive knot called the Spanish Mustache, or the Spanish Mustache with Goatee, in his horse's tail during the fall, winter, and spring months. In the summer, the tail is left open for switching flies. When I asked Mackey Hedges why buckaroos did this, his response was, "Just to show that they can." Carl Hammond described the knot as a "mustanger's knot" and said that its purpose was to keep the tail out of the way when chasing wild horses. In other words, although there might be some practicality in such an action (i.e., keeping a horse's tail free from burs), the main reasons are tradition and aesthetics. A linked superstition is that if you turn your horse loose at night without untying the knot, the devil will ride him all night long.

Californios, like buckaroos, were excellent ropers who constantly practiced difficult and tricky, but always potentially usable, throws. They used braided rawhide riatas (of four, six, or eight strands with three-eighths inch being the most popular diameter). Their ropes ranged in length from 65 to 110 feet. Mora himself had witnessed running catches at the end of an 85-foot riata, which means that the roper was at least sixty feet from the steer's horns when he threw. He also notes that Californios were artists with a rope, taking great pride in form and valuing unusual loops over speed.

A favorite sport of the Californio was using his riata to rope a grizzly bear, a dangerous, and inhumane, activity. One horseback game involved picking up a coin from the ground at a full gallop, while another involved pressing a coin between each knee and the saddle while maneuvering at high speed over a complicated course, then coming to a sudden stop without losing the coins. One game, the *carrera del gallo*, involved grabbing the neck of a live rooster and pulling him out of the ground where he had been buried. Other sports were tailing down bulls (the *colear*), racing horses, and fancy roping.

CATTLE IN BUCKAROO COUNTRY

Unlike the great sweeping region from Canada to Mexico where bison had once cropped the rich grasses of the Great Plains, the Great Basin had not been the habitat of any major herds of large native grazers, according to James A. Young and B. Abbott Sparks. Only antelope could be found there in any sort of numbers before the advent of cattle and the growth of the herds of feral horses that followed white settlement. The first cattle in the region were draft animals on the immigrant

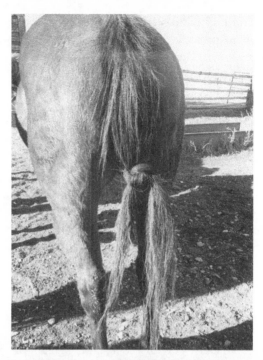

Two versions of knots in horses' tails—the Spanish Mustache tied by Mackey Hedges (Jim Hoy photo) and a more simple design in the tail of Dwight Hill's horse (Lawrence Clayton photo).

George Smiraldo working rawhide at his shop in Elko, Nevada, 1997.

trail to California that branched off from the Oregon Trail at Fort Hall, thence following the Humboldt River across northern Nevada. Often along major trails in the West, such as the Santa Fe Trail, an enterprising man might establish a trading station, generally termed a ranch, where he would offer lodging, sell supplies and stock feed, and exchange rested draft oxen for sore-footed ones. The first ranching venture in northern Nevada, established by Peter Haws near Humboldt Wells in 1854, seems to have been an establishment of this type. According to Young and Sparks, Haws attempted to increase his profits by encouraging the Indians to steal back the animals he had traded, a circumstance that soon forced him out of business—and out of the area.

Real ranching began in earnest in buckaroo country during the 1860s and became fully established in the following two decades. Two major factors contributed to the success of ranching in the Great Basin. One was the discovery of gold and silver in Idaho and Nevada in the early 1860s. The other was the building of the transcontinental railroad later in the decade. The former event provided a large local demand for beef, while the latter provided a means by which to ship excess cattle both to California and to markets east of the Rocky Mountains.

The first Longhorns, some 3,500 head, to come into the region were driven in 1858 from California to pasture in western Nevada near present-day Reno. Six years later a severe drought in California caused an exodus of stock and stockmen into northern Nevada. Contracts for Nevada beef from California buyers in 1865 provided an impetus for cattlemen to move into the Great Basin, and another drought occurred in 1871. These events, along with the establishment of a California fence law in 1873 that spelled the end of the open range there, solidified the position of northern Nevada as a major ranching center. Large ranching operations, such as the Miller and Lux and the Sparks and Tinnin, interspersed with smaller independent ranchers, became the pattern in northern Nevada. By 1883 the Sparks-Tinnin ranch, which covered northeastern Nevada and southwestern Idaho, ran 70,000 cattle and branded 17,000 calves. It was considered the largest in the country, with its owners labeled the "cattle kings of the west."

In addition to Spanish-derived Longhorns from California, those from Texas also had a notable influence on the development of the Great Basin cattle industry. Gold and silver strikes in Idaho from 1860 to 1863 had resulted in cattle of California ancestry being driven into the area from Washington Territory to provide meat for miners. However, as early as 1867, Stanke notes, Cornelius "Con" Shea headed for Texas at the behest of Idaho businessman John Catlow with instructions to hire a crew, buy beef steers, and drive them back to Idaho. In the Raft River country, before clearing Idaho, Shea encountered a herd of Texas cattle belonging to George Miller and Sol Walters. He bought the steers from them and pushed the herd on west, while Miller and Walters returned to Texas for more cattle. In 1869 Shea and a number of other men went to Texas and bought fourteen hundred steers, bringing them back in two herds along a route that began near Belton (between Waco and Austin) and angled northwest across northeastern New Mexico, the southern half of Colorado, northeastern Utah, and southwestern Idaho. In both 1871 and 1873 David Shirk, who had earlier worked for Con Shea, made trips to Texas and brought back herds of over fifteen hundred head, following a route that headed north from Belton, through Fort Worth, across Indian Territory to Dodge City and thence to Scottsbluff, Nebraska, then west through Wyoming to Bruneau, Idaho. By the early 1870s the range cattle industry was well established in the Owyhee Desert country of southwest Idaho.

Although Texas cattle from Idaho also found their way into southeastern Oregon, the first major stocking of those ranges, according to Richard Slatta, seems to have come from western Oregon where, in 1869, John Devine had some three thousand head driven into Harney County. These cattle were probably the descendants of cows driven from California into Oregon as early as 1837. The foreman for Devine's drive was renowned vaquero Juan Redon, who in the 1880s became a cow boss for the Miller and Lux ranches. He is remembered by Waltzy Elliott as "one of the great cowboys of Miller and Lux days," one who could throw and catch at the end of a hundred-foot rawhide riata.

THE BUCKAROO HALL OF FAME

Back in the mid-1980s, Carl Hammond, the son and grandson of buckaroos, began to think about instituting a Buckaroo Hall of Fame and Heritage Museum to honor the memories of, as he has put it,

> ... those old buckaroos who were very good at what they did. Nobody seemed to care; some of them didn't even have money enough to get buried with. But the tradition they carried on, from the vaqueros of Mexico, helped to establish their own type of character and the buckaroo became part of the heritage of Western America.

Hammond, who ranches near Golconda, Nevada, had earlier, in 1982, started the Western Art Round Up, now held annually over Labor Day weekend in Winnemucca. By the late 1980s, Hammond had put together a number of exhibits of Great Basin ranch life and buckaroo paraphernalia, which went on display in downtown Winnemucca in 1989. The City of Winnemucca had cooperated by providing exhibition space in an old casino, and the Humboldt County Fair and Recreation Commission helped financially. Hammond had also solicited members for a Hall of Fame organization, from which was drawn a governing board whose duties included giving direction to the new organization, taking nominations for honorees, and selecting those to be inducted. Hammond's wife, Helen (who is well known for her skill in making horsehair mecates), serves as secretary and nonvoting board member.

The first induction was held on the Saturday before Labor Day, 1990. Each of the four charter inductees—Tom Minor, Fred Raker, Shorty Riffe, and Glenn Walcott—met the four personal requirements: he had been born before 1900 or was at least ninety years old, was known as a buckaroo who had earned his living on horseback, had worked as a buckaroo within a two-hundred-mile radius of Winnemucca, and was well known for such buckaroo lifestyle skills as old-time buckaroo-style bronc riding, rawhide braiding, dally roping with the long riata, and horse- and cow-handling abilities. Those making a nomination had to submit a biography and a photograph of the nominee.

Many of the lifestyle skills, such as roping and rawhide work, have been discussed earlier, but not old-time buckaroo-style bronc riding. This style stands in contrast to ordinary rodeo contest bronc riding, which uses an association saddle, a halter, and a buck rein. According to Hammond:

> The old style, you'd just take them right out in the middle of
> the corral and saddle them and the guy just gets on and pulls
> the blind and uses not necessarily a hack rein but just a bit or a
> hackamore or a snaffle or whatever and rides with a quirt in his
> free hand.

The saddle would be the buckaroo's everyday slick-fork, single-cinch riding saddle, and he would ride without any time limit. This style of riding was done in competition, but often right on the ranch and not necessarily in a rodeo arena. Perhaps for Sunday afternoon entertainment a buckaroo would put on a show, or, perhaps to settle a boast, two buckaroos would vie against each other. Again, according to Hammond:

> The hardest horse to ride in the remuda is the one they picked out and usually two guys went out and whoever rode the longest won, and if they both rode, they'd pick another one until one rider got thrown. That's the way they contested it.

The requirement of having worked within two hundred miles of Winnemucca describes what people who live there think of as the Great Basin and does, in fact, clearly delineate the boundaries of buckaroo country. Those men who have been thus far inducted are not concentrated in one particular area or state but instead have worked on ranches throughout the Great Basin. They also represent the range of ethnicity found among buckaroos: Anglo, European, African American, Hispanic, and Indian. Following is a brief synopsis of some of the more interesting episodes in the lives of some of the honorees, which both summarizes the essence of buckarooing and reveals the variety of men who have pursued the occupation. A complete list of the honorees, by year, appears at the end of this chapter.

In appearance Oscar "Leppy" Arnold was typical of the buckaroo: he rode a Walker saddle with a narrow-forked Weatherly tree, wore chaps, a small hat, Levis, and a chambray shirt with a black vest, in the pocket of which he always carried a sack of Bull Durham tobacco. He was an excellent horseman who was especially adept at roping the stallions that would try to break away from a herd of wild horses being driven into a pen. The word around the ranches for which he worked, which included the Miller and Lux and the Goodman in Oregon and the Quarter Circle A and the 96 in Nevada, was that if a horse got too rank for the other hands, "Give him to Leppy."

John Crow, who is one of the few living men to have been taken into the Hall of Fame, demonstrates the toughness required for the dangers of buckarooing in the remote regions of the high desert range. Once, when he was roping a sick cow twenty miles from the main ranch, he got his hand caught in his dallies when his horse began to buck. Two fingers were torn off and a third broken. He has also broken his back three different times. On the third break he not only made it back to his Crow's Nest Ranch near the Malheur National Wildlife Refuge in Oregon, he also drove himself to Portland for treatment, stopping at Madras on the way to buy a clean shirt and Levis. On the way he had to push his pickup out of the snow in order to put chains on it. He did buy and drink a fifth of whiskey on the way in order to help with the pain, but he refused to take any of the pain pills prescribed by the doctors who treated his back. One of Crow's more unusual jobs, as related by Rick Steber in *Roundup*, was as a "tule rooter" when he and some other buckaroos were hired by Pete French in 1922 to catch hogs that had run wild and multiplied. Crow describes the process thus:

> Get a loop around a hog and drag it fighting and screeching and squealing to a high-sided wagon where ground men would tackle the critter, knock off the tusks with a hammer, toss it into the wagon. When they had a load the wagon would head for the railroad siding at Crane. Believe it or not but we shipped out better than 2,000 hogs that summer.

Another example of stoic buckaroo toughness was Emery "Shorty" Riffe. Once when he was gathering cattle in the rocky Owyhee Desert, a rattlesnake, coiled on top of one of the upright boulders, struck him as he rode by. Shorty loped and trotted some forty miles to Golconda, Nevada, where he caught a train to Winnemucca and a doctor.

Another rattlesnake story concerns Bob Ward who, in the summer of 1935, was riding with Tom Pedroli when they saw a big rattler. Tom wondered if Bob, who was carrying a gun, was going to shoot it, but Bob said, "No, let it go. I'm not going to be around much longer anyway, so he's not going to bother me." Ward died in early December of that same year.

Ross Dollarhide rode for most of the big ranches in the Great Basin: the Whitehorse, the P, the Roaring Spring, the Rock Creek, the Diamond, the New Diamond, the ZX, and the MC. His riding ability was proven at the 1914 Pendleton Round Up when he rode a previously unridden bronc. His riding skills were put to use during World War I when he moved to Miles City, Montana, to break horses for the army. His son Ross, Jr., was a successful rodeo performer during the 1940s and 1950s. Some buckaroos, because of the loneliness of the job, can tend toward the eccentric or the loner sensibility, but Dollarhide was a gregarious, friendly man, that rarity who was said to have had no enemies.

Several early buckaroos were heavily involved in mustanging. Arthur Drummond, known as the King of the Mustangers, generally operated out of Owyhee County, Idaho. Drummond ran horses throughout the three-state region, and between 1915 and 1937 he shipped out thousands of wild horses from the railroad pens at Winnemucca. Among other early buckaroos involved in mustanging was Glenn Walcott, who as a boy hired on with Drummond to round up wild horses in the Owyhee Desert. One time Glenn rode into a herd of mustangs coming off water and captured three of them all by himself. He roped one and tied it down with his mecate, roped another and tied it down with his riata strap, then roped the third and tied it down with his riata.

Robert Henry "Bob" Wilkinson also spent much of his life running mustangs on the Owyhee Desert. Wilkinson liked to gamble in the high-stakes poker games of the area (fifteen thousand dollars on the table was not an uncommon sight at that time), and he was often seen heading out for the mustang ranges after a long, and bad, night in town. Wild horses sold for chicken feed brought from three to five cents a pound, while a broke horse could bring from two hundred to two hundred fifty dollars. In contrast, big steers at the time brought three cents a pound. Wilkinson operated his wild-horse business much like a cattle rancher, rounding up mustangs, culling out the bad ones and cutting out those ready for market, castrating the colts, then turning them out to let them grow up. In 1928 Wilkinson made two drives of about five hundred horses each to Winnemucca. When the buyers would not take the colts from one drive, Bob turned them loose in the streets of town. As a result, every kid in town that year had a pony, if he or she wanted one.

Ed Ducker learned his riding and roping skills from the Mexican vaqueros near his home in Modesto, California. At the age of seventeen, he moved to Nevada to begin buckarooing, and for some fifteen years he worked for various wagon outfits. In the evenings, he would go off by himself and read from his volume of Shakespeare or his Blackstone law books. One time an older buckaroo, accompanied by his buddies, threatened Ducker with a revolver: "Hey, kid, I think you'd make a better dancer than a lawyer. Get up and start practicing!" punctuating his remark with a shot near Ducker's outstretched foot. The youngster calmly replied, "Oh, I can dance all right," as he laconically pulled himself to his feet, then quick as a cat landed a stunning blow to the chin of his unsuspecting tormentor. Ducker then pulled his own gun and made the rest of the onlookers do some dancing of their own. No one ever interrupted his reading again, and when he was thirty-two he was admitted to the Nevada Bar, where he eventually became a Justice of the State Supreme Court.

Jack Frusetta was born in New York to Swiss and Irish parents, but his family moved to San Benito County, California, when he was just a boy. Like many buckaroos, Jack was fond of fancy gear: a Walker Visalia saddle, silver-mounted bridles, and elaborate spade bits. His death defines the rigors of buckaroo life in the high desert. In May of 1937 Jack was representing the IL Ranch at the Circle A roundup. On June 4 he headed across the Owyhee Desert with seventeen IL cattle and his string of horses. On June 17 Jack's horse turned up at the CS Ranch, the saddle turned under its belly and a cut rope around its neck. Searchers discovered his packhorse, some items of clothing, and a dress boot. They also found a pile of brush about two feet high and eight feet long where Jack had apparently tried to build a mound so that he could mount his horse with a broken leg. Failing that, he had cut the horse loose and started crawling, traveling miles through rocks, brush, and mud before finally succumbing to his injury and to thirst. He had crawled under some tall brush to die, neatly laying his spurs on his gloves next to his body and covering his face with his hat before dying. His fancy dress Blucher boots are on display at the Hall of Fame.

Frank Hammond, the great-uncle of Carl Hammond, had a reputation as the best all-around buckaroo in Nevada. He was a top buckaroo-style bronc rider, a skilled trainer of reining cow horses, and an excellent roper. Once at the YP Ranch he forefooted twenty-three horses in a row before missing a throw. His buckarooing was cut short when he lost a leg in an automobile accident in the early 1940s, but in 1943 he became sheriff of Lander County, an office he held for twelve years.

Ambrose Maher buckarooed and ranched his entire life. He always rode a good bridle horse, and he kept three bands of mares for raising horses. On two bands he ran thoroughbred-type stallions and on the third a percheron-type. He had a reputation for being able to set broken bones, as well as for spinning horsehair mecates, braiding rawhide riatas, and working with silver. And he would entertain around the buckaroo camp with his fiddle.

Tom Minor was a top horse breaker and rodeo bronc rider. He began buckarooing at age eleven, herding mares for the DH Ranch near Paradise Valley. A year later he became the horse wrangler for the Hoppin Brothers Ranch. At sixteen he hired on, for fifty dollars a month, as the full-time horse breaker for the Spur Ranch near Trout Creek, Oregon, where he once broke a hundred horses in a month. During the four and a half years that he worked for the P Bench Ranch, he was bucked off only three times.

William "Bill" Nelson demonstrated his riding ability to his eleven children by hanging from a crossbar in a corral full of untamed horses, then jumping onto their backs one at a time as each was turned out, riding with a mane hold for a quarter of a mile or so, then jumping off and coming back to get on another one. He had learned to ride by breaking remount horses for the cavalry. It is said that he kept seven men busy saddling for him as he showed horses to army officials. Nelson used a shorter rope than most buckaroos because of an episode that occurred one time when he had roped a mustang stallion with a new hundred-foot rawhide riata and his arms and neck got tangled in the rope. He escaped injury, but once the storm was over he took out his pocket knife and cut the rope half in two, saying: "Fifty feet is enough for anyone."

Many buckaroo horse breakers took the edge off horses in rough fashion—rope them, saddle them, get on them, and let them buck. Fred Raker, however, was a forerunner of the currently popular method of gentling horses rather than breaking them. He would enter a corral with an untamed horse, talk to it, and walk around it until the horse would let him pet it, even if it took many attempts and lots of time. Then he would halter the horse and lead it around the corral before putting on a snaffle bit and saddle. After about an hour he would catch the horse and ease himself on. Rarely would the horse buck but instead would trot around the corral with Fred on its back. Fred would then move into a larger corral and take down his rope, rubbing it all over the horse's back, belly, and legs. Once the horse was used to the rope, Fred would build a loop and catch a coal-oil can sitting in the corral, then drag it slowly toward the horse, which would at once turn to face this strange object. Staying relaxed and keeping the reins loose, Fred would slowly pull the can to the horse and lift it up to the horse's shoulder, then take the rope off and throw the can away. After that, the horse would never be afraid of anything on the end of a rope.

More is known about the skills than the lives of the non-Anglo members of the Buckaroo Hall of Fame. Not even the birth or death dates are known for Lawrence Jackson, the only black buckaroo in the Hall of Fame. He left home at fifteen to work on ranches in Wyoming, Idaho, Nebraska, and Colorado, turning up in Elko, Nevada, in 1921, where he began some fifty years of working for the big ranches: the Spanish, the Double Square, John G. Taylor, and Abel and Kurtner. Nor is much known about Lolo Muñoz, the only Hispanic in the Hall of Fame, who might have been born in 1877 or else in 1882. He began work on the Spanish Ranch in 1924, where he claimed that he had been on his own since age eleven. He worked as a buckaroo until well over the age of eighty and claimed that his longevity was the result of drinking a shot of whiskey every day. Albert Skedaddle, a full-blood Paiute, worked many years for the 96 Ranch in Paradise Valley where, for a time, he was buckaroo boss of an all-Indian crew. He worked quietly around cattle and was especially known for his ability to "mother up" calves with the right cows.

Other honorees of the Buckaroo Hall of Fame are Frank Joseph Button, Nathan Pierce "Pete" Kershner, Francis "France" Hammond (Carl Hammond's father), Taft Miller, Paul Sweeney, Quentin Lee "Stub" Curry, Samuel Waltzy Elliott, William Warren "Bill" Thomson, Frank Leon "Jumper" Jones, Marvin Myers, Sr., Pete Foredyce, Joseph John "Joe Boy" Bankofier, and Thomas Edward "Tom" Hayes. Up to six men can be named to the Hall of Fame each year, although the actual number of inductees has usually been either three or four annually. If, as is planned, the Hall of Fame is able to construct its own building within the next decade, which will allow for a greater display area and also room for archives, then Carl Hammond's dream of providing a permanent facility for honoring the heritage of the buckaroo will be fully accomplished.

THE BUCKAROO TODAY

Awareness of, and fascination with, the buckaroo have become more widespread today than when Carl Hammond began thinking about establishing a Hall of Fame because, as he said, "Nobody seemed to care." This greater appreciation is the result of varying degrees of exposure of the buckaroo to the country at large via, in particular, television and cowboy poetry gatherings. Also contributing to greater attention is the striking artwork of, among others, Dave Holl and William Matthews and the photographs of C. J. Hadley, John Land LeCoq, Kurt Markus, and David Stoeklein.

One consequence of this heightened exposure—similar to that which occurred because of the media-disseminated image of the cowboy of the railroad cowtown days over a century ago—is that youngsters from other parts of the country and beyond are attracted by the romanticism of the buckaroo image. These youngsters, when they come to the Great Basin and become buckaroos, come with a preconceived notion of what a buckaroo looks like, if not precisely what he does. This, too, recalls an earlier period when the actual working cowboy of the Great Plains found himself adapting his clothing and gear so that he matched the image being projected by wild west shows, rodeo, film, and dime novels. So, too, has today's buckaroo deliberately affected an appearance that is even more distinctive than that of the original buckaroos who, by the early 1900s, had developed from the California vaqueros.

Many of today's buckaroos, for instance, roll up the legs of their blue denim jeans (usually, ironically, Wranglers rather than the more traditional Levis) into a large cuff, a style that was popular in the 1920s and 1930s, when blue jeans were first coming into widespread use in ranch country. Many buckaroos grow handle-bar mustaches of exaggerated length, whereas facial hair was not particularly common among the earliest buckaroos. Small straight-brimmed hats of Spanish styling, or snap-brimmed fedora styling, are growing in popularity over the larger ten-gallon types. Wild rags are nearly ubiquitous, as are chinks, whereas photographs from the 1920s show many buckaroos with open-collared shirts and either shotgun or batwing chaps. Angora woolies for winter chaps are no longer museum pieces for those buckaroos who can afford them. And the silver. In the words of Carl Hammond:

> My dad always felt that the buckaroos of his era and this area
> didn't really believe that you had to have all that silver. But
> say the last ten to twenty years, a lot of these books written on
> buckaroos of the Great Basin show them pretty much dressed up
> with great big wild rags and big handle bar mustaches and lots
> and lots of silver on their rigging.

Whether from affectation or from exaggerated imitation, today's buckaroo undoubtedly presents a more spectacular facade than did the original.

Many of the attributes of the original buckaroo, in other words, have been intensified among their successors today, who have become deliberate throwbacks to an earlier era. But the emphasis on certain aspects of external appearance does not mean that today's buckaroo is not a good horseman, is not skilled with the riata, is less adept at rawhide braiding and horsehair weaving, nor is any less drawn to the openness of the landscape or to a love of the lifestyle than his predecessors.

Buckaroos, like cowboys and vaqueros, may change in appearance and may adapt to new technologies, but so long as cattle are grazed in large numbers in open pastures, all three types of herders will continue to maintain their long traditions, distinct but intermingled.

1990 Thomas F. "Tom" Minor (1871–1937)
George Fredrick Raker (1895–1951)
Emery "Shorty" Riffe (1884–1953)
Glenn Walcott (1888–1970)

1991 Arthur Drummond (1874–1938)
Frank L. Hammond (1886–1960)
Ambrose A. Maher (1880–1955)
Robert Henry "Bob" Wilkinson (1874–1929)

1992 Frank Joseph Button (?–?)
Edward Augustus Ducker (1870–1946)
Thomas Edward "Tommy" Hayes (1899–1963)

1993 William "Bill" Nelson (1859–1948)
Albert Skedaddle (1902–1981)
Louis Robert "Bob" Ward (ca. 1870–1935)

1994 Oscar "Leppy" Arnold (1874–1961)
John Crow (b. 1902)
Ross Dollarhide (1886–1974)

1995 Lawrence Jackson (?–ca. 1970)
Nathan Pierce "Pete" Kershner (1903–1958)
Lolo Muñoz (ca. 1880–ca. 1960)

1996 Quentin Lee "Stub" Curry (1906–1993)
Samuel Waltzy Elliott (b. 1905)
Jack Frusetta (1878–1937)
Francis "France" Hammond (?–?)

1997 Taft Miller (1893–1982)
Paul Sweeney (b. 1910)
William Warren "Bill" Thomson (1883–1958)

1998 Frank Leon "Jumper" Jones (1885–1958)
Marvin Myers, Sr. (1913–1985)
Pete Foredyce (1906–1986)
Joseph John "Joe Boy" Bankofier (1880–1949)

1999 Lawrence Ralph Stanford (1890–1972)
Benjamin (Bennie) Earl Jordan (1908–1999)
Jim Dorrance (1900–1990)
Tom Pedroli (1913–)
Lynn Kimball (1909–1976)

2000 Juan Redon (1850–?)
Hillery Barnes (1903–1996)
Louis Willford Rueker (1917–)

2001 Cory Smythe (1883–1948)
Henry Dave (1885–1980)
Powder River Lee Reborse (1887–1953)
Jay Fowler (1914–1999)
Dave Castro (1906–1973)

CONCLUSION

The central purpose of the mounted herders discussed here is, as it has long been, to look after the stock around which their lives gravitate. How this work is done, how the person is dressed, how he or she lives, and other traits of the work, as well as which region of North America is the home range—all of these factors and more determine whether the term *vaquero, cowboy,* or *buckaroo* accurately describes the individual and the culture that has fostered that way of life.

To outsiders, it really matters little which label is applied. To the individuals involved, however, it is of crucial importance. To apply the wrong term is an affront, proof that the observer does not understand the culture at all.

In both discussion and graphic depictions, we have striven to delineate as exactly as possible just how these three cultures are different. At the same time we have revealed their enormous similarity in appearance, philosophy, and work habits. Obviously, all of these cultures have their own biases, even prejudices, in the way they face life.

Ramirez believes that the vaquero and the cowboy differ in significant ways. Whereas the early cowboy was often a drifter moving from one range to another according to season or wages, the vaquero tended to be married and settled on a permanent range. One of the reasons for a vaquero's staying at one ranch was to continue to use the horses he had trained for the work. The cowboy seldom had that kind of attachment to the horses he rode, many times green-broke stock parceled out by the foreman to be rebroken to tolerate the rider each spring (p.49). The vaquero's life centered on the horses, developing fiesta games that included daring actions on horseback—throwing bulls down and roping bears—that showcased his ability to ride and train his horses. The cowboy was more prone to ride bucking horses into submission than to fine tune the animal in the work.

That the buckaroo followed in the vaquero tradition is apparent in his attitude toward horses. Ramirez says that the main difference in the two types is the attitude toward the stock (p. 50). The cowboy rides in doing his work but sees the horse as a tool for that work. The buckaroo, like the vaquero, is principally a horseman who does the cow work in order to work his horses.

All three types take pride in their gear and tack, but the buckaroo is apt to spend more on flashy ornamentation than the cowboy or the vaquero. At heart, however, they are the same, they do their work a little differently, they dress a little differently, but they are the same. Frank Graham says that they all do the work; it is just a different way to do it.

The folk culture of these people has enriched the world in which we live and helped us cope because of how they have adjusted to a way of life that has been changing since its inception and continues to undergo transition forced on it by factors over which the individuals have little or no control. They follow the life they love, an existence that still centers around the horse. Often as they grow older they must seek other ways to make a living and support their families. That has not changed. In their minds, however, they are still people of the great outdoors. Even more, in one very real sense, they are the Centaur that is part man, part horse. They have melded the wily, resourceful human and the beautiful, athletic horse into one figure, just as Native Americans thought when they first saw the mounted conquistadors.

As long as these men and women work with their horses and chase cattle across the plains or out of the brush, we will continue to admire the life because it is so different from that lived by the mass of humanity caught, often by choice, in jungles of brick, concrete, asphalt, and steel. We may envy the life of relative freedom these people enjoy, but at the same time we realize the personal, financial, and physical sacrifices they make to do this work and experience this existence. Often miles from town and the customary social amenities, the families of these herders nonetheless adjust to the life and thrive or leave it. We are thankful for the ones who have stayed and made a hand.

GLOSSARY

The following terms are found in one or more of the three cultures. Many are relevant to all. Those specific to one or more of the groups are coded with the appropriate letter(s): v for vaquero, c for cowboy, and b for buckaroo. Those common to all three bear no identifying code.

A-FORK SADDLE See *slick-fork saddle.*

AMANSADOR One who trains horses to ride. See also *bronc stomper.* v

ANDALUSIAN Spanish horses of the kind brought by the conquistadors.

ANNUAL CYCLE The various seasonal events and chores considered collectively required to take care of cattle during each year.

ARABIAN A breed of horses developed in Arabia; this particular breed, which is usually swift and compact in build, has endurance but little innate cow sense.

ARMAS Large pieces of heavy leather mounted on the saddle to protect the rider's legs from thorns or weapons. v

ARMITAS Apron-style chaps, forerunner of chinks. v b

ATAJO A small number of cattle. See also *herd.* v

AUCTION RING A complex of pens and buildings where stock is auctioned to the highest bidder, usually one day a week, known locally as Sale Day.

BACK CINCH See *flank girth.*

BAJA Low or lower, as in *Baja* California (feminine form). v b

BAJÍO Spanish for low country. v

BATWING CHAPS A style of leather covering for a rider's legs. The chaps have full legs and flap almost like wings when the man walks.

BEDROLL The cowboy's bed composed of a tarp used as an outer cover for sleeping and for enclosing blankets, clothing, and personal effects. See also *soogan*.

BED WAGON Extra wagon used to haul bedrolls on large ranches. See also *hoodlum wagon*.

BELL-SHAPED STIRRUPS Stirrups that measure four inches or more across the bottom. B

BERBERS An ancient North African tribe, known as "Blue Men of the Desert" because of a dye used in their clothing, conquered by the Arabs in the seventh century A.D. and an important part of the culture that dominated Spain.

BIT A metal device for controlling a horse by putting pressure on its mouth. The side bars are attached by a bar that goes through the horse's mouth. A "low" or "shallow" port has a gentle or small curve in the center; a "high port" has a sharp, high curve. There are numerous variations of the basic bit.

BORDERLANDS The term originated by Herbert E. Bolton in 1921 to include the states of Florida, Louisiana, Texas, New Mexico, Arizona, and California. Some scholars do not include Florida and Louisiana but define it narrowly, including only those U.S. states that touch Mexico (Texas, New Mexico, Arizona, and California).

BOSAL A band made of plaited rawhide, horsehair, or fiber, often reinforced with wire, that fits over the horse's nose about eight inches from the animal's muzzle. A rope or reins are attached to it to control the horse if the bosal is used as a part of a hackamore. Often referred to as a nose band.

BOTAS Leather coverings for the lower part of a rider's legs. v

BRAND (v) To burn into an animal's hide an identifying mark of a ranch. (n) The mark itself.

BRANDING IRON A metal device with a handle three feet long or longer with the emblem representing the ranch reversed on the end of the bar so that the burned mark on the hide can be read normally.

BRASADA A Spanish term to describe the thick growth of thorny brush found in South Texas. v

BRAVEMAKER Whiskey. B

BREAST COLLAR OR HARNESS A strap of leather, or, less often, of mohair, attached to the front cinch rings of the saddle and encircling the chest of the horse. The breast collar is most useful for keeping the saddle from slipping to the rear when the roper is pulling an animal by a lariat attached to, or dallied around, the saddle horn. c

BRIDLE (*la brida*) The device composed of a headstall, bit, and reins that gives the rider control of the horse's head.

BRIDLE CHAINS See *slobber chains.* B

BRIDLE HORSE An older, well-trained horse; one having gone through stages of training with hackamore and snaffle bit. B

BRINDLE Coloration pattern on a cow in the form of black stripes, usually vertical, on a background of cream or red.

BRONC Also *bronco;* unbroken horses. See also *brutos.* c

BRONC STOMPER Also *bronc rider;* a cowboy who forces an unbroken horse to accept a rider.

BROW BAND That part of the headstall that fits around the top part of the horse's head above the eyes and below the ears.

BRUSH A far-reaching term describing small trees, shrub-like plants, and cacti that choke many ranges. B c

BRUSH POPPER A rider who rides in the brush, breaking or "popping" limbs as he goes. c

BRUTOS Unbroken or wild horses. See also *bronc.* v

BUCKAROO BOSS Foreman. B

BUCKAROO WAGON Chuck wagon. B

BUCKING ROLLS Leather swells strapped onto the pommels of a slick-fork saddle to provide a grip for the thighs of the rider. Often found on A- or slick-fork saddles, they are also called squaw tits. B

BUNKHOUSE A sparsely furnished building where bachelor cowboys live when not working off the wagon. c

BUTTON Decorative braided rawhide knot on a quirt or reins. B

CABALLERO A gentleman on horseback. v

CABALLO Spanish for horse. v

CABALLO CORRIENTE A common horse. v

CABALLO DE TRABAJO A common horse used for ranch work. v

CABALLO FINO A fine horse, spirited and well trained. v

CALF CRADLE A term sometimes used to identify a working table.

CALF FRIES See *mountain oysters.*

CALIFORNIA SADDLE See *center-fire rig.*

CAMP Usually a barn, corrals, horse pasture, facility for storing feed, and a house where a cowboy and his family live. The man is usually responsible for the pastures that surround the residence. c

CANTLE (*la teja*) The rear part of the seat of the saddle. It may be short, with the leather "rolled" back for a rolled cantle, or it may rise up several inches to form a straight cantle.

CANTLE PLATES Metal, usually silver, strips, often decorated with designs or initials, fastened to the cantle of the saddle.

CAPORAL The Spanish equivalent of foreman and cow boss. v

CAPRIOLAS One of the best outfitters of mounted herders. It has long been located in Elko, Nevada, and is an excellent source of buckaroo gear and tack. B

CASCABEL Knot at the end of a riata, from the Spanish for the rattles of a rattlesnake. B

CASTRATION To remove the testicles from a male animal.

CATTLE PROD Battery powered electrified stick used to move cattle by giving them a mild shock. Also called *hot shot.*

CAVVY Short for *cavyyard,* a Spanish term, indicating a herd of saddle horses on a ranch. See also *remuda.* B

CENTAUR WISH The notion of being one with the horse. v

CENTER-FIRE RIG Saddle with a single cinch attached in the center, directly under the stirrup leathers. B

CHAPARRERAS The Spanish (and thus original) term for chaps. v

CHAP GUARDS On some spurs, a part of the shank designed to keep the bottom of the chaps from touching the rowel on the spur.

CHAPS Coverings for a herder's legs. Made of a soft but durable leather, chaps resemble pants with the seat cut out. Also called *leggings.* See also *woolies, shotgun chaps, batwing chaps,* and *chinks.*

CHARRO In early Spanish history, a man from the country or country man outside of the city. Modern use indicates a Hispanic rodeo performer who has a superbly trained horse and is skilled with the lasso. v

CHELINO Ring bit, Spanish-style. v b

CHEYENNE ROLL The low cantle on the back of a saddle.

CHIHUAHUA SPUR A Mexican spur with a large spoke rowel. v

CHINKS Leather leggings, usually fringed, that reach below the knee. B

CHIN STRAP A small strap of leather, chain, or other material attached to the bits and fitted under the horse's jaw. It helps control the horse.

CHUCK WAGON A horse-drawn wagon outfitted with a storage box, the back of which folds down to make a working surface for the range cook. The box has drawers and bins for storing foods and utensils. This rolling kitchen, first built by Charles Goodnight, is the range cowboy's home away from home.

CHUTE 1. An area two to three feet wide between two strong fences. This area may be several yards long. The chute is used to force cattle to form a single line in order to be worked or sorted. The various working tables can be attached to one end of the chute, and the cattle will be driven into the chute from the other end. 2. The narrow confines from which bucking stock is released for that eight-second ride in a rodeo arena.

CINCH (*la cincha*)(n) The braided band of mohair or horsehair, or in buckaroo culture even of burlap, that passes beneath the horse's stomach to hold the saddle in place. See also *girth*.(v) To pull the latigo tighter to hold the saddle on the horse more securely. This is called "tightening the girth" or "cinching up."

CINCH RING (*la argolla*, or, for buckle, *el hebjon* or *hebillon*) The rings, either round or D-shaped, through which the cinch or girth is tightened.

CIRCLE HORSE A leggy horse used for rodearing cattle. **B**

CONCHO (*la concha*) Silver medallion used for decorating chaps, saddles, bridles, and other gear.

CONQUISTADOR Spanish explorer; these explorers conquered and helped colonize parts of North America. Their presence prompted the existence of the vaquero.

COOL-BACK PAD A heavy saddle pad used under a Navajo blanket.

CORRAL (n) One of the names for a set of pens, or just one pen, for holding or working stock. (v) To drive cattle into a set of pens.

COW (v) The instinctive and trained response of horses to the movements of cattle while working in a pasture or pen.

COW BOSS The man in charge of the crew of herders; the equivalent of the cowboy's foreman. See also *buckaroo boss, caporal, major domo,* and *mayordomo.* **B**

COW-CALF OPERATION A ranch devoted to breeding cows and raising calves. See also *steer operation.*

COW CAMP A temporary or semipermanent setup of cowboys for the purpose of working cattle. It may be only the chuck wagon and the bedrolls with or without various kinds of tents. Cow camps are still used when the range to be worked is a great distance from the headquarters or the crew desires to emulate an earlier day of their kind of work.

COW HORSE A horse trained to work cattle. It will have cow sense.

COW SENSE Innate tendencies, found especially in Quarter Horses, to do cattle work with little or no training. A good cowman has this sense as well.

COYOTE An omnivore prevalent on the ranges across the West generally. Its melodious howls at sundown are the music of the range. The animals prey on small game and young deer as well as mice and rats and consume carcasses of dead animals. They have been known to kill small calves and even disabled cows unable to fight them off.

CRANKY Term used to describe "bronk," or unruly, horses. B

CREASE The pattern impressed into the crown or top of a hat.

CREW The assembly of men and women whose job it is to work livestock for a given period. It may include temporary hands (day workers) and others from nearby ranches who are neighboring.

CUFF PROTECTORS Leather bands from six to twelve inches long that fasten around a buckaroo's forearms to protect his wrists. Usually, the leather is heavy and heavily tooled. B

CULL (n) An animal no longer productive. (v) To cut out undesirable animals to sell.

CURB CHAIN A piece of small chain or leather strap that fits on the back of the bits and passes just above the horse's lip. See also *chin strap.*

CUT (v) 1. To castrate male animals. 2. To separate cattle from a herd. (n) The cattle removed and held separately from a larger herd.

CUT A HERD To separate specific categories of animals from a larger collection of stock. Also, to remove a number of animals from a herd.

CUTTING ALLEY A long chute designed to facilitate the separating of animals.

CUTTING HORSE The "ballet dancers" of the horse world, the intelligent, agile animals adept at separating and keeping animals separated (the cut) from a herd.

DALLY From the Spanish *dar la vuelta,* meaning to wrap the lariat around the saddle horn when roping stock. The alternative is to tie the rope to the horn. See also *hard and fast.*

DAR LA VUELTA To give or take a turn around something; to take turns of a rope around a saddle horn. See *dally.* v

DAY WORK Doing ranch work by the day rather than being hired by the ranch on a full-time basis.

DINNER-PLATE SADDLE HORN A large, flat-top style of the horn of a saddle.

DOUBLE-RIGGED SADDLE A "Texas style" saddle with two girths—one attached to the saddle below the fork or swell and the other below the cantle. This style is still preferred by plains cowboys. Also called "rimfire" saddle. See also *center-fire rig, three-quarter rigged saddle,* and *seven-eighths rigged saddle.*

DOVE WINGS A single strap of leather for holding spurs on the wearer's boots.

EAR TAG (v) To attach a piece of plastic to an animal's ear for identification or other purpose. (n) The tag itself.

EL CAMPO The camp of the vaquero. **V**

ENCOMIENDA A grant of Indians and land made by the Spanish monarchy to some deserving Spaniard in North America, generally for agricultural purposes. It was the second system used by the Spanish to settle the frontier. **V**

ENTRADAS Mounted expeditions into the New World by Spanish explorers. **V**

FEEDERS Cattle of the right age and weight to fatten for slaughter.

FEEDLOT Enclosure in which feeder cattle are confined and fed to fatten them for slaughter.

FEED ROUTE See *feed run.*

FEED RUN The route followed in distributing feed to cattle during the winter.

FIADORE Rope used to make a headstall and reins; also called *thedore.*

FIELD Buckaroo term for a pasture. **B**

FLANK GIRTH (*la barriguera*) A heavy leather strap attached to the rear cinch rings on a double-rigged saddle. It passes beneath the horse's stomach and keeps the rear of the saddle from being pulled up by a taut lariat holding an animal located in front of the horse. Also called *back cinch.*

FLANKER A cowboy whose job it is to throw the calves to the ground for working when the crew is roping and dragging.

FLANKING CALVES The technique a herder uses to throw calves to the ground in order to work them. The man grasps the rope around the calf's neck with his left hand and the loose skin in front of the right hind leg with his right hand, and lifts the calf off the ground in order to throw the animal to the ground.

FOREMAN The man in charge of the cowboys on a ranch. He gets his orders from the owner or manager. See also *buckaroo boss, caporal, cow boss, major domo,* and *mayordomo.*

FORK That part of the saddle that forms the front. These can be slick (with no swell) or swelled (with a noticeable swell).

FORMANDO A method of training horses to line up against a rope and stand to be caught and saddled. v

FRONTERA Spanish for *frontier.* v

GAL-LEG SPUR A spur with a shank in the form of a female leg.

GANADEROS Cattlemen or cattle breeders. v

GANADO LIVIANO Spanish for wild cattle. v

GATHER (v) Collecting cattle from a given area by men on horseback. (n) The cattle so driven together. See also *rodear.* c

GELDING A male horse that has been castrated.

GIRTH The braided band of mohair that holds the saddle in place. The front girth is so called to denote its location; the flank girth is attached to the rear cinch rings. The term is pronounced "girt" in some sections. See also *cinch.* c

GOOSENECK SPUR A spur whose shape is long and graceful like a goose's neck. The pin holding the rowel may have a small stone that serves as the eye of the goose.

GOOSENECK TRAILER A device pulled by a truck and characterized by a hitch that attaches to the bed of the truck over the rear axle and arches over the tailgate. This arching tongue resembles the neck of a goose—hence the name of this style of trailer.

GRAZER BIT A bit on which the shanks bend back toward the horse in order to allow him to graze. The shanks on a buckaroo bit are straight and prevent grazing. Also called grazier bit. c

GREEN-BROKE Describes a horse willing to accept the saddle but otherwise untrained.

GUMMER An aged cow whose teeth are bad or missing.

HACIENDA Large, privately owned estate, usually embracing smaller properties and employing many families in raising crops or livestock. The establishment of haciendas was the third system used by the Spanish to settle the frontier. v

HACIENDADO Owner of a hacienda, or large estate, in Mexico or on the Northern Frontier of New Spain. v

HACKAMORE (*la jáquima*) Headgear used for training young horses, made of a bosal and a leather strap for a headstall. For the buckaroo, the term may describe only the nosepiece or bosal.

HAIR PAD A protective covering usually placed between the horse's back and the saddle blanket to protect from saddle sores caused by rubbing of the saddle during riding. The hair pad is constructed of soft animal hair sewn to a sturdy cloth back.

HARD-AND-FAST The cowboy style of attaching the lariat to the saddle horn by tying the rope, half-hitching it, using a slip-knot made especially for the purpose, or employing a *honda*. The alternative style is the dally method. See also *dally*. c

HEAD AND HEEL The method of roping an animal first by the head by one roper and then by the hind leg or legs (called the heels) by a second roper. Larger animals may be roped by the head and heel method and thereby thrown to the ground.

HEADQUARTERS The residence of the boss and the foreman as well as the central offices, main horse herd, the bunkhouse, and other centrally significant ranch operations. "Branch offices" for the ranch are usually called "camps." See also *la casa grande*. c

HEADSTALL The part of the bridle that attaches to the bit and goes over the horse's head. It may have a brow band, nose band, and throat latch.

HERD (n) A number of cattle held together. See also *atajo* and *partida*. (v) To watch over or move cattle by men on horseback.

HIDALGO A man on the low end of the upper-class social and economic scale in Spain. v

HIGH PORT BIT A bit on which the cross bar has a high curve or port.

HOBBLES Leather, rope, or rawhide straps used to secure the front legs of a horse to keep it from straying.

HOCKING KNIFE A curved knife attached to a long pole; used to cut the hamstring of an animal, thus crippling it to make slaughtering easier. v

HONDA 1. A metal ring used to form a slip knot to fasten the lariat to the saddle horn. 2. The small loop of rope, metal, or rawhide on the end of a lariat rope through which the rest of the rope is passed in order to make a loop for throwing.

HOODLUM WAGON The wagon used to haul bedrolls, tents, and other gear on roundups if the chuck wagon cannot hold all of the baggage. See also *bed wagon*. c

HOOLIHAN A type of loop used most often to rope a horse. It is thrown backward from the regular loop and has the advantage of reaching its target at a ninety-degree angle with the ground; hence the loop is upright, and the opening is at its largest when going over the horse's head. Adams gives the spelling *hooley-ann*.

HORSE JEWELRY Fancy rawhide and silver gear. B

HORSEHAIR ROPE A rope made of twisted mane or tail hair from a horse; used as lead rope or reins, not as a lasso. VB

HOT SHOT See *cattle prod.*

IMPLANT To inject growth hormones into a calf or weanling.

JÁQUIMA A hackamore. V

JERK CINCH (*la barrigueros*) The back cinch on a double-rigged saddle. C V

JERKY Lean meat preserved by drying in strips.

JINETA. See *la jineta.*

JINGLE BOY The buckaroo equivalent of the cowboy term *wrangler.* B

JINGLE THE HORSES To round up and bring the remuda to the corral or other locations so that mounts can be selected for the day's work. An equivalent phrase is to "wrangle" the horses.

JINGLE-BOBS Formed pieces of metal hung on spur rowels to provide a chiming noise. See also *la mota.* B

JUNTA DE VACAS A gathering of cattle. See also *roundup* and *rodear.* V

KILLING GROUND That area to which vaqueros drive cattle to slaughter them. V

KINÉÑOS Vaqueros who have for generations worked on the King Ranch in South Texas. V

LA BRIDA I. a bridle. 2. A style of riding a horse with the rider's legs straight. V

LA CASA The house, or a bunkhouse. V

LA CASA GRANDE The headquarters of the ranch. V

LADINO An outlaw bovine, especially a bull. V

LA JINETA A style of horseback riding with the rider's knees pulled up, like a modern jockey. V

LA MOTA Tassel on the end of metal hung on spurs to create a chiming noise. B

LARIAT Also called simply rope, the lariat is one of the basic tools of the cowboy's trade. The variety used by cowboys is usually thirty or so feet in length and made of three-eighths-inch nylon. See also *riata.* C

LASS (v) To lasso or rope an animal. B

LASS ROPE A lariat. B

LASSO (n) A lariat. (v) To rope an animal.

LATIFUNDIO A landholding usually composed of two or more haciendas. The term was used in the early period in Mexico; now rarely used in the United States. V

LATIGO The leather (less often nylon) strap used to tighten the girth of the saddle to hold it securely on the horse's back.

LAZO The Spanish word from which *lasso*, the lariat, stems. v

LECHUGUILLA A semidesert plant of the agave group; fibers of the lechuguilla are twisted to make lariats. v

LEPPY Orphan calf, or dogie. B

LEYENDA NEGRA "Black Legend" of the English, repeated by many American historians, indicating that the Spanish were not true colonizers, but only interested in God, glory, and gold. Oakah L. Jones, Jr. (in *Los Paisanos*, p. 4) discusses the fact that the Black Legend is at least partly false and proves there were many Spanish settlements on the northern frontier of New Spain. The English also used the term to suggest that their enemy of long standing, the Spanish, were ruthless, corrupt, and inferior people. v

LLANO The Spanish word for land; this term often conveys a sense of reverence for the vast open plains. v

LONAS Chaps fashioned from canvas instead of leather. v

LOOPED REIN A single strand of rope or other fiber, each end of which is secured to the bottom ring of the bits.

MAGUEY A rope made from the fibers of a plant by the same name. v

MAJOR DOMO Early term for the foreman of a buckaroo crew. Replaced in early twentieth century by buckaroo boss. B

MANADA See *mare band*. v

MAN OF THE NORTH The man on the frontier of northern Mexico who developed special traits of character. v

MARE BAND The herd of brood mares for raising colts on a ranch. The Spanish equivalent is *manada*.

MARKET A generic term in English to indicate a place where cattle are taken to be sold.

MASCADA Scarf. See also *wild rag*. v

MAVERICK An unbranded animal, usually a bovine. See also *oreana*.

MAYORDOMO The Spanish term for an estate manager, or a top hand (Ramirez p. 85). v

MECATE Rope, usually horsehair, used as reins and lead rope on a hackamore; also called mecarty, McCarty, McCardy.

MECHANICAL HACKAMORE The headgear without a bit, usually with a noseband and jaw chain, for controlling a horse.

MESQUITE A parasitic thorny perennial plant, ranging from bush to tree size, with a huge appetite for moisture. Because of its nature, it is all but impossible to eradicate unless the base is dug up. The plant produces a bean palatable to livestock and, for Indians, the source of a kind of beer as well as a flour for bread.

MESTEÑOS Source of the English word *mustang*. A broad expression meaning wild horses and cattle without owners. v

MISSION The earliest form of settlement used by the Spanish to control the frontier. v

MOCHILLA A tanned leather covering placed over a Mexican saddle to protect the rider from horse sweat and the horse from the elements. v

MOORS People of mixed Arab and Berber blood who conquered and occupied Spain for eight hundred years.

MOTA See *la mota*.

MOUNTAIN OYSTERS Calf testicles cleaned and cooked, usually dipped in corn meal and fried. These are considered a range delicacy. Also called *calf fries* and *prairie oysters*.

MULE HIDE A strip of tough but soft leather an inch and a half wide and five feet long used to protect the saddle horn from the dallied lariat. It allows the roper to give slack to the animal. B

MUSTANG A feral horse running free in the wild. Mustangs served as the basis for transportation in early ranching days. See also *mesteños*.

NAVAJO A brightly colored wool saddle blanket. The sturdy blankets may or may not be made by Navajo Indians, but the term traces from a time when these typically were made by Navajos.

NEIGHBORING A time-honored practice of the cowboys on one ranch helping a neighbor work cattle on the neighbor's ranch. C

NIGHT HORSE A horse kept in a corral over night so that the wrangler can ride the animal to gather the remuda in the early morning. It is often the only horse kept in a pen overnight.

NORTEÑOS People of northern Mexico. v

NYLON Lariat rope of this material.

OREANA Unbranded steer, maverick. B

OUTLAW CATTLE AND HORSES Animals that refuse to be gathered and worked with the other stock on the ranch. The best treatment for an outlaw is to sell it. See also *ladino*.

OXBOW A style of stirrup of iron, wood, or fiberglass characterized by a round rather than flat bottom. It allows the rider to insert his foot into the stirrup up to the heel of the boot. It is known as a "widow maker," because it is difficult for the rider to remove the foot if thrown from the horse.

PACKERS Footwear evidencing a cross between a cowboy boot and a lumberjack lace-up boot. Being laced up tightly on the wearer's ankle and lower calf, this kind of boot is especially good for working on the ground. B

PALPATING A method of determining if a cow or mare is pregnant.

PARATHA The animals removed from a larger herd and held separately, the cut. B

PARTIDA A large bunch of cattle. For the buckaroo, a bunch of tame horses into which mustangs were run in order to slow the wild horse down and direct them into a corral. See also *herd*. V B

PARTING CATTLE Separating cattle or cutting the herd. B

PARTING OUT Sorting cattle; cutting out cattle from a herd. B

PELICAN SADDLE HORN A style of saddle horn flat on top but swooping downward on the underside to resemble the bill of a pelican. B

PEN (n) A corral. (v) To put cattle into a corral. C

PEON The Mexican peasant. V

PIGGING STRING Short rope used to tie the legs of an animal.

POLY ROPE A lariat made of polypropylene. B

POPPER Single or double strip of leather attached to the end of a quirt or romal.

POST A riding technique in which the rider moves up and down in rhythm with the trotting gait of a horse. B

POST HORN A saddle horn that rises straight up from the center of the swell and is the same size from top to bottom. It may or may not have an ornate metal cap. It is particularly suited for dally roping and is common on buckaroo saddles. B

POUR To put liquid insecticide on the back of a cow.

PRICKLY PEAR A variety of cactus characterized by fleshy pads covered with both long sharp thorns and numerous clusters of small thorns. Wildlife and cattle eat some of these spiny but water-rich plants.

PROD As in the expression "on the prod," meaning agitated. See also *snuffy*.

PROWLING The practice of mounted cowboys riding slowly through a pasture looking for signs of danger, illness, strays, or other problems in the pasture. C

PUEBLO Indian villages in the southwestern United States in which the inhabitants lived in apartments made of dried mud bricks, or adobe. The Spanish coined the name. v

PUNCHY A slang term to describe a person or event epitomizing cowboy life; from *cowpuncher*. c

QUARTER HORSE The preferred breed of horse for cattle work. These horses are characterized by stocky conformation and well-developed hindquarters and are known for quickness, agility, speed over short distances, and innate cow sense.

QUIRT (*warta*) A short whip, often of braided rawhide, attached to a handle, used by horsemen.

RANCH HORSE Any horse raised, trained, and used on a ranch. A horse so called may well be of mediocre quality, that is, not highly trained to rope, cut, or perform other specific work; often called a "using horse." See also *caballo de trabajo, caballo corriente,* and *bridle horse.*

RANCH RODEO Contested skill-based events between teams of ranch cowboys as opposed to the traditional rodeo where professional rodeo cowboys compete as individuals. c

RANCHO In Mexico, a small, privately owned farm or ranch for raising crops, livestock or both; a subsistence-type farm; in New Mexico, a small settlement or place with few dwellings; in the American Southwest, especially in California and southern Texas, slang for *ranch.* v

RANGE CUBES A round or cubed piece of compressed protein-rich feed ranging from one-half inch to two inches or more in length and an inch or less in thickness. These cubes are dumped from feeders or sacks onto the ground where the cattle pick them up and eat them.

RATTLESNAKE A poisonous reptile found on many ranches and throughout the West. The snake has a pair of fangs for injecting venom into its prey—usually mice and small rabbits—and "rattles" on its tail. The whirring of these rattles causes fear to anyone or any beast familiar with this deadly creature.

RAWHIDE The untanned hide of an animal with the hair removed. Rawhide is very strong and tough but softens when exposed to water.

REIN (v) To give directions to a horse through pressure applied by the reins; (n) The strips of leather, rope, rawhide, or horsehair attached to the bits to guide the horse.

REMUDA The herd of horses, usually geldings, kept on the ranch for the cowboys to ride. For the vaquero, it is *la remuda*. C

REMUDERO The man who keeps the remuda. See also *wrangler, jingle boy*, and *wrangle boy*. V

REP Representative for a ranch helping out at roundups or neighboring ranches to assure that each ranch got back any cattle that might have strayed from the home ranch.

RIATA A rope made of plaited strips of rawhide; also *reata*. V B

RIDING PASTURE (v) Checking cattle. See also *prowling*.

RIGGING A general term to indicate the girth, saddle tree, and other parts of the saddle used to hold the saddle in place.

RINGY A cow that is *snuffy*.

RODEAR, RODEER (v) To round up cattle. (n) The herd of cattle so rounded up. B

RODEO (n) A competition between professional rodeo cowboys in such events as calf roping, bareback and saddle bronc riding, bull riding, and steer wrestling. See also *ranch rodeo*. (v) To compete in rodeos.

ROLLED CANTLE See *Cheyenne roll*.

ROLLER Small copper wheel in the mouthpiece of a high-port or spade bit.

ROMAL Braided rawhide quirt attached to a pair of braided rawhide reins used with a California-style spade bit. B

ROPE A lariat or lasso of plant fiber, rawhide, or nylon.

ROPE AND DRAG The method of roping a calf by the neck or heels and dragging it to a crew waiting to work it.

ROPE CORRAL A pen formed by a group of cowboys holding their lariats to form a loose pen for holding the remuda while a designated roper catches horses to be ridden for the day's work.

ROPER BOOTS Boots (also called simply *ropers*) with flat, low heels, round toes, and short (usually eight- to ten-inch) tops. This kind of boot is especially good for working on the ground. B C

ROSETTE (*la rosetta*) A cut piece of leather, often in a round design, used to facilitate tying a leather string on a saddle or bridle.

ROSIN JAW Ranch hand hired to do non-buckaroo jobs on a ranch. B

ROUND SKIRTS A saddle skirt cut so that it rounds up sharply toward the back of the saddle.

ROUNDUP A general term indicating the gathering of livestock for any purpose. See also *gather, rodear*, and *junta de vacas*. C

ROWEL The round spike-like piece of metal attached to the shank of the spur. It is the part that touches the horse when the cowboy spurs the animal.

"RUNNING" CATTLE Not necessarily moving cattle at a run. The expression most often refers to the number of grazing cattle on the ranch, as in the expression, "We are running eight hundred head of cattle on the ranch."

RUNNING IRON A straight or curved piece of steel attached to a steel handle. Rustlers used these to alter brands when stealing cattle. A heated cinch ring held by two green sticks can accomplish the same task and is less obvious when not in use.

SADDLE (*la silla*) The throne of the herder. Many styles of saddles have been developed to suit specific needs. See *double-rigged, center-fire rig, seven-eighths rig,* and *rimfire.*

SADDLE HORN (*la cabeza*) The part of the saddle protruding upward from the fork or swell. It serves to secure or dally the lariat.

SADDLE HORSE A horse trained for riding. A saddle horse may or may not be a trained cow horse.

SADDLE HOUSE A small building where saddles and related gear are kept. "Tack house" and "tack room" are equivalent terms.

SADDLE PAD (*el suadero*) A cloth pad that protects a horse's back from the saddle.

SADDLE TREE The wooden base to which the saddle leather is attached. The best are still made of wood (hence, tree) and covered with rawhide for strength.

SAGE Any one of a variety of plants common on ranges of the West.

SANDALS Footwear common to early vaqueros; these sandals were of the type called *guaraches.* v

SCARF The name for the cloth usually worn around a cowboy's neck. See also *wild rag* and *mascada.* c

SEGUNDO The second in command of a crew of vaqueros. v

SERAPE (*sarape*) The blanket-like covering worn by a vaquero; it also can serve as a saddle blanket or a covering at night. v

SET A number of calves, steers, cows, or other such groupings of approximately equal size, weight, or quality. c

SEVEN-EIGHTHS RIGGED SADDLE A saddle with the front girth set back slightly to the rear of the fork. The saddle will likely have a flank girth as well.

SHADOW RIDER Buckaroo with fancy equipment and clothes who rides along looking at his own shadow. B

SHALLOW PORT BIT The bit preferred by cowboys. The raised part of the bar that passes through the horse's mouth rises only an inch or less. See also *spade bit*. c

SHIPPING PASTURE A pasture used only for holding the collected herd ready for shipping to market. c

SHOO-FLY A switch of horsehair suspended under a horse's jaws to keep flies from biting the animal. b

SHOT The toss of the lariat in an attempt to catch an animal. b

SHOTGUN CHAPS Leather leg coverings with long, cylindrically shaped leg pieces resembling the barrel of a shotgun; hence the name. Long zippers are used to open and close the pieces for each leg. c

SKIRTS That part of the saddle on which the seat, cantle, and swell sits. The fleece lining is sewed to the underside of the skirts. See also *round skirts* and *square skirts*.

SLICK-FORK SADDLE A saddle made on a tree without swells. b

SLICKER Raincoat made for wearing while riding a horse.

SLOBBER CHAINS Lengths of chain attached to the bottom of the bits on a bridle. The reins are attached to the other end of the chains. The metal chains save the rawhide or leather reins from getting wet from horse saliva (slobber) or from becoming wet when the horse drinks; they also keep the reins from applying direct pressure to the bit. b

SNAFFLE BIT A type of bit characterized by a large ring on each side of the horse's mouth and a hinged bar across the animal's mouth. When the rider pulls on the reins, the snaffle applies pressure on the sides of the horse's mouth, not on the roof of its mouth, as does the *spade* bit.

SNUFFY Describes an agitated bovine looking for some human being to charge and hurt. The term may derive from the expulsion of air from the animal's nose when about ready to charge. The phrase "on the prod" also describes such an animal.

SOMBRERO The straw, leather, or felt hat, usually having a flat crown and straight brim, worn by a vaquero; slang for a cowboy's hat. v

SOOGAN Also called *sugan* or *sougan*. See *bedroll*.

SORTING CATTLE The act of separating a herd into desired categories for any special purpose. For example, at shipping time, the marketable calves are separated from their mothers and may be sorted by weight to form the best set of calves for the buyer.

SPADE BIT A metal device to fit into a horse's mouth to control it. This style has a high port and often includes rollers and other devices. v b

SPANISH MUSTACHE Decorative knot tied into a horse's tail. B

SPLIT REINS Two usually leather reins, six feet or more in length, typical of the cowboy. Each rein is tied to one side of the bits to control the horse. See also *looped rein.*

SPOON BIT Type of high-port, Spanish-style bit. B

SPUR (*la espuela*) A steel device attached to the cowboy's boot heel by a leather strap. The spur consists of a band of steel fitted around the heel of the boot, a shank attached to the rear of the band, and a rotating rowel attached to the end of the shank.

SPUR LEATHERS Also referred to simply as spur straps. Usually two leather straps attached to the heel bands on each side and fastened by a buckle positioned on the outside of the wearer's foot. See also *dove wings.*

SQUARE SKIRTS A saddle skirt cut so that it extends backward and downward at the rear of the saddle.

SQUAW TITS The crude term for *bucking rolls.* B

STAMPEDE STRING Leather, rawhide, or horsehair strap that fits under the chin to help hold on a rider's hat. B

STEER OPERATION A ranch devoted to buying steers, grazing them on grass for a few months, and then selling them. See also *cow-calf operation.*

STIRRUP LEATHERS (*la ación* or *las aciones*) The sturdy pieces of leather that hold the stirrups on a saddle.

STOCKERS Cattle, usually yearlings, not yet large enough to be ready for feeding for slaughter. See also *feeders.*

STOCKYARDS Pens used for holding cattle. C

STOVEPIPE BOOTS Cowboy boots, the tops of which are straight, without the traditional scallops in front and back. C

STRAIGHT CANTLE The raised rear part of the seat of the saddle. It rises some four to six inches or more rather than being laid over in the style called rolled cantle.

STRING 1. Slang for lariat rope. 2. The (string of) assigned to a cowboy to ride in regular rotation. The string may include from three to as many as twelve horses, depending upon the amount of riding done, the amount of feed given the horses, and the roughness of the terrain.

SWAPPING HELP The practice of exchanging cowboys between ranches on heavy working days such as roundup or shipping days. See also *neighboring.*

SWELL The term used to describe the front part of the saddle to which the saddle horn is attached.

TACK Horse-related gear that include saddles, parts of the bridle, blankets, pads, stirrups, girths, latigos, and the like.

TACK ROOM Room in a barn where saddles, bridles, and other riding gear is kept. See also *saddle house.*

TAPADEROS Leather coverings over the front of a stirrup, sometimes in buckaroo culture with flaps extending twenty-eight or more inches below the stirrup. Also called "taps" and "toe fenders."

TAPA-OJOS Blinders used on a green horse for ease in mounting. **B**

THOROUGHBRED A tall, slender, long-legged horse bred for racing, sometimes crossbred with Quarter Horses for speed. Blood from the breed is preferred in buckaroo country because of the long *gathers* or *rodears* often found there.

THREE-QUARTER RIGGED SADDLE A saddle with the front girth set to the rear of the fork. This saddle likely also has a flank cinch as well.

THROAT LATCH That part of the headstall that goes over the top of the horse's head behind the ears and fastens, usually with a buckle, under the throat. Its purpose is to hold the bridle securely on the horse's head.

TIE-DOWN A leather strap attached to the bosal around the horse's nose, run through a ring on the front of the breast collar, and then attached to a ring on the front side of the front girth. This girth is attached by a short leather strap to the flank girth.

TIE ON To attach the rope to the saddle horn in preparation for roping an animal. **C**

TOE FENDER See *tapaderos.*

TOUGH RAG See *wild rag.* **B**

TRAP A small pasture used to hold cattle or horses on a temporary basis.

TURK'S-HEAD Also turk-head. A decorative turban-shaped knot at the end of a mecate.

TWINE Slang term for a lariat rope. **C**

VACCINATE To administer medications to animals to prevent disease.

WAGON BOSS On large ranches the man in charge of the cattle-working crew. He gets his orders from the foreman or manager, who does not accompany the crew when doing the actual work. The term derives from the practice of managing the men who work "on the wagon" on a large ranch.

WEANER Also weanling. A calf recently removed from its mother.

WILD RAG Silk kerchief worn around the neck (also called tough rag) B

WOOLIES Angora, mohair, or bearskin chaps used in winter by buckaroos and Northern Plains cowboys.

WORK CATTLE (v) A general term describing any of the several routine practices necessary to move through the annual cycle; includes vaccinations, ear tagging, castration, branding, palpating, sorting, and the like.

"WORK ON THE WAGON"—An expression designating the routine of a group of men who live for varying periods around a chuck wagon. They sleep, eat, and spend their free time far from the *headquarters*. The chuck wagon is their home away from home.

WORKING TABLE A device constructed of metal sheeting and pipe to trap, hold, and lay the animal on its side for ease in working it by the cowboys. See also *calf cradle*.

WRANGLE BOY See *wrangler*. B

WRANGLE THE HORSES To round up and bring in the remuda to the corral or other location so that mounts can be selected for the work day. Sometimes called "jingle the horses."

WRANGLER The person whose job it is to bring in the remuda, separate the horses needed for the day's work, and feed the horses early enough that they have finished eating before the men arrive before break of day to saddle up. C

WRANGO (n) Horse wrangler. (v) To wrangle horses. B

WRECK A term describing any of the numerous accidental falls, kicks, and other injuries common to working cowboys, spilling cattle, or generally descriptive of anything going wrong.

YEARLY Weaned calf of around one year of age. See also *stockers*.

COMPARATIVE CHART

Vaquero, Cowboy, and Buckaroo Characteristics

Trait or Characteristic	VAQUERO	COWBOY	BUCKAROO
SADDLES			
Fork	(*la campana*) Slick (*juste*); more recently, a swelled fork extending past the rider's knees.	Swelled, rarely with the swell extending past the rider's knees.	Slick or A-fork, often with bucking rolls.
Cantle	(*la teja*) Straight.	Rolled or straight.	Straight.
Rigging	(*equipo*) Single, with leather straps around horn; may be double rigged on newer models.	Double (front and back), rimfire.	Three-fourths or center-fire with single cinch.
Skirts	Round.	Usually full cut.	Round.
Horn	(*la cabeza*) Round or straight, wooden, with a 45-degree cut on top with no rawhide or leather covering; may have metal cap.	Tapered with enlarged cap, 3 to 5 inches tall, covered with leather; no metal caps.	Post 4 inches tall, covered with leather; wrapped with "mule hide"; some ornate metal caps.
Stirrups	(*estribo*) Width 2 to 3 inches; made of wood bolted at the top; may be metal bound, tied to tapaderos with *los*.	Width 2 to 3 inches; made of wood reinforced with metal and covered with leather, either	Width 4 inches; metal-covered bell-shaped, or oxbow; often with ornamentation.

Trait or Characteristic	VAQUERO	COWBOY	BUCKAROO
	tientos (ties).	tanned or rawhide; or oxbows with initials, brands, or bars.	
Tapaderos	(*tapaderas* or *estrivos*) Plain with little or no flap.	Those with no flaps in brush country to none in open country; called toe fenders.	Flaps measuring 28-inches, called "eagle-wings."
Blanket	(*suadero*) May be a wool serape or a thick pad made of cotton (*fibra de algodón*).	Hair or wool pad next to body; ornate wool blanket (often called "a Navajo") or saddle pad under saddle.	Hair or cool-back pad with wool "Navajo" blanket.
Girthing components (front)	(*la cincha*) Mohair or horsehair cinch; *látigo* may not have holes for use with a cinch ring with a tongue.	Leather latigo and mohair girth ("girt"); latigo has holes to use with a cinch ring with a tongue.	Leather latigo with holes for tongued cinch belt of mohair or horsehair.
Girthing components (back)	No back cinch, except on some newer saddles; when present, called *vrageno*.	Heavy leather tightened with buckles; called "flank girth" or "cinch."	Back cinch rare.

OTHER TACK

Trait or Characteristic	VAQUERO	COWBOY	BUCKAROO
Bits	(*el freno de la bridona*) Spade, high port (*buenas portadas*) with rollers (*rodillos*) and ring or snaffle.	Snaffle or grazing, shallow port; stainless, or steel that will form rust patina; some ornamentation on side bars.	Steel, silver, and copper snaffle and fixed bit, both with high port with rollers and spade with ornate side bars silvered; Spanish- or Old-California-style spade bits, short, straight shank.
Breast collar	Uncommon.	Widely used.	Rarely used.
Reins	Two reins (*de dos*	Two split leather	Single rein of

Trait or Characteristic	VAQUERO	COWBOY	BUCKAROO
	riendas) of twisted horse mane-hair, rope, or plaited rawhide; some use of a single looped rein.	reins, 7 to 8 feet long, ½ to 1 inch wide.	braided rawhide with attached romal, twisted horsehair mecate forming a single rein and lead rope, often with slobber chains.
Spurs	Chihuahua or similar style with large spoked rowels (*estrellas*); some with silver mounting for decoration.	Short shanks with some ornamentation; small rowel, infrequently jingle-bobs; stainless, or steel that will form rust patina.	Ornate, heavily blued or rustable steel, large rowels; California drop shank with jingle-bobs; lots of decoration.
Ropes	Rawhide, lechuguilla, or maguey fiber riata; less often, nylon for lasso, twisted horsehair for lead ropes; length varies.	Made of nylon, 30 to 35 feet long; may have a horn knot on the rear to make tying hard and fast quick and convenient.	Rawhide or nylon riatas, 60 to 80 feet long.

ACCOUTREMENTS

Hats	Hat of straw (*unpajizo*); others, of felt or of heavy fabric, have drawstrings (barbiquejo) that come under the chin.	Felt, 4- to 6-inch brim, rolled, various crushes, black color commonly preferred; some straw in summer; drawstrings rare.	A variety, including old Spanish style low crown and flat brim, also fedoras and caps in earlier years; felt, flat brim, full height crown, or flat crown, often with "stampede string."
Neckerchief	Not common.	Cotton bandanna, usually plain or no slide, tied in square knot.	"Wild rag" of silk, ornate slides often of decorated silver.
Boots	(*botas*) Ankle-high (*botines*) or high-	Scalloped or stovepipe tops, to	High topped scalloped, high

Trait or Characteristic	VAQUERO	COWBOY	BUCKAROO
	(*botines*) or high-top boots, often with rubber soles; poor vaqueros may wear sandals (*guaraches*).	the knees with spur ridge on heel; tall heel; Leddy name is highly respected.	heeled; Paul Bond and Blucher preferred; some high-heeled lace-up packers.
Chaps	Cut full with leather "buttons" to close the back; called *las chaparreras* if made of cowhide, or *las chivarras* if made of goat hide.	Usually full length shotgun with zippers; growing use of chinks for use in hot weather; batwings common in earlier times.	Knee-length chinks; "woolies" for winter use.

CLOTHING

Trait or Characteristic	VAQUERO	COWBOY	BUCKAROO
Shirts	(*camisas*) Cotton in various colors.	Sturdy cotton, often denim, with pearl snaps, western yoke in back.	Cotton, western or dress style with buttons or snaps.
Pants	(*pantalones*) Denims; name brands rarely available.	Levi or Wrangler blue denim jeans, often worn with legs tucked inside boot tops.	Blue denim jeans, usually Levis or Wranglers, sometimes with a cuff turned up one turn.
Belts	(*cinturones*) Sometimes worn, sometimes not; design is often geometric and painted in bright colors (*disenas pintadas*); *faja* and *cinto* are other words for belt.	Leather with tooling, usually no name but may have brands.	Leather with tooling; suspenders may be worn instead of belt.
Buckles	(*hebillas grandes*) Pass-through buckle or trophy-style, often with fighting roosters design.	Trophy or large silver types common, often handmade with brands or initials.	Silver, western style, with tongue.

Trait or Characteristic	VAQUERO	COWBOY	BUCKAROO
Vest	(*chaleco*) Not common.	Down-filled nylon, leather, or sheepskin-lined denim.	Wool, suit style with silk back and buttoned front.
Coat	Made of brown canvas.	Short, made of denim or brown canvas lined with wool cloth.	Made of duck or denim, sometimes lined; in cold weather, long heavy coats of wool.
Raincoat	Not special made.	Yellow plastic slicker.	Yellow slicker or olive duster.
Gloves	Short, leather (cowhide), no cuffs or fringe.	Thin, leather, no cuffs or fringe.	Leather, often used with cuff protectors.

WORKING METHODS

Roping	Dally around a wooden, uncovered horn; may tie hard and fast if saddle will withstand the strain; play of rope can cause friction heat to make the wood smoke.	Tie hard and fast; younger cowboys and arena ropers will dally; horn is usually wrapped with rubber strips from tire inner tube to hinder rope from slipping.	Dally; saddle horn may be wrapped with long piece of "mule hide," a soft but strong leather that allows rope to slip.
Branding	Wrestle animal down in branding pen, or head and heel, or just head and wrestle down.	Head *or* heel calves; use cradle or working tables; may wrestle down; usually separate cows from calves to work.	Heel, or head *and* heel, often on unfenced range depending on size of calves and terrain; cattle held loosely, calves unseparated from cows.
Corrals	Made of mesquite timbers laid sideways, pipe, wire, or even pits dug into ground; older pens made of a	Made of planks, net wire, or, in oil-producing areas, 2-inch pipe.	Made of materials on hand; rocks, sagebrush, willow lattice, poles either upright stockade style or horizontal.

Trait or Characteristic	VAQUERO	COWBOY	BUCKAROO
	lattice of timber around upright posts, called *corrales de leña.*		

HORSES

Trait or Characteristic	VAQUERO	COWBOY	BUCKAROO
Type and breeding	Plain horses, called *caballos de trabajo* or *caballos corrientes.*	Medium to large Quarter Horse, sometimes with Thoroughbred cross for size, depending on terrain.	Large horses to cover the terrain; some Thorough-bred blood likely or even, in earlier years, a trace of draft blood.
Breaking horses to ride	Often broken at five years of age; young horses broken with a bosal, older ones with bosal and snaffle bit; work with bosal for first several months.	Usually broken at two to three years of age; use snaffle bit from the start; transition to shallow port bit within a few weeks or months.	Full training may last several years; use rawhide bosal (hackamore) for breaking, then snaffle, then fixed bit.
The group of horses ridden by the herders		String.	String or cavvy.

THE HERDER

Trait or Characteristic	VAQUERO	COWBOY	BUCKAROO
The Best of His Kind	*(vaquero completo)* Complete vaquero.	Top hand.	Good hand, good baquero, good buckaroo.

BIBLIOGRAPHY

GENERAL PUBLICATIONS

Adams, Ramon. *Western Words.* Rev. ed. Norman: University of Oklahoma Press, 1968.

Ahlborn, Richard E., ed. *Man Made Mobile: Early Saddles of Western North America.* Washington, D.C.: Smithsonian, 1980.

Beatie, Russel. *Saddles.* Norman: University of Oklahoma Press, 1982.

Brown, Mark Herbert, and W. R. Felton. *Before Barbed Wire.* New York: Holt, 1956.

Dary, David. *Cowboy Culture: A Saga of Five Centuries.* New York: Avon Books, 1981.

Dobie, J. Frank. *The Longhorns.* 1941. Reprint, Austin: University of Texas Press, 1985.

Dykstra, Robert. *The Cattle Towns.* 1968. Reprint, Lincoln: Bison Books, 1983.

Fehrenbach, T. R. *Lone Star: A History of Texas and the Texans.* New York: American Legacy Press, 1983.

Grant, Bruce. *How To Make Cowboy Horse Gear.* Centreville, Maryland: Cornell Maritime Press, 1956.

Jordan, Terry G. *North American Cattle-Raising Frontiers: Origins, Diffusion, and Differentiation.* Albuquerque: University of New Mexico Press, 1993.

McCoy, Joseph. *Cattle Trade of the West and Southwest.* 1874. Reprint, Readex Microprint, 1966.

Miller, Joaquin. "Kit Carson's Ride." In *Best Loved Poems of the American West,* edited by John J. Gregg and Barbara T. Gregg. Garden City: Doubleday, 1980.

Pattie, Jane. *Cowboy Spurs and Their Makers.* College Station: Texas A&M University Press, 1991.

Rice, Lee M., and Glenn R. Vernon. *They Saddled the West*. Cambridge, Maryland: Cornell Maritime Press, 1975.

Russell, Charles. *Trails Plowed Under*. New York: Doubleday, 1927.

Slatta, Richard. *Comparing Cowboys and Frontiers*. Norman: University of Oklahoma Press, 1997.

Wellman, Paul I. *The Trampling Herd: The Story of the Cattle Range in America*. 1951. Reprint, New York: Cooper Square, 1974.

VAQUEROS

Allen, John Houghton. *Song to Randado*. Dallas: Kaleidograph Press, 1935.

Bannon, John Francis. *The Spanish Borderlands Frontier, 1513–1821*. Albuquerque: University of New Mexico Press, 1974.

Bolton, Herbert Eugene. *Padre on Horseback*. 1931. Reprint, Chicago: Loyola University Press, 1963.

———. *Rim of Christendom: A Biography of Eusebio Francisco Kino, Pacific Coast Pioneer*. Reprint. Tucson: University of Arizona Press, 1984.

Cisneros, José. *Riders across the Centuries: Horsemen of the Spanish Borderlands*. El Paso: Texas Western Press, 1984.

Curtis, P. S., Jr. "Spanish Songs of New Mexico." In *Happy Hunting Ground*. Publications of the Texas Folklore Society no. 4. Austin: Texas Folklore Society, 1925.

Davidson, Harold G. *Edward Borein, Cowboy Artist: The Life and Works of John Edward Borein, 1872–1945*. Garden City: Doubleday, 1974.

Denhardt, Robert M. *The Horse of the Americas*. Norman: University of Oklahoma Press, 1975.

Díaz Castillo, Bernal. *The Conquest of New Spain*. Translated and with an Introduction by J. M. Cohen. New York: Penguin Books, 1963.

Dobie, J. Frank. *Vaquero of the Brush Country*. 1929. Reprint. Austin: University of Texas Press, 1957.

———. "Versos of the Texas Vaqueros." In *Happy Hunting Ground*. Publications of the Texas Folklore Society no. 4. Austin: Texas Folklore Society, 1925.

Espinosa, Aurelio M. *The Folklore of Spain in the American Southwest*. Norman: University of Oklahoma Press, 1985.

Espinosa, Paul. "The Rich Tapestry of Hispanic America Is Virtually Invisible on Commercial Television." *Chronicle of Higher Education*, October 3, 1997, p. B 7.

Fehrenbach, T. R. *Fire and Blood: A Bold and Definitive Modern Chronicle of Mexico*. New York: Bonanza Books, 1985.

Fuentes, Carlos. *The Old Gringo*. Translated by Margaret Sayers Peden and Carlos Fuentes. New York: Farrar, Straus and Giroux, 1985.

Gonzalez, Jovita. "Tales and Songs of the Texas-Mexicans." In *Man, Bird, and Beast*. Publications of the Texas Folklore Society no. 8. Dallas: Southern Methodist University Press, 1930.

Graham, Joe S. *El Rancho in South Texas*. Denton: University of North Texas Press, 1994.

———. "Vaquero Folk Arts and Crafts in South Texas." In *Hecho en Tejas: Texas-Mexican Folk Arts and Crafts*. Edited by Joe S. Graham. Publications of the Texas Folklore Society no. 50. Denton: University of North Texas Press, 1991.

Graham, R. B. Cunninghame. *The Horses of the Conquest*. Norman: University of Oklahoma Press, 1949.

Haley, J. Evetts. *Charles Goodnight, Cowman and Plainsman*. Norman: University of Oklahoma Press, 1936.

Harris, Charles H., III. *A Mexican Family Empire: The Latifundio of the Sánchez Navarro Family 1765-1867*. Austin: University of Texas Press, 1975.

Jackson, Jack. *Los Mesteños: Spanish Ranching in Texas 1721-1821*. College Station: Texas A&M University Press, 1986.

Jones, Oakah L., Jr. *Nueva Vizcaya: Heartland of the Spanish Frontier*. Albuquerque: University of New Mexico Press, 1988.

———. *Los Paisanos: Spanish Settlers on the Northern Frontier of New Spain*. Norman: University of Oklahoma Press, 1979.

Kelton, Elmer. *Manhunters*. New York: Ballantine, 1974.

Lamoreau, Stephen. "The Road North—The Oñate Trail." *Texas Journal of Ideas, History and Culture* 9, no. 2 (Spring 1987): 22–23.

Lea, Aurora Lucero-White. *Literary Folklore of the Hispanic Southwest*. San Antonio: Naylor, 1953.

Lea, Tom. *King Ranch*. 2 vols. Boston: Little, Brown, 1957.

———. *The Hands of Cantú*. Boston: Little, Brown, 1964.

———. *Randado*. El Paso: Carl Hertzog, 1941.

Leon-Portilla, Miguel. "The Norteño Variety of Mexican Culture: An Ethnohistorical Approach." In *Plural Society in the Southwest*. Edited by Edward Spicer and Raymond Thompson. Albuquerque: University of New Mexico Press, 1960.

Lister, Florence C., and Robert H. Lister. *Chihuahua: Storehouse of Storms*. Albuquerque: University of New Mexico Press, 1966.

Machado, Manuel A., Jr. *Centaur of the North: Francisco Villa, the Mexican Revolution, and Northern Mexico*. Austin: Eakin, 1988.

———. *The North Mexican Cattle Industry 1910-1975: Ideology, Conflict, and Change*. College Station: Texas A&M University Press, 1981.

McLean, Malcolm D. *Fine Texas Horses: Their Pedigrees and Performance, 1830-1845*. Fort Worth: Texas Christian University Press, 1966.

McNeil, [Norman] "Brownie." "Corridos of the Mexican Border." In *Mexican Border Ballads*. Publications of the Texas Folklore Society no. 21. Dallas: Southern Methodist University Press, 1946.

Meinig, D. W. *Imperial Texas: An Interpretive Essay in Cultural Geography*. Austin: University of Texas Press, 1969.

Monday, Jane Clements, and Betty Bailey Calley. *Voices from the Wild Horse Desert*. Austin: University of Texas Press, 1997.

Mora, Jo. *Californios: The Saga of the Hard-Riding Vaqueros, America's First Cowboys*. Garden City: Doubleday, 1949.

Myres, Sandra L. *The Ranch in Spanish Texas, 1691–1800*. El Paso: Texas Western Press, 1969.

Noyes, Stanley. *Los Comanches: The Home People, 1751–1845*. Albuquerque: University of New Mexico Press, 1966.

Paredes, Américo. "Folklore and History." In *Singers and Storytellers*. Publications of the Texas Folklore Society no. 30. Dallas: Southern Methodist University Press, 1961.

———. "The Mexican Corrido: Its Rise and Fall." In *Madstones and Twisters*. Publications of the Texas Folklore Society no. 28. Dallas: Southern Methodist University Press, 1958.

———. *A Texas-Mexican Cancionero*. Urbana: University of Illinois Press, 1976.

———. *With His Pistol in His Hand: A Border Ballad and Its Hero*. Austin: University of Texas Press, 1958.

Ramirez, Nora Ethel. "The Vaquero and Ranching in the Southwestern United States, 1600–1970." Ph.D. dissertation. Indiana University, 1979.

Remington, Frederic. *Frederic Remington's Own West, Written and Illustrated by Frederic Remington*. Edited by Harold McCracken. New York: Dial Press, 1960.

Robb, John D. *Hispanic Folk Music of New Mexico and the Southwest: A Self-Portrait of a People*. Norman: University of Oklahoma Press, 1980.

Roemer, Ferdinand. *Roemer's Texas, with Particular Reference to German Immigration and the Physical Appearance of the Country*. Translated by Oswald Mueller. San Antonio: Standard Printing Co., 1935.

Rojas, Arnold R. *The Vaquero*. Charlotte, North Carolina: McNally and Loftin, 1964.

Sandoz, Mari. *The Cattlemen, from the Rio Grande across the Far Marias*. New York: Hastings House, 1958.

"Vaqueros Completos." *Cattleman Magazine* 80, no. 7 (1994): 10.

Weber, David J. *The Mexican Frontier 1821–1846: The American Southwest under Mexico*. Albuquerque: University of New Mexico Press, 1982.

————. *The Spanish Frontier in North America.* New Haven: Yale University Press, 1992.

Wittliff, William D. *Vaquero: Genesis of the Texas Cowboy.* San Antonio: Institute of Texan Cultures, 1972.

Wyllys, Rufus K. *Pioneer Padre: The Life and Times of Eusebio Francisco Kino.* Dallas: Southwest Press, 1935.

COWBOYS

Abbott, E. C. ("Teddy," "Blue"), and Helen Huntington Smith. *We Pointed Them North.* 1939. Reprint, Norman: University of Oklahoma Press, 1955.

Adams, Andy. *Log of a Cowboy.* 1903. Reprint, Lincoln: University of Nebraska Press, 1964.

Adams, Ramon. *The Cowboy and His Humor.* Austin: Encino, 1968.

Brackman, Barbara, Jennie A. Chinn, and James F. Hoy. *Cowboy Boots: The Kansas Story.* Topeka: Kansas State Historical Society, 1994.

Capps, Benjamin. *The Trail to Ogallala.* 1964. Reprint, with an Afterword by Don Graham. Fort Worth: Texas Christian University Press, 1985.

"Case History of the Longhorn." Manuscript, Barker Center Collection, University of Texas at Austin.

Cashion, Ty. *A Texas Frontier: The Clear Fork Country and Fort Griffin, 1849–1887.* Norman: University of Oklahoma Press, 1996.

Clayton, Lawrence. "At Home after Life on the Range." *Mesquite: A Journal of Ideas, History, and Culture* 4 (1992): 36–39.

————. *Clear Fork Cowboys: Contemporary Cowboys along the Clear Fork of the Brazos River.* Abilene: Cowboy Press, 1985.

————. "The Contemporary Cowboy: 1941–Present." *Concho River Review* 1 (Spring 1987): 51–62.

————. "Contemporary Cowboy Music in Texas: Red Steagall, Don Edwards, and Michael Martin Murphey." *Journal of Popular Culture* 33, no. 3 (Winter 2000): 29–35.

————. "The Cowboy: Some Views on the Area of His Origin." *Heritage of the Great Plains* 31, no. 2 (Fall 1998): 5–12.

————. *Cowboys: Ranch Life along the Clear Fork of the Brazos River.* Austin: Eakin, 1997.

————. "Cowboys and Buckaroos: Two Faces of the Same Figure." *West Texas Historical Association Yearbook* 64 (1988): 107–112.

————. "Evolution of the Cowboy." In *The Catch Pen: Proceedings of the National Cowboy Symposium.* Edited by Len Ainsworth and Kenneth Davis. Lubbock: Texas Tech University Press, 1991.

————. *Historic Ranches of Texas.* Austin: University of Texas Press, 1993.

————. *Longhorn Legacy: Graves Peeler and the Texas Cattle Trade.* Abilene: Cowboy Press, 1994.

————. *Ranch Rodeos in West Texas.* Abilene: Four-O-Imprint, Hardin-Simmons University Press, 1988.

————. "The Second Period of Cowboy Life in the Southwest: The Recollections of Charlie Cone." *Concho River Review* 6 (1992): 66–79.

————. "Today's Cowboys: Coping with a Myth." *West Texas Historical Association Yearbook* 60 (1984): 178–184.

————. *Watkins Reynolds Matthews: Biography of a Texas Rancher.* Austin, Eakin, 1994.

Clayton, Lawrence, Kenneth W. Davis, and Mary Evelyn Collins. *Horsing Around: Contemporary Cowboy Humor.* Lubbock: Texas Tech Press, 1999.

Cone, Charlie. See Clayton, Lawrence. "The Second Period of Cowboy Life in the Southwest."

Dobie, J. Frank. *The Longhorns.* Boston: Little, Brown, 1941.

Erickson, John. *The Modern Cowboy.* Perryton, Texas: Maverick Books, 1981.

————. *The Catch Rope.* Denton: University of North Texas Press, 1994.

Ford, John Salmon. *Rip Ford's Texas.* Edited by Stephen B. Oates. Austin: University of Texas Press, 1987.

Haley, J. Evetts, Jr., ed. *Cowboys Who Rode Proudly.* Midland, Texas: Haley Library, 1992.

Horgan, Paul. *Great River.* 1954. Reprint, Austin: Texas Monthly Press, 1984.

Horton, Thomas F. *History of Jack County, Being Accounts of Pioneer Times, Excerpts from County Court Records, Indian Stories, Biographical Sketches, and Interesting Events.* Jacksboro, Texas: Jacksboro Gazette-News, 1933.

Hough, Emerson. *North of 36.* New York: Appleton, 1923.

Hoy, Jim. *Cowboys and Kansas.* Norman: University of Oklahoma Press, 1995.

Hunter, J. Marvin. *The Trail Drivers of Texas.* 2 vols. 1923. Reprint: New York, Argosy-Antiquarian, 1963.

Jordan, Terry G. *Trails to Texas: Southern Roots of Western Cattle Ranching.* Lincoln: University of Nebraska Press, 1981.

Limerick, Patricia. *The Legacy of Conquest: The Unbroken Past of the American West.* New York: Norton, 1987.

Lomax, John A., and Alan Lomax. *Cowboy Songs and Other Frontier Ballads.* 3d ed. New York: Macmillan, 1938.

London, G. D. *Through the Years: A Collection of Cowboy Stories.* Throckmorton, Texas: Privately Printed, 1997.

Marsh, Lois Cambern, comp. *They Came to Stay: Cambern, Kutch, and Bell Families.* Quanah, Texas: Nortex Press, 1974.

Massey, Sarah. *Black Cowboys of Texas.* College Station: Texas A&M University Press, 2000.

Matthews, Sallie Reynolds. *Interwoven: A Pioneer Chronicle.* 1936. Reprint, College Station: Texas A&M University Press, 1982.

McMurtry, Larry. *Lonesome Dove.* New York: Simon & Schuster, 1985.

Nelson, Barney. *Voices and Visions of the American West.* Austin: Texas Monthly Press, 1986.

Pound, Louise. *Poetic Origins and the Ballad.* New York: Macmillan, 1921.

Rector, Ray. *Cowboy Life on the Texas Plains: The Photographs of Ray Rector.* College Station: Texas A&M University Press, 1982.

Rollins, Philip Ashton. *The Cowboy: An Unconventional History of Civilization on the Old-Time Range.* 1936. Rev. ed. Albuquerque: University of New Mexico Press, 1979.

Saunders, Tom B., IV. *The Texas Cowboys.* Photographs by David R. Stoecklein. Privately printed, 1997.

Schreiber, Martin H. *Last of a Breed: Portraits of Working Cowboys.* Austin: Texas Monthly Press, 1982.

Sims, Orland L. *Cowpokes, Nesters, and Such.* Austin: Encino, 1970.

Siringo, Charles. *A Texas Cowboy, or Fifteen Years on the Hurricane Deck of a Spanish Pony.* 1950. Reprint, Lincoln: University of Nebraska Press, 1966.

Slatta, Richard. *Comparing Cowboys and Frontiers.* Norman: University of Oklahoma Press, 1997.

Smith, Erwin E., and J. Evetts Haley. *Life on the Texas Range.* Austin: University of Texas Press, 1952.

Tinkle, Lon, and Allen Maxwell, eds. *The Cowboy Reader.* New York: David McKay, 1959.

Tinsley, Jim Bob. *He Was Singin' This Song.* Orlando: University Presses of Florida, 1981.

Ward, Fay. *The Cowboy at Work: All about His Job and How He Does It.* 1958. Reprint, Norman: University of Oklahoma Press, 1987.

Webb, Walter Prescott. *The Great Plains.* Waltham, Massachusetts: Blaisdell, 1959.

White, Richard. *"It's Your Misfortune and None of My Own": A New History of the American West.* Norman: University of Oklahoma Press, 1991.

Wister, Owen. *The Virginian.* 1902. Reprint, New York: Signet, 1979.

Worchester, Don. *The Chisholm Trail: High Road of the Cattle Kingdom.* Lincoln: University of Nebraska Press, 1980.

Adams, Mildretta. *Owyhee Cattlemen 1878–1978: 100 Years in the Saddle.* Rev. ed. Homedale, Idaho, 1979.

Cannon, Hal, and Thomas West, eds. *Buckaroo.* New York: Simon & Schuster, 1993.

Capriola, J. M., Company Catalogue. Elko, Nevada, 1997.

Elliott, Waltzy. Oral history transcript (1992), Humboldt County Library, Winnemucca, Nevada.

Hadley, C. J. *Trappings of the Great Basin Buckaroo.* Reno: University of Nevada Press, 1993.

Hanley, Mike, with Ellis Lucia. *Owyhee Trails: The West's Forgotten Corner.* Caldwell, Idaho: Caxton Printers, Ltd., 1973, reprinted 1988.

———. *Tales of the I.O.N. Country.* Desert Graphics, 1998.

Hedges, Mackey. *Last Buckaroo.* Salt Lake City: Gibbs-Smith Publisher, 1995.

Markus, Kurt. *After Barbed Wire: Cowboys of Our Time.* Pasadena, California: Twelvetrees Press, 1985.

———. *Buckaroo: Images from the Sagebrush Basin.* Boston: Little, Brown, 1987.

Marshall, Howard W., and Richard E. Ahlborn. *Buckaroos in Paradise: Cowboy Life in Northern Nevada.* Washington, D.C.: American Folklife Center, 1980; Lincoln: University of Nebraska Press, 1981.

Matthews, William. *Cowboys and Images.* San Francisco: Chronicle Books, 1994.

McLaury, Buster. "Chasing the Wild Bovine." *Western Horseman,* October, 1994, pp. 74–78, 80, 82; November, 1994, pp. 26–29; December, 1994, pp. 39–43, 46.

Mendieta, Tony. Oral history transcript (1988), Humboldt County Library, Winnemucca, Nevada.

Mora, Jo. *Californios: The Saga of the Hard-riding Vaqueros, America's First Cowboys.* Garden City: Doubleday, 1949.

———. *Trail Dust and Saddle Leather.* 1946. Reprint. Lincoln: University of Nebraska Press, 1987.

Morris, Ernest. *El Buckaroo.* Flagstaff, Arizona: Northland Graphics, 1995.

———. *El Vaquero.* N.p., 1989.

Russel, Charles M. *Trails Plowed Under.* 1927. Reprint, University of Nebraska Press, 1996.

Slatta, Richard W. *Cowboys of the Americas.* New Haven: Yale University Press, 1990.

Stanford, Omer. "Cattle Drives." *Owyhee Outpost* no. 2 (April 1971): 15–24. Owyhee Historical Society, Murphy, Idaho.

Stanke, Jerry. "Con Shea and His Sister." *Owyhee Outpost* no. 2 (April 1971): 1–14. Owyhee Historical Society, Murphy, Idaho.

Starrs, Paul F. *Let the Cowboy Ride: Cattle Ranching in the American West.* Baltimore: Johns Hopkins University Press, 1998.

Steber, Rick. *Roundup.* Prineville, Oregon: Bonanza Publishing, 1996.

Stewart, Leslie J. Oral history transcript (1993–1994), Humboldt County Library, Winnemucca, Nevada.

Stoecklein, David R. *Cowboy Gear.* Ketchum, Idaho: Dober Hill, 1993.

———. *Don't Fence Me In: Images of the Spirit of the West.* Ketchum, Idaho: Dober Hill, 1996.

———. *The Idaho Cowboy.* Ketchum, Idaho: Dober Hill, 1991.

Visalia Stock Saddle Company Catalogue No. 22. Facsimile reprint, Pitman's Treasurers & Co., San Gabriel, California, 1989.

Walters, Keith. "Buckaroo Hat Styles." *Western Horseman,* May 1987, p. 91.

Young, James A., and B. Abbott Sparks. *Cattle in the Cold Desert.* Logan: Utah State University Press, 1985.

ORAL SOURCES

INTERVIEWS BY LAWRENCE CLAYTON

Alonzo, Arturo. (With Jerald Underwood.) Uvalde, Texas. October 22, 1996.

Amezquita, Victor. Abilene, Texas. May 6, 1997.

Atkinson, Don. Kerrville, Texas. March 22, 1988.

Baldeschwiler, Barney. Hebbronville, Texas. October 21, 1996.

Barton, Bill. Abilene, Texas. July 21, 1987.

Campbell, John. Kingsville, Texas. February 22, 1996.

Cantú, Roy. Hebbronville, Texas. October 20, 1996.

Díaz Sánchez, José "Pepe." San Antonio, Texas. September 27, 1997.

Edgar, Sonny. Nail Ranch, Albany, Texas. Numerous interviews, 1985–1988.

Graham, Frank. Kingsville, Texas. February 21, 1997.

Gray, Ted. Alpine, Texas. August 10, 1996.

Huerta, David. Alpine, Texas. August 10, 1996.

Keefe, Joe. Victoria, Texas. July 19, 1996.

Ledbetter, Morris. Albany, Texas. March 21, 1991.

Leech, Glenn. Albany, Texas. January 5, 1993.

Matthews, Watt. Lambshead Ranch, Shackelford County, Texas. Numerous interviews, 1985–1987.

Pate, Jack. Albany, Texas. March 15, 1985.

Peacock, Benny. Albany, Texas. Numerous interviews, 1985–1997.

Peacock, George. Albany, Texas. Numerous interviews, 1985–1997.

Perkins, Litt. Fort Griffin, Texas. Several interviews, 1977–1979.
Reynolds, Jimbo. (By telephone.) Sheridan, Wyoming. January 16, 1993.
Sánchez, Ismael. Abilene, Texas. March 20, 1987.

INTERVIEWS BY JERALD UNDERWOOD

Ortiz, Cirildo. Uvalde, Texas. November 6, 1987.
Vásquez, Félix. (With Arturo Alonzo.) Uvalde, Texas. October 10, 1994.

INTERVIEWS BY JIM HOY

Amos, Charley. Paradise Valley, Nevada. November 21, 1995.
Bengochea, Gary. Winnemucca, Nevada. November 1995.
Dodge, Caleb Newt. McDermitt, Nevada. November 1995.
Durham, Griff. (By telephone.) Reno, Nevada. January 12, 1998.
Evans, Charles. Lamoille, Nevada. November 19, 1995.
Farmer, Don. Elko, Nevada. November 18, 1995.
Galyen, Mark. Jordan Valley, Oregon. November 21, 1995.
Griswold, Stanley. Elko, Nevada. November 19, 1995; August 15, 1997.
Hall, Chuck. Bruneau, Idaho. August 13, 1997.
Hall, Tom. Bruneau, Idaho. August 13, 1997.
Hammond, Carl. (By telephone.) Golconda, Nevada. February 22, 1996.
———. Winnemucca, Nevada. August 14, 1997.
Hanley, Mike. Jordan Valley, Oregon. August, 13, 1997.
Hedges, Mackey, and Candy Hedges. Woodruff, Utah. November 25, 1995.
———. Grant, Montana. August 8, 1997.
Marvel, Pete. Paradise Valley, Nevada. November 20, 1995.
McQuery, Rod. Elko, Nevada. November 18, 1995.
Smiraldo, George. Elko, Nevada. November 19, 1995; August 15, 1997.
Wallis, Sue. Elko, Nevada. November 18, 1995.

INDEX

Page numbers in **boldface** indicate illustrations.

Abbott, Teddy "Blue," 77, 132
Abel and Kurtner Ranch, 157, 219
Adams, Andy, 77, 117
Adams, Ramon, 133
a-fork saddle. *See* slick-fork saddle
African Americans: as buckaroos,
    207, 215, 219, 222; as cowboys on
    cattle drives, 74; as vaqueros, 2
Africans: horseback culture of the
    Moors, 4; influence on Texas cattle
    ranching, 71
Alonzo, Arturo, 56–58
amansador, 208; defined, 225. *See
    also* bronc stomper
Amarillo, Texas, 111, 134, 154
American Indians, 73; as buckaroos,
    207, 220, 222; *encomienda* system
    and, 13; Spanish mission system
    and, 11–13, 207–208; as vaqueros,
    2, 8. *See also* Native Americans
American Quarter Horse Heritage
    Center and Museum, 134
Amezquita, Victor, xx, **1**, **33**, 46–53,
    46
Andalusian: defined, 225
annual cycle: defined, 225
antelope: roping, 199
Apache, 7, 11, 12, 15, 19
Arabian, 90, 195; defined, 225
Arizona: borderlands, 2; Spanish ex-
    peditions to, 10; Spanish mission
    system in, 11–12
armas: defined, 225

armitas, 168, 169; defined, 225
Arnold, Oscar "Leppy," 215, 222
atajo: defined, 225
auction ring: defined, 225
Autry, Gene, 134
Aztec, 7, 15

B. K. Johnson Ranch, **43**, 56
back cinch. *See* flank girth
baja: defined, 225
bajío, 15; defined, 225
Baldeschwiler, Barney, 143–146, **144**
bandanas. *See* neckerchief
Bankofier, Joseph John "Joe Boy," 220,
    222
Barnes, Hillery, 222
bear: roping a, 199, 209
bear trap saddle, 170
bedroll, 79, **82**, 139, 148, 196; defined,
    226. *See also* soogan
bed wagon: defined, 226. *See also*
    hoodlum wagon
belts: comparative traits of, among
    vaqueros, cowboys, and buckaroos,
    248; cowboy style, 106, **108**, **109**;
    vaquero style, 52, **52**
Berbers: Blue Men of the Desert, 3;
    defined, 226; horseback culture of,
    3–4, 5
Big Loop rodeo, 170, 200
bit: buckaroos and, 179–180; as
    collectors' items, 131; compara-
    tive traits of vaqueros, cowboys,

and buckaroos, 246; cowboys and, 26, 127, **127**, 129, **130**, 131, **131**; defined, 226; Half-breed, 179; Las Cruces style, 179, 208; Santa Barbara, 179, 208. *See also* snaffle bit

Black Angus, 72, 73, 87

blacks: as buckaroos, 207; as cowboys, 74; and horseback culture of Moors from Africa, 4; *Morisco* description, 7; as slaves of conquistadors, 7; as vaqueros, 8, 68. *See also* African Americans

blanket: comparative traits of vaqueros, cowboys, and buckaroos, 246. *See also* Navajo blanket

boots, 218; buckaroo style, 161, 163–164, **165**; comparative traits of vaqueros, cowboys, and buckaroos, 247–248; cowboy style, 107, 110–111, **110**, 115

borderlands, 2, 5, 9, 18; defined, 226

bosal, 31, 127, **129, 132**; defined, 226

bosalillos, 208

botas, 20; defined, 226

Boyd, William (Hopalong Cassidy), 134

Brahman, 49, 54, 72

brand: defined, 226

branding: buckaroos and, 188–189, **189**, 193; comparative traits of vaqueros, cowboys, and buckaroos, 249; cowboys and, 75, **80, 81**, 94, 139; defined, 226

branding iron, 50; defined, 226

brasada, **16, 21**, 68; defined, 226

bravemaker: defined, 226

breaking: and comparative traits among vaqueros, cowboys, and buckaroos, 250; of horses, 50, 140, 141–142, 144–145

breast collar (or harness): buckaroo style, 177; comparative traits of vaqueros, cowboys, and buckaroos, 246; defined, 226–227

breeding: of horses, and comparative traits among vaqueros, cowboys, and buckaroos, 250

Brennan, Walter, 134

bridle (*la brida*), 126–127, **126**; defined, 227

bridle chains. *See* slobber chains

bridle horse, 185–186; defined, 227

bronc: defined, 227. *See also brutos*

bronc rider (*also* bronc stomper), 151, 208; buckaroo-style bronc riding, 214–215

bronc stomper (*also* bronc rider): defined, 227

brow band, 180–181; defined, 227

Brown Ranch, 94

Brummett, Curt, 158

brush: defined, 227

brush jacket, **17, 22**, 107

brush popper, 107; defined, 227

brutos: defined, 227. *See also* bronc

buckaroo boss: defined, 227

Buckaroo Hall of Fame and Heritage Museum 157, 192, 206–207, 213–220, 222

buckaroos, xv–xvii, 94, 95, 125, 135, **160**, 223–224; accoutrements, 247–248; African Americans as, 207, 215, 219, 222; American Indians as, 207; artwork of, 220; bits, 179–180, **183**; boots, 161, 163–164, **165**; branding and, 188–189, **189**, 193, 249; breaking horses, 127, 250; bridle horses, 185–186; bronc riding, 214–215; buckaroo wagon, 193, 204, 227; Californios and, 207–209; cattle ranching, 203–204, 209, 212–213; characteristics of, 187–193; Chinese, 169, 204, 207; chinks, 158, 167, 168–169, 170, 187; clothing, 165–170, 221, 248–249; comparative traits of, with cowboys and vaqueros, 245–250; concept of time and aesthetics and, 187–193; corrals of, 249; daily ranch life, 193–197, **194–197**; as distinguished from cowboys, 156–158; evolving from the California vaquero, 189–190; Garcia spurs, 179; gentling horses, 219; geographical influence of the Great Basin region, 190–191; handle-bar mustache, 221; hats, 160–161, **162, 163**, 221; horse breeding, 250; horses, 191–192, 195, **196, 197**, 202–203; individualism and, 192–193; leisure time,

199–200, 205–206; literature on, 159–160, 170, 187; "Man of the Northwest," 3; Mexican, 207; modern-day buckaroos, 220–221; multiculturalism, 206–207, 215; music, 199; mustanging, 216–217; in the 1920s, 193–201; origin of the term *buckaroo*, 71, 156–157; poetry and, 136, 199; ranching and, 193–201, **194–197**; ranch rodeos, 200–201; revivalists, 170; riata artistry, 192; rodear, 194–197; roping, 177–178, 199–200, 249; roping and dragging, 188; saddle-bronc riders, 200; saddlery and tack, 170–187, 245–247; shadow riders, 186–187; silver décor of, 177, 187; spurs, 179–180, **180, 181**; stirrups, 174, **175**, 176; as top-notch herders, 250; unique characteristics of, 187–193; vaquero origin of, 189–190, 207–209; wild rag, 164–165, 187, 221; women and ranching, 204–205, 206; working methods, 249–250

buckaroo wagon, 193, 204; defined, 227. *See also* chuck wagon

bucking rolls: defined, 227

buckles: comparative traits of vaqueros, cowboys, and buckaroos, 248; cowboy style, 106, **108, 109**

buffalo, **146**; slaughter of, 73

bunkhouse: defined, 227

Burnett, Burk, 134

button: defined, 227

Button, Frank Joseph, 220, 222

caballero, 2, 8, 69; defined, 227

caballo: defined, 227

caballo corriente, 43, 56; defined, 227

caballo de trabajo, **48**; defined, 227

caballo fino, 56; defined, 227

calf cradle: defined, 227

calf fries. *See* mountain oysters

California: borderlands, 2; Californios, 207/-209; conquistadors in, 10; early vaqueros in, 167, 180, 189, 207–209, 221; Longhorns in, 212; missions in, 11, 12, 207

California saddle. *See* center-fire rig

Californios: origin of buckaroos, 207–209

camp: defined, 227

cantle (*la teja*), 117; comparative traits of vaqueros, cowboys, and buckaroos, 245; defined, 228

cantle plates: defined, 228

caporal, 63; defined, 228

Capps, Benjamin, 63, 77, 136

carrera del gallo, 209

cascabel, defined, 228

Cashion, Ty, 73

Castillo, Bernal Díaz, 6–7

castration: defined, 228

Castro, Dave, 222

Castro, Fred, 207

cattle drives, 147; end of open-range practices, 78; to Kansas railheads, 74/-77; modern-day cattle driving, 84, 143–144

cattle prod (also called *hot shot*): defined, 228

cattle ranching, **16**, 89; beef markets, 74; birth of cattle culture in Mexico, 8; black horsemen and, 8; branding, 139; breeds of cattle, 72; British cultural influence theory on, 69–70, 72; buckaroos and, 203–204, 209, 212–213; cattle barons, 72; cattle cars, **85**; cattle pens, 84, 86; electronic video auctions, 197; feeding cattle, 88–89; fencing of cattle, 84–85, **87, 88**, 149–150; fever tick and, 72; helicopters used in, 151; line maneuver, 89; markets for hides and tallow, 74; mestizo horsemen and, 8; modern-day economics of, 87–89; mountain cattle in Mexico, 49–50; mulatto horsemen and, 8; Native American horsemen and, 8; pickup trucks and trailers, 88, 143–144, 150; post–Civil War, 74; railroads and, 76, 212; in Rancho Nueva, Mexico, 53, 54; roping, 53–54; screwworm, 92, 139; Spanish introduction of cattle in Americas, 7; Spanish-Mexican influence in Texas on, 72; Spanish mission system and, 11–13; theories on origins of cowboy life and ranching in Texas, 68–73;

wheel maneuver, 89; women and, 188, 204–205, 206; work horses and, 88–94, **89, 90, 93;** "working" the cattle, 57, 58, 59, 94, **97**

Cauble, Bill, 103

cavvy: defined, 228. *See also remuda*

"Centaur Wish," of vaqueros, 18, 224; defined, 228

center-fire rig, 177, 179; defined, 228

chaparreras, 37; defined, 228

chap guards, 111; defined, 228

chaps (also called *leggings*), 107, 115, **116, 118, 119,** 145; batwing, 167, 169, 221, 225; chinks, 167–169; comparative traits of vaqueros, cowboys, and buckaroos, 248; defined, 228; shotgun, 167, 169, 221; woolies, 167, **168**

charreada: defined, 2

charro: charro contests, 45, 190; defined, 228; distinguished from vaquero, 2, 45; tradition of, 190

chelino: defined, 228

Cheyenne roll, 170–171; defined, 228

Chihuahua spur, **40;** defined, 228

Chinese: as buckaroos, 207; as ranch hands in buckaroo country, 169, 204

chin strap: defined, 228

chinks: buckaroos and, 158, 167, 168–169, 170, 187, 221; defined, 228

Chisholm, Jesse, 74

Chisholm Trail, 74

chuck wagon, 54; cook (*cocinero* or *coosie*) of, 99, 102, **102,** 103; cowboys and, 75, 79, **82,** 98–99, 138, 143, 147–148; defined, 228–229; work on the wagon, 244. *See also* buckaroo wagon

chute chinks: defined, 229

cinch (*la cincha*): defined, 229. *See also* girth

cinch ring (*la argolla*), **120,** 229

Circle A Ranch, 157, 218

circle horse, 195; defined, 229

Cisneros, José, 63

Clarkson, Harry, 207

Clayton, Lee, 107

Clayton, Sonia Irwin, 135

clothing and accoutrements: comparative traits of vaqueros, cow-

boys, and buckaroos, 247–249. *See also* buckaroos; cowboys; vaqueros

cock fighting, 44, 52

Colonizer of the Rio Grande. *See* José de Escandón

Colorado Springs, Colorado: cattle grazing in mountainous areas, 86; cowboy museum in, 134; Goodnight-Loving Trail and, 74

Columbus, Christopher: introduction of cattle in New World and, 7

Comanche, 11, 26

concho (*la concha*), 177, 187; defined, 229

Cone, Charlie, 98, 105, 137–141, **138,** 148, 152, 153

conquistador: defined, 229; *encomienda* system in New Spain and, 13; and Spanish expeditions in the Americas, 5–11

cook (*cocinero* or *coosie*): of chuck wagons, 99, 102, 103

cool-back pad: defined, 229

Cooper, Gary, 134

corella de toros, 44, 52

Coronado, Francisco de, 9

corral, 150; comparative traits of vaqueros, cowboys, and buckaroos, 249–250; defined, 229; origin of *corral,* 71

corrales de leña, **51**

corridas, 59, 60, 63, 64

Cortés, Hernán, 5–7

cow boss: defined, 229

cowboys, xv–xvii, **67, 76, 91,** 223–224; advertising images of, 135; belts and buckles, 106, **108, 109;** black cowboys, 74; boots and spurs, 107, 110–111, **110, 112–115,** 115; branding methods, 249; breaking horses, 127, 250; brush poppers, 107; buckaroos distinguished from, 156–158; Cajun, 71; chuck wagons, 75, 98–99, 102, **102,** 103; clothing and accoutrements, 103–107, **108–110,** 110–111, **112–115,** 115, 131–132, 141, 247–249; comparative traits of, with buckaroos and vaqueros, 245–250; corrals of, 249; as cultural icon, 68; diet of, 75, 97–99, 102–103, 138–139, 148, 149;

defined, 68; distinguished from vaqueros, 71, 223–224; guns of, 132–133; and horse breeding, 250; lingo of, 133; literature depicting cowboy life, 68, 76–77; magazines on cowboy life, 134; "Man of the West," 3; museum collections and archives, 133–134, 135; music and song, 77, 134–137; photograph collections of cowboy life, 135; pickup trucks and trailers, 84, 88, 97; poetry and, 135, 136; roping and dragging, 95; roping methods, 29, 249; saddlery and tack, 116–117, **121, 122,** 133, 141, 245–247; tepees, 79, **83;** theories on the origin of, 68–73; as top-notch herders, 250; vaquero influence on, 68, 69; working methods, 249–250. *See also* cattle drives; cattle ranching; Texas

cow-calf operation, 229. *See also* steer operation

cow camp, 99; defined, 229

cow horse: defined, 229

cow sense: defined, 230

coyote: defined, 230; roping, 199

cranky, 172, 202; defined, 230

crease: defined, 230

crew: defined, 230

Crow, John, 200, 215–216, 222

cull: defined, 230

curb chain: defined, 230. *See also* chin strap

Curry, Quentin Lee "Stub," 220, 222

cut a herd: defined, 230; cutting alley cut defined, 230; cutting horse cut defined, 230

dally, 28–29, 33, 54, 178; defined, 230. *See also* hard and fast

dar la vuelta, 28; defined, 230. *See also* dally

Dave, Henry, 222

day work: defined, 230

De León, Alonso, 10, 12

Dewees, W. B., 156–157

Diamond Ranch, 216

Díaz, Pepe, 33, 42–45, **44**

dinner-plate saddle horn: defined, 231

Dobie, J. Frank, 2, 12, 68, 69, 71, 134

Dodge, Caleb "Newt," **162, 164,** 198–199

Dollarhide, Ross, 200, 216, 222

Dorrance, Jim, 222

double-rigged saddle, 117, 141, **173,** 176; defined, 231. *See also* center-fire rig; seven-eighths rigged saddle; three-quarter rigged saddle

Double Square Ranch, 219

dove wings: defined, 231

Drummond, Arthur (King of the Mustangers), 216–217, 222

Ducker, Edward Augustus "Ed," 217, 222

Durham, 72, 78, 203

Durham, Griff, 169, 171

ear tag: defined, 231

Edgar, Sonny, **151,** 152–153

Edwards, Don, 136

el campo: defined, 231

Elliott, Samuel Waltzy, 169, 199–200, 201–207, 213, 220, 222

encomienda: conquistadors and, 13; defined, 231; in New Spain, 13–14

entradas, 9; defined, 231

Erickson, John, 135, 137

Escandón, José, 16

Evans, Dale, 134

Farmer, Don, 161, 185–186

feed route. *See* feed run

feeders: defined, 231

feedlot: defined, 231

feed run: defined, 231

fiadore: defined, 231

field: defined, 231

flanker: defined, 231

flank girth (*la barriguera*): 117; defined, 231. *Also called* back cinch

flanking calves: defined, 231

Ford, Glenn, 134

Foredyce, Pete, 220, 222

foreman: defined, 231–232. *See also* buckaroo boss; *caporal; cow boss; major domo; mayordomo*

fork, 117; comparative traits of vaqueros, cowboys, and buckaroos, 245; defined, 232

formando: 38; defined, 232

Fowler, Jay, 222
Frazier, R. T., (saddler), 143, 171
French, Pete, 207, 216
frontera: defined, 232
front girth *(also known as* girt), 117
Frusetta, Jack, 178, 217–218, 222

Galyen, Mark, 158, 200–201
ganaderos: defined, 232
ganado liviano: defined, 232
Garvey Ranches, 157–158
gather: defined, 232. *See also rodear*
gauchos, xvi, 64, 157
gelding, 219; defined, 232
girth: defined, 232. *See also* cinch
girthing: comparative traits of va-
    queros, cowboys, and buckaroos,
    246
Goodman Ranch, 215
Goodnight, Charles, 73, 134; chuck
    wagon and, 229
Goodnight-Loving Trail, 74
gooseneck spur: defined, 232
gooseneck trailer: defined, 232
Graham, Frank, 34, **34,** 71, 92, 107,
    137, 224
Graham, Joe, 69
Gray, Ted, 90
grazer bit: defined, 232
Great Basin: cattle ranching in,
    209, 212–213; and early Euro-
    pean settlers, 206–207; and elec-
    tronic video cattle auctions, 197;
    geographical boundaries of, 156;
    geographic influence on bucka-
    roos, 190–191; ranch rodeos, 200–
    201; Spanish influence on cattle
    ranching in, 157; wild horses, 203
green-broke: defined, 232
Green Ranch, **150**
Griswold, Stanley, 169, 205–206
gummer: defined, 232
guns: and cowboys, 132–133

hacienda: defined, 232
haciendado: defined, 232
hackamore (*la jáquima*), 31, **31,** 127,
    128, 129, 141, 180, 181, 183, 208;
    defined, 232
Hadley, C. J., 220
hair pad: defined, 232–233

Haley, J. Evetts, 134
Hall, Chuck, 158, 200
Hall, Tom, 158, 176
Hammond, Carl, 157, 161, 169, 170,
    195, 200, 206, 209, 213–215, 218,
    220, 221
Hammond, Francis "France," 220, 222
Hammond, Frank L., 218, 222
handmade spurs, 111
Hanley, Mike, 157, 170, 177, 201, 204,
    206, 207
hard-and-fast: defined, 233. *See also*
    dally
Harmon, Del, 203
Harris, Charles H. III, 14
hats: buckaroos and, 160–161, **162,**
    163, 166, **166;** comparative traits of
    vaqueros, cowboys, and buckaroos,
    247; cowboys and, **91,** 103–104;
    Montana Poke style, 104; Stetson,
    104, 160, 166; Tom Mix–style, 161
Haws, Peter, 212
Hayes, Thomas Edward "Tommy,"
    220, 222
head and heel, **96;** defined, 233
headquarters: defined, 233. *See also la*
    casa grande
headstall, 126, **132,** 180; defined, 223
Hearst, Bill, 207
Hearst, William Randolph, 15
Hedges, Mackey, xiii, 159–161, **163,**
    166, 174, 176, 187, 188, **190,** 192–
    193, 194, 195, **196, 197,** 198, 199,
    209, **210**
herd: defined, 233
Hereford, 54, 57, 72, 73, 78, 87, 203
hidalgo, 6; defined, 233
high port bit: defined, 233
Hill, Dwight, 154, **155, 210**
Hispanics. *See* Mexican Americans
Hittson, Jesse, 72
hobbles, **120,** 123; defined, 233
hocking knife: defined, 233
Holl, Dave, 220
honda, 95, **100, 101;** defined, 233
hoodlum wagon, 148; defined, 233. *See*
    also bed wagon
hoolihan hoop, **89, 190;** defined, 233
Hopalong Cassidy. *See* Boyd, William
Hopkins Brothers Ranch, 218
horn, 117, 170–171, 172, 178, **178, 179;**

comparative traits of vaqueros, cowboys, and buckaroos, 245
horsehair rope: defined, 234
horse jewelry: defined, 234
horses: Andalusian, 225; Arabian, 90, 195, 225; breaking to ride, 50, 91, 140, 141–143, 144–145, 250; bridle horse, 185–186; buckaroos and, 191–192, 195, **196, 197;** bucking, 202–203; *caballo finos*, 56; cattle ranching and, 88–94, **89, 90, 93,** 93–94; circle horse, 195; comparative chart of, among vaqueros, cowboys, and buckaroos, 250; cowboys and, 88–94, **89, 90, 93,** 140–147; cranky, 202; feral, 203, 209; gentling, 219; Morgan, 195; mustang horses, 60; Percheron, 195; Quarter Horse, 44, 56, 195; Randado Ranch and, 30; rodearing, 194–197, 239; saddlery and tack, 31–37, 245–247; slaughter horses, 31–37, 94; Spanish introduction of, to the Americas, 5–7; Spanish mission system and, 11–12; Spanish Mustache, 209, **210,** 242; Spanish Mustang, 56; sports and games, 209; Standard-bred cross, 195; Thoroughbred, 195; utility horses (*caballos corrientes*), 56; vaquero culture and, 30–31, 56–57; work horses, 140, 146–147. *See also remuda*
Horton, Thomas, 103, 132
hot shot. *See* cattle prod
Hot Springs Ranch, 157
Hough, Emerson, 77
Huerta, David, 33, 53–55, **53;** vaquero saddlery of, **35–37, 56, 57**
Hunt, Ray, 91
Hunter, Marvin, 77

IL Ranch, 205, 206, 218
implant: defined, 234
India: Brahman cattle breed in Texas, 72
Irwin, John Chadbourne, 72
Irwin, John G., 72

Jackson, Lawrence, 207, 219, 222
James, Walt, 199

James, Will, 134
jáquima: defined, 234
jerk cinch: defined, 234
jerky: defined, 234
Jersey bulls, 87
jineta. See la jineta
jingle-bob, 111, 179; defined, 234. *See also la mota*
jingle boy: defined, 234
jingle the horses: defined, 234
John G. Taylor Ranch, 219
Johnson, Ben, 134
Jones, Buck, 134
Jones, Frank Leon "Jumper," 220, 222
Jordan, Benjamin "Bennie" Earl, 222
Jordan, Terry: and theory on the emergence of cattle-raising culture in Texas, 69–72
Juárez, Benito, 14
junta de vacas, 50; defined, 234. *See also rodear; roundup*

Kansas: cattle drives to, 74–77; Dodge City, 76, 110
Kelton, Elmer, 64
Kenedy, Mifflin, 134
Kenedy Ranch, 145
Kershner, Nathan Pierce "Pete," 200, 220, 222
Kickapoo, 57
killing ground: defined, 234
Kimball, Lynn, 222
Kinéños, 16; defined, 234
King, Richard, 16, 74, 134. *See also* King Ranch
King of the Mustangers. *See* Arthur Drummond
King Ranch (South Texas), 16, **17,** 18, **18, 20, 21, 23, 24, 56,** 63, 81; vaquero tales of, 63–64
Kino, Eusebio Francisco, 10–12, 134
Klapper, Billy, 111, 131
Kleberg, Robert J., 63, 134

La Bahía Mission, 13
la brida: defined, 234
la casa: defined, 234
la casa grande: defined, 234
ladino: defined, 234
la jineta: defined, 234
Lambshead Ranch, **89,** 103

la mota: defined, 234
lariat, 25, 45, 54; cowboys, **91**, 95, **99**, 141; defined, 234. *See also* riata
la riata, 19
lariata larga, 25
lass: defined, 234
lasso, 45, 95; defined, 234
lass rope: defined, 234
latifundio, 14; defined, 234
latigo: defined, 235
lazo, 25, 70, 95; defined, 235
Lea, Tom, 2, 65, 134
lechuguilla (lasso), **27,** 45, 54, 57, 247; defined, 235
LeCoq, John Land, 220
Ledbetter, Morris, 92
Leddy, James, 107, 110
Leech, Glenn, 147–149, **148**
leppy: defined, 235
Levi jeans, 58, 60, 105, 165, 166, 215, 216, 221
leyenda negra: defined, 235
Limerick, Patricia, 70
literature: buckaroo culture in, 159–160, 170, 187; cowboys portrayed in, 76–77; vaqueros portrayed in, 63–64
llano, 70; defined, 235
lonas: defined, 235
London, G. D., 141–143, **142**
Long X Ranch, 146–147, **146**
Longhorn, xv–xvi, **16;** cowboys and, 70, 72, 74, **77,** 87; and Great Basin cattle industry, 212–213; origin of breed, 7; Texas ranching and, 68, 72, **77,** 87; in the West, 212. *See also* cattle ranching
looped rein: defined, 235
Lorenzana, Frank, 205
Louisiana: origin of open-range ranching and, 70, 72, 73
Loving, Oliver, 72, 74, 134
Lux, Charles, 201

Machado, 14
Mackenzie, Ranald, 73
maguey, **28,** 45, 247; defined, 235
Maher, Ambrose, 218, 222
major domo, 157; defined, 235
manada. See mare band
"Man of the North," defined, 235

mare band: defined, 235
market: defined, 235
Markus, Kurt, 220
Martin, Granville, 192
Marvel, Joe, 200
Marvel, Pete, 158
Marvel, Tom, 200
mascada: defined, 235. *See also* wild rag
Massey, Sarah, 135
Matador Ranch, 73, 81
Matthews, John A., 72
Matthews, Joseph Beck, 72
Matthews, Watkins R., 134
Matthews, William, 220
maverick: defined, 235. *See also* oreana
mayordomo: defined, 235
McCarty (or McCardy), 183. *See also* mecate
McClure, Walter, 202, 205
McCoy, Tim, 134
McCrea, Joel, 134
McLaury, Buster, 104
McLean, Malcolm D., 25
McMurtry, Larry, 77, 78
McQuery, Rod, 158, 188, 191, 192
MC Ranch, 216
Meanea, (saddler), 171
mecate (also called mecarty, McCarty, McCardy), 183; defined, 235
mechanical hackamore: defined, 235
Mendieta, Galo, 157
mesquite: defined, 235–236
mesteños: defined, 236. *See also* mustangs
mestizos: as vaqueros, 8
Mexican Americans: as buckaroos, 207, 219–220, 222
Mexicans: as buckaroos, 207, 219–220, 222; as vaqueros, xvi, 2, 14, 19, **24,** 25–26, 56, 62–63, 157, 207
Mexico, 69; Aztecs, 8; birth of cattle culture in, 8; conquistadors in, 7; contemporary vaqueros in, 46–53, **46,** 53–55, **53, 56,** 58–61; independence from Spain, 14; "Man of the North," 235; Mexico City, 8, 15; northern, 15–16; ranching and, 14–16; silver mining in, 15–16; Spanish conquistador Hernán Cor-

tés in, 5–7; Spanish introduction of cattle and horses in, 5–7
Miller, Charlie, 201
Miller, George, 213
Miller, Henry, 201
Miller, Joaquin, 18
Miller, Taft, 220, 222
Miller and Lux, cattle empire, 157, 158, 201–204, 207, 212, 213, 215
Minor, Tom, 200, 214, 218, 222
mission: defined, 236; cattle ranching and, 11–13; missionaries training Native Americans in the art of horsemanship, 207–208
Mission Dolores, 11
Mitchell, Waddy, **166**, 199
Moberly, Terry, **89**
mochilla: defined, 236
Monahan, Little Joe, 206
Moors: defined, 236; horsemanship and influence on vaqueros, 3–5; *Morisco,* 7
Mora, Jo, 28, 189, 192; on Californios, 207, 209; on origin of chinks, 167, 169
Morgan horse, 195
Morocco: Moorish horsemanship influence on vaqueros, 3–5; Moriscos, 7
Morris, Ernest, 157, 174, 194
mota. See la mota
mountain oysters, 59; defined, 236
mulattos: and cattle ranching in Mexico, 8; as vaqueros, 8
mule hide: defined, 236
Muñoz, Lolo, 219–220, 222
Murphy, Michael Martin, 136
music and song: buckaroos and, 199; cowboys and, 77, 134–137
mustang, 60; defined, 236. *See also mesteños*
mustanging: buckaroos and, 216–217
Myers, Marvin, Sr., 220, 222

Nail Ranch, **84, 88, 92,** 94, 102, **149**
Nampa Stampede, 200
National Cowboy Hall of Fame, 133–134
Native Americans, 11; Californios and, 207–209; cattle ranching in Mexico and, 8; Spanish conquista-

dors and, 7–8. *See also* American Indians
Navajo blanket, 126, **177, 178;** defined, 236
Navarro, José Miguel Sánchez, 14
neckerchief: buckaroo's "wild rag," 164–165, 187, 221; comparative traits of vaqueros, cowboys, and buckaroos, 247; cowboy style, 104–105
neighboring: defined, 236
Nelson, Barney, 135
Nelson, William "Bill," 218–219, 222
New Diamond Ranch, 216
New Mexico: borderlands, 2; first Spanish settlement in North America in, 9–10; Goodnight-Loving Trail and, 74; Spanish mission system in, 11, 12
New Spain, 5, 8; *encomienda* system in, 13–14; establishment of missions in, 11–13; Spanish expedition of, 9–11. *See also* California; Mexico
New West Historians, 70–71
night horse: defined, 236
96 Ranch, 157, 168, **195,** 215, 220
norteños: defined, 236
North Africa: Arab horsemen in, 3–4, 5; Berbers in, 3–4; Moorish horsemanship influence on vaqueros, 3–5
Northup, Tex., 195
nylon: defined, 236

Oñate, Juan de, 9
oreana: defined, 236
Oregon Trail, 212
Ortega, José Francisco, 208
Ortiz, Cirildo, 61–62, 64
outlaw cattle and horses: defined, 236. *See also ladino*
oxbow, 123, **123, 124,** 141, 174; defined, 236–237

packers: defined, 237
Paiute, **195,** 205, 207, 220
palpating: defined, 237
Panhandle-Plains Museum, 134
paratha, 194; defined, 237
Paredes, Américo, 64

partida, 203; defined, 237. *See also* herd
parting cattle: defined, 237
parting out: defined, 237
Pate, Jack, **152**
P Bench Ranch, 218
Peacock, Benny, 150–152, **150**
Peacock, George, **92**, 94, 96, 97, 102, 149–150, **149**
Peacock, Sue, 102
Pedroli, Tom, 216, 222
pelican saddle horn: defined, 237
pen: defined, 237
Pendleton Round Up, 200, 216
peon: defined, 237
Pierce, Shanghai, 74
pigging string: defined, 237
pita belt, 52, **52**
Pitchfork Ranch, 81, 91
piteadas, 60
Poco Bueno, 151
poetry: buckaroos and, 136, 199; cowboys and, 135, 136; Pioneer Arts Folklife Festival and, 199
poly rope: defined, 237
popper: defined, 237
Portolá, Gaspar de, 10, 12
post: defined, 237
post horn: defined, 237
pour: defined, 237
P Ranch, 216
prickly pear: defined, 237
prod: defined, 237. *See also* snuffy
Pro-Rodeo Hall of Fame and Museum of the American Cowboy, 134
prowling: defined, 237
pueblo, 10; defined, 237–238
Pueblo Indian Revolt, 12
punchy: defined, 238

Quarter Circle A, 215
Quarter Horse, 44, 56, 89–90, 140, **148**, 195; defined, 238
quirt (*warta*): defined, 238

railroads: influence on cattle ranching and beef industry, 212; and trail drives, 76
Raker, Fred, 214, 219, 222
Rambo, Clay, 169, 207
Ramirez, Nora Ethel, 71, 94, 223, 224

ranch horse: defined, 238. *See also* bridle horse; *caballo de trabajo*; *caballo corriente*; horses; *remuda*
ranching: corporate ownership of ranches, 81; Spanish introduction of, in the Americas, 7; women and, 188, 204–205, 206. *See also* cattle ranching; horses; *and names of individual ranches*
rancho: defined, 238
Rancho Nuevo, 53, 54
ranch rodeo: and buckaroos, 200–201; defined, 238
Randado Ranch, 30
range cubes: defined, 238
Range Riders Museum, 182
rattlesnake: defined, 238
rawhide, 45, 247; defined, 238
Rawlins, Rawhide, xvi
Reborse, Powder River Lee, 222
Rector, Ray, 135
Redon, Juan, 207, 213, 222
Reeves, Frank, 135
reins, 126, 127, 129, 182; comparative traits of vaqueros, cowboys, and buckaroos, 246–247; defined, 238
Remington, Frederic, 15, 63
remuda (also *la remuda*): cowboys and, **89, 90,** 91, 94, 143, 145, 147; defined, 239. *See also* cattle ranching; horses
remudero: defined, 239. *See also* jingle boy; wrangle boy; wrangler
rep: defined, 239
Reynolds, Barber Watkins, 72
Reynolds, George T., 72, 134
Reynolds, Jimbo, 146–147, 153
Reynolds, W. D., 72
riata, 29, 57, 178; as artistic medium of the buckaroo, 192; defined, 239
riding pasture: defined, 239. *See also* prowling
Riffe, Emery "Shorty," 214, 216, 222
rigging: comparative traits of vaqueros, cowboys, and buckaroos, 245; defined, 239
ringy: defined, 239. *See also* snuffy
Roaring Spring Ranch, 216
Rock Creek Ranch, 216
rodear: buckaroos and, 194–197; defined, 239

rodeo: defined, 239. *See also* ranch rodeo
Roemer, Ferdinand, 26–27
Rogers, Roy, 134
rolled cantle, 117. *See also* Cheyenne roll
roller: defined, 239
Rollins, Philip Ashton, 104, 105
romal, 182; defined, 239
rope and drag: defined, 239
rope corral: defined, 239
roper boots: defined, 239
ropers: cowboys, 79–80, **79, 80,** 95, **96,** 145–146
ropes, 54, **54,** 60; of buckaroos, 173–174; comparative traits of vaqueros, cowboys, and buckaroos, 247; defined, 239; Oregon crossover, 173. *See also* lariat; lazo; *lechuguilla*; maguey
roping and dragging, 188; buckaroos and, 199–200; in California, 28–29; comparative traits of vaqueros, cowboys, and buckaroos, 249; cowboys and, **79,** 95, **96;** dally, 28–29, 95; dangers of, 95; in Texas, 29; vaqueros and, 25–30, **26–30**
rosette (*la rosetta*): defined, 239
rosin jaw: defined, 239
round skirts: defined, 239
roundup, 148; defined, 239. *See also* gather; *junta de vacas*; rodear
rowel, 111; defined, 239–240
Rueker, Louis Willford, 222
running cattle: defined, 240
running iron: defined, 240
Russell, Charles M., xvi, xvii, 187

saddle (*la silla*), xvi, 60–61; bear trap, 170; bronc, 34, 117; of buckaroos, 33, 170–173, **171–173,** 176–177, **176, 177,** 178–179, 245–246; cantle, 245; Capriola, 171, 228; charro, 36–37, **38, 39;** of cowboys, 33, **91,** 116–117, **121, 122,** 124–125, 141, 143, 245–246; defined, 240; fork, 245; horn, 245; Mexican, 116; rigging, 245; single-rigged, 116; skirts, 245; slick-fork, 143; stirrups, 245–246; Texas-cowboy model, 33, 34; three-quarter, 117; Tipton, 171;

Tunstall, 143; of vaqueros, 31–37, **32–37,** 245–246; Visalia, 169, 171, 205, 218. *See also* center-fire rig; double-rigged; seven-eighths rigged
saddle-bronc riders, 200
saddle horn (*la cabeza*), 95, **99,** 116, 125; defined, 240
saddle horse: defined, 240
saddle house: defined, 240
saddle pad (*el suadero*): defined, 240
saddle tree: defined, 240
sage: defined, 240
San Antonio de Valero, 13
Sánchez, Ismael, 58–61, **59**
sandals: defined, 240
San Francisco de los Tejas, 12
San José de Bavicora Ranch, 63
San Juan de los Caballeros, 9
San Xavier del Bac, 11
Saunders, Tom B. IV, 135
Schreiber, Martin, 135
Schreiner, Charles, 134
Scott, Randolph, 134
segundo, 75; defined, 240
serape (*sarape*): defined, 240
Serra, Junipero, 12
set: defined, 240
seven-eighths rigged saddle, 117; defined, 240
shadow rider, 186–187; defined, 240
shallow port bit: defined, 240–241. *See also* spade bit
Shea, Cornelius "Con," 212–213
shipping pasture: defined, 241
Shirk, David, 213
shoo-fly, **185;** defined, 241
Shoshone, 205, 207
shot: defined, 241
shotgun chaps, **116,** 143, 145, 167, 169; defined, 241
silver conchos, 177, 187
single-rigged saddle, 116, **172, 177**
6666 Ranch, 81, 91
Skedaddle, Albert, 220, 222
skirts, 124; comparative traits of vaqueros, cowboys, and buckaroos, 245; defined, 241. *See also* round skirts; square skirts
Slatta, Richard, 70, 71, 213
Slaughter, John H., 134

Slaughter Ranch, 139
slicker: defined, 241
slick-fork saddle, 143, 170, 172;
    defined, 241
slobber chains, 180, **184;** defined, 241
Smiraldo, George, 167, 169, 185, 186,
    205, **211**
Smith, Erwin, 135
Smythe, Cory, 222
snaffle bit, 127, 131, **131,** 180, **182,** 183;
    defined, 241
snuffy: defined, 241
sombrero, 20, **25,** 60, 104; defined, 241
soogan (also called *sugan* or *sougan*),
    138. See also bedroll
sorting cattle: defined, 241
South Texas Ranching Festival, **83**
Southwest: Spanish introduction of
    cattle and horses, 5–7
Southwest Collection, 134
spade bit: defined, 241
Spade Ranch, 81, 87, 90
Spain: conquistadors in the Ameri-
    cas, 5–11; influence on Great
    Basin ranching, 157; influence of
    Moorish horsemanship on, 4–5;
    Mexican independence from, 14;
    mission system in New Spain, 10,
    11–13; slaves in the New World,
    7. See also Mexico; mission; New
    Spain
Spanish Mustache, 209, **210;** defined,
    242
Spanish Ranch, 219
Sparks, B. Abbott, 209, 212
Sparks-Tinnin Ranch, 212
split reins, **91,** 127, **132,** 183; defined,
    242. See also looped rein
spoon bit: defined, 242
Spraberry, Tommy, 111
spur (*la espuela*), 51, 131, 141, 143; of
    buckaroos, 179; in Chihuahua,
    40, 228; as collectors' items, 131;
    comparative traits of vaqueros,
    cowboys, and buckaroos, 247;
    of cowboys, 111, 115, **112–115;**
    defined, 242; drop-shank, 179; fa-
    mous makers of, 111; gal-leg, 232;
    Garcia, 179; OK spur, 111
spur leathers: defined, 242. See also
    dove wings

Spur Ranch, 218
square skirts: defined, 242
squaw tits, 172; defined, 242. See also
    bucking rolls
Stagg, Sam, 171
stampede, 75, 136
stampede string: defined, 242
Stanford, Lawrence Ralph, 222
Steagall, Red, 136
Steber, Rick, 203, 207, 216
steer operation: defined, 242. See also
    cow-calf operation
Stewart, James, 134
Stewart, Leslie, 157, 168–169, 195
stirrup leathers (*la ación* or *las
    aciones*): defined, 242
stirrups: bell-shaped, 226; of bucka-
    roos, 174, **175,** 176; comparative
    traits of vaqueros, cowboys, and
    buckaroos, 245–246; of cowboys,
    120, 123–124, **123.** See also oxbow
Stockard, Gerald, 111
stockers: defined, 242. See also feed-
    ers
stockyards: defined, 242
Stoeklein, David, 135, 220
stovepipe boots: defined, 242
straight cantle: defined, 242
string: defined, 242
swapping help: defined, 242. See also
    neighboring
Sweeney, Paul, 220, 222
swell: defined, 243
Swenson Ranch, **78–82, 91, 102**
S-Wrench brand, 201

tack, **176;** defined, 243. See also
    saddlery and tack
tack room: defined, 243. See also
    saddle house
Taham, Jim, 207
Taham, Moe, 207
tapaderos: and buckaroos, 246;
    buckaroo style, 176; bulldog, 176;
    comparative traits of vaqueros,
    cowboys, and buckaroos, 123, **125,**
    141; defined, 243; monkey-face,
    176; vaquero style, 33, 35, **37,** 53
tapa-ojos, 182; defined, 243
Terrazas, Luis, 14–15
Texas Expedition, 27

Texas: Abilene, 97, 107; borderlands, 2; breeds of cattle in, 72; contemporary vaqueros in, 42–45, **44**, 56–58, 58–61, 61–62; French settlement in, 10; influence on Great Basin cattle industry, 212–213; Longhorns and, 68, 72, 73–75, **77**, 87; Randado Ranch, 30; South Texas "diamond" region, 68, 69, 70, 75; Spanish expeditions to, 10; Spanish-Mexican influence, 72; Spanish mission system and cattle ranching in, 10, 12–13; theories on origins of cowboy life and ranching in, 68–73; trail drives, 74–75. *See also* cattle ranching; cowboys; King Ranch; Longhorn; vaqueros

Thomson, William Warren "Bill," 202, 220, 222

Thoroughbred, 94, 143, 195; defined, 243

three-quarter rigged saddle, 117; defined, 243

throat latch: defined, 243

tie-down, 127; defined, 243

tie on: defined, 243

Tinsley, Jim Bob, 71–72

toe fender. *See tapaderos*

tough rag. *See* wild rag

trail drives, 136; Chisholm Trail, 74; cowboy traditions developed on, 78–81; Goodnight-Loving Trail, 74; impact of railroads on, 76; modern-day, 84; Santa Fe Trail, 212; stampedes and, 75, 136; Western Trail, 74. *See also* cattle drives; cattle ranching

trap: defined, 243

Turk's-head: defined, 243

twine: defined, 243

vacas sierras, 49–50

vaccinate: defined, 243

Van Riper, Leslie, 202

vaqueros, xv–xvii, **1**, 60, 94, 95, 125, 144, 223–224; accoutrements, 247–248; *armas*, 167–168, 225; *armitas*, 168, 225; branding methods, 249; breaking horses, 50, 127, 250; Californios, 207–209; "Centaur Wish" of, 18, 224; chinks, 167; clothing and riding gear of, **17**, 19–20, 22, **22, 23,** 37–38, 45, 52–53, **52,** 57–58, 60, 248–249; comparative traits of, with cowboys and buckaroos, 245–250; contemporary 42–62, **43, 44, 46, 53, 55, 59;** corrals of, 249–250; cultural images of, 63–65; daily work of, 43–44; description of, 2–3; distinguished from charro, 45; distinguished from cowboys, 71, 223–224; early history of vaquero tradition, 3–5; early vaqueros as black Moorish slaves, 7; *encomienda* system and, 13–14; handmade roping and riding gear, 44–45; herbal remedies and, 60; horse breeding, 250; horse gear, 50–52, 55, **55;** horse roping, 45; horses of, 30–31; housing of, 43, 46, 58; influenced by horseback cultures of North Africa and Spain, 3–5; influence on cowboys, 68, 69; King Ranch and, 16, **17,** 18, **18, 20, 21, 23, 24;** leather chaps and, 107; leisure activities of, 44, 52; in literature, song, and film, 62–65; machinery and, 61; "Man of the North," 3; ranch diet of, **21, 23,** 46–47, 54, 58–59; ranching in Mexico and, 14–16; riding gear of, 19, **19,** 25, **26,** 27–29, **27, 28,** 30–37, **30–41;** roping and riding style of, 18–19, **24,** 25–27, 38–40, 249; roping gear of, **26,** 27–29, **27, 28;** saddlery and tack, 31–37, **32–39,** 245–247; saints and home remedies, 60; Spanish California vaqueros, 167, 180, 189, 207–209, 221; Spanish conquistadors in the Americas, 5–11; Spanish missions and, 11–13; temporary shelters of, 22, 25; as top-notch herders, 250; working methods, 249–250; working songs of, 64

Vásquez, Félix, 40

Villa, Pancho, 63

Villalobos, Gregorio de: first conquistador to bring cattle to Mexico, 7

Waggoner, Daniel, 134

Waggoner Ranch, 142, 150–152

wagon boss: defined, 243
Walcott, Glenn, 200, 214, 217, 222
Walker, Eldon, 199
Wallis, Sue, 188
Walters, Sol, 213
Walther, Jack, 199
Ward, Louis Robert "Bob," 202, 216, 222
Wayne, John, 134
weaner: defined, 244
Webb, Walter Prescott, 68, 69, 70, 71, 75
White, Richard, 70
Whitehorse Ranch, 216
wild rag, 164–165, 187, 221; defined, 244. *See also* neckerchief
Wilkinson, Andy, 189
Wilkinson, Robert Henry "Bob," 217, 222
Williams, Bob, 111
Wilson Ranch, 202

Winecup Ranch, 205
Wittliff, Bill, 2, 63, 65, 69
women: and buckaroo culture, 204–205, 206; ranching and, 188, 205, 206
Wood, Bill, **162**
woolies, 167, **168,** 221; defined, 244
working table: cowboys and, 94, **97, 98;** defined, 244. *See also* calf cradle
work on the wagon: defined, 244
wrangle boy. *See* wrangler
wrangler: cowboys, 93–94, 140, 145; defined, 244
Wrangler jeans, 58, 60, 105, 165, 221
wrangle the horses: defined, 244
wrango: defined, 244
wreck: defined, 244

yearly: defined, 244. *See also* stockers
Young, James A., 209, 212

ABOUT THE AUTHORS

LAWRENCE CLAYTON'S books, articles and reviews focused largely on life and literature on the American West, especially on the contemporary cowboy and ranch life. His *Historic Ranches of Texas* is from the University of Texas Press. He was past president of the West Texas Historical Association, Texas Folklore Society, and the Western Literature Association. He served as Dean of the College of Liberal Arts at Hardin-Simmons University in Abilene, Texas, where his wife, Sonja Irwin Clayton, still lives. She also runs their Lazy C Ranch near Ft. Griffin.

JIM HOY is a trustee of the American Folklife Center at the Library of Congress and is past president of the Kansas Folklore Society, the Mid-America Medieval Association, and the Kansas State Historical Society. He writes about the folklife of ranching, a topic on which he has lectured in England, Germany, New Zealand, and Australia. On several occasions he has served as a judge for the Kansas Championship Ranch Rodeo. He and his wife, Catherine Thompson Hoy, live near Emporia, Kansas, where he is a professor of English at Emporia State University.

JERALD UNDERWOOD'S interest in the vaquero has resulted in two papers on the subject: "The Vaquero: Forerunner and Foundation of the American Cowboy" published by the Ranching Heritage Center at Texas Tech University (1991). His 1992 paper, "The Vaquero in South Texas with an Interpretation by John Houghton Allen" was published in the *West Texas Historical Association Year Book*. He and his wife, Dorothy Eads Underwood, live in Uvalde, Texas, where he is retired from Southwest Texas Junior College, after many years as a dean.

CPSIA information can be obtained
at www.ICGtesting.com
Printed in the USA
LVHW041314310322
714807LV00002B/70